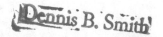

SOCIAL TRANSITION IN CHINA

ZHANG Jie and LI Xiaobing

Editors

University Press of America,® Inc.
Lanham • New York • Oxford

Copyright © 1998
University Press of America,® Inc.
4720 Boston Way
Lanham, Maryland 20706

12 Hid's Copse Rd.
Cummor Hill, Oxford OX2 9JJ

Library of Congress Cataloging-in-Publication Data

Social transition in China / Zhang Jie and Li Ziaobing, editors
p.   cm.
Collection of papers presented at the International symposium on
Socio-Economic Transition and Cultural Re-construction in China at
Georgia Southern University on May 2-4, 1997.
Includes bibliographical references.
1. China—Social conditions—1976- 2. China—Economic
conditions—1976 3. China—Rural conditions. I. Zhang, Jie, 1955-
. II. Li, Xiaobing, 1954- . III. International Symposium on Socio-
Economic Transition and Cultural Re-construction in China (1997 :
Georgia Southern University)
HN733.5.S64 1998   306'.0951—dc21   98-20008   CIP AC

ISBN 0-7618-1146-X (cloth: alk. ppr.)
ISBN 0-7618-1147-8 (pbk: alk. ppr.)

Contents

Acknowledgments

This volume is a product of the International Symposium on Socio-Economic Transition and Cultural Reconstruction in China held at Georgia Southern University, Statesboro, Georgia May 2-4, 1997. This book would not have been possible without the support of many people and institutions. The editors wish to thank Professor TU Weiming, Director of the Harvard-Yenching Institute of Harvard University, and Professor CAO Siyuan of the Chinese Academy of Social Sciences in Beijing. Their strong support for this first interdisciplinary scholarly effort is deeply appreciated.

A special appreciation goes to the 1995-1997 Board of Directors of the Association of Chinese Professors of Social Sciences in the U.S. (ACPSS), who organized the international symposium at its Second Annual Conference. Our deep gratitude goes to Dr. TIAN Guoqiang, ACPSS President and Professor of Economics at Texas A & M University, and Dr. HONG Zhaohui, ACPSS Executive Vice President and Director of the Asian-Pacific Study Committee at Savannah State University.

We thank Georgia Southern University for its efforts in hosting the conference. Our special thanks go to Dr. Nicholas L. Henry, President of the University, and Dr. Zia H. Hashmi, Director of the University's Center for International Studies.

We also thank the China Development Foundation, the China Time Foundation, and the Ford Foundation, which have been very supportive of ACPSS scholarly projects like the international symposium held at Georgia Southern University. The ACPSS partially financed the symposium proceedings and made the volume's publication possible.

The editors are grateful to the professional support from their colleagues and staff members at the University of Central Oklahoma and SUNY College at Buffalo. Drs. Donald Duffy and Wayne Stein at the University of Central Oklahoma read and commented on part of the manuscript. Mr. Christian J. Kull and Ms. LU Xuehong rendered assistance in the computer work. Our thanks also go to Nancy Ulrich and

Helen Hudson, editors at the University Press of America. Their professionalism and commitment to academic excellence has helped make this publication a success. Without their help, this volume would not have been possible.

Last but not least, we wish to make explicit our debt to the contributors to this volume. They are the authorities in the field. We thank them for their contributions.

Editors
March 1998

Note on Transliteration

The new "*pinyin*" romanization system is applied to Chinese names of persons, places, and terms. The transliteration is also used for the titles of Chinese publications. Some popular names have traditional Wade-Giles spellings appearing in parentheses after the first use of the "*pinyin*." However, traditional spellings for a few names of prominent persons like Sun Yat-sen, widely known places like Taipei, and names of persons in Taiwan and Hong Kong are not within the "*pinyin*" system.

As a convention in this volume, total transliteration is employed for the Chinese personal names, in which surnames are in front of given names, exactly as they are in Chinese. Surnames, when put before given names, are in capital letters. For example, in the name of DENG Xiaoping, DENG is the surname, and Xiaoping is the given name.

Editors
March 1998

Chapter 1

Introduction: Social-Economic Transition and Cultural Reconstruction in China

LI Xiaobing

The summit in October 1997 between Bill Clinton and JIANG Zemin, President of the People's Republic of China (PRC), once again put China's future in the spotlight.[1] Debate over the viability of the Chinese government, which started immediately after the 1989 Tiananmen Square crackdown, aroused now even more concerns and criticism from the politicians, public, and media in the United States. A "broad-based" "anti-China wave" and the upsurge of criticism of the Clinton administration's "strategic partnership" and "constructive engagement" with China "has tended to politicize China policy in a way not seen since the McCarthy period of the 1950s."[2] While the sharp criticism "reached beyond the Washington beltway and foreign policy elite well into the country,"[3] nationwide attention also demands a new re-assessment of the major issues between the two countries, and the overheated China debate needs more intellectual engagement.

Current problems of the U.S.-China relationship have stirred a strong research interest among American scholars. Some of them are cheerful about the solid, "if less than epochal" accomplishments of the summit and are optimistic about the future of U.S.-China relations, as Harry Harding pointed out at a recent symposium.[4] Others look at the event in a different way. They believe that "this summit showed how far apart the United States and China remain on fundamental issues, not how much they have come together."[5] Among the other major issues are human rights, Tibet,

Taiwan, imbalanced trade, weapon sales, and nuclear proliferation. Yet what might be considered the fundamental *problem* may not be the issue with which the China debate is primarily concerned. In their recent co-edited book, Thomas Metzger and Ramon Myers suggest that the key to the debate should be "the decisions determining which questions to debate."[6] Although people often discuss alternative answers to U.S. China policy issues, the key issue we should address today is "far from obvious."[7]

The Key Issue

Most scholars likely agree that the future relationship between America and China mainly depend upon China's internal development. Andrew Nathan emphasizes that China becomes more and more important to the United States because it has become more important itself in the world.[8] The major development decisive to the direction of U.S.-China relations is China's own democratization, which should take place during its economic reform and modernization. The democratization will transform the government from an authoritarian to a democratic form. Democracies tend not to fight one another. As John Gaddis states in his book, democratic governments are "less likely than their authoritarian counterparts" to confront against each other.[9]   Henry Kissinger emphasized this point during a recent conference at the University of Oklahoma. The question about the relationship is not whether the U.S. can impose democracy on China, Kissinger said, but whether "the most populous and the most technologically advanced nations have a basis for cooperation."[10] Nevertheless, a democratic form of government does not necessarily nor automatically result from economic growth. Gaddis examines some cases and concludes that "The relationship between democratization and economic growth is by no means exact: prosperity in South Korea, Taiwan, and Singapore did not evolve under the most scrupulous democratic procedures...."[11]

China's economic reform that DENG Xiaoping started in the late 1970s has changed the face of China and made it one of the fastest growing economies in the world. Unfortunately, its economic growth neither significantly contributes to the PRC's political stability nor to a democratic transformation. It has been argued that economic development and modernization may lead to political instability.[12] The most known causes accounting for China's political instability are the increasing political dissatisfaction, anti-government minority revolts, and widespread complaints of corruption among party and governmental officials. Jiang certainly knows these situations. He confessed to an American reporter that he can not get to sleep sometime since there are so many "brain-breaking questions and problems" in China. The PRC President, however, is "very confident about the future" because he believes that "in the past few years the Chinese people have scored very exciting achievements" in the social transition.[13]

How is China's social transition? What does it mean to China's democratization? Can the Chinese Communist Party (CCP) survive the Tiananmen Square events without a major political reform? What kinds of problems does China have during its social transition? How is Beijing's regime handling these problems--with political repression such as arrests and terror, or by other methods? The further intellectual debate should focus on China's social transition as the key issue and as an important indicator of its modernization and democratization. The new assessment of China's reform and of U.S.-China relations should be able to explore the new reality by answering these crucial questions.

However, when China experts begin their new research on China's social transition, they soon find out that neither established schools nor existing forums can answer these questions by merely revisiting the old debate. They wonder why some Western theories do not work very well on China's issues, or whether the PRC would be an "exception" to the fall of communism worldwide.[14] They were even more disappointed by Jiang's state visit to the U.S. (October 26 to November 3, 1997) since the summit has brought more questions than answers to the decade-long debate. Jiang has realized this problem and said that "it is no easy task for the people of our two countries to really understand each other."[15] A major re-assessment of China's social transition requires not only exploring a new research opportunity, but also developing new analytical approaches and conceptual frameworks and opening new forums.

Research problems and difficulties in understanding China's situation challenge Chinese scholars of social sciences in America. As a new generation of social sciences and humanities experts, Chinese scholars have a unique position to study Chinese society. They were born and educated in mainland China and then received their professional training and advanced degrees in America and other Western countries. Currently working as university professors or institute researchers, many of them are China experts in their disciplines as well as witnesses of China's transition themselves. Their personal experience is in fact part of the result of this transition either as beneficiaries or victims. Having exploited their obvious advantages, they open up new sources of first-hand information to an unprecedented degree and have been stimulated by a large and enthusiastic audience in America for their research. They have quite different answers to our questions since their cross-cultural background and expertise in a wide range of fields help them see what many people can not see and say what others would not say. Their views are much needed to be heard in a collective way by both American and Chinese peoples as well as their governments.

To make new efforts and enter their input, the Chinese scholars open a new forum for the debate. On May 2-4, 1997, the Association of Chinese Professors of Social Sciences in the United States (ACPSS) sponsored the "International Symposium on Socio-Economic Transition and Cultural Re-construction in China" at Georgia Southern University. The symposium addressed important topics on China's economy, politics, and society from a multi-disciplinary perspective and explored cooperative interdisciplinary research efforts among Chinese scholars interested in the subject. Their scholarship makes a significant contribution through multi-faceted components (including six keynote speeches, 42 paper presentations, and 12 panel discussions) attended by more than 70 Chinese scholars from different fields such as political science, economics, history, sociology, psychology, military, diplomacy, education, communication, information science, and environmental science. These Chinese academics are establishing new critical mass through their scholarly contributions. TU Weiming, Director of the Harvard-Yenching Institute of Harvard University, noted in his opening remarks that the symposium provided well-balanced perspectives and the insight of China's economic reforms and social transition because the participants had a comprehensive understanding of Chinese society through their unique personal experience and extraordinary research efforts.[16]

This book is the collection of the symposium papers. It offers American people a chance for the first time to view China's internal situation and problems from a Chinese perspective and makes an important contrast between the two very different cultures. It presents a new examination of many current issues and controversial points. The contributors conduct a wide-ranging discussion and look at the key issues from different perspectives of their own disciplines. Their distinctive multi-disciplinary approach has blown fresh air into the study of contemporary China and shed new light on many important questions. This extraordinary research volume surely fills in some major gaps in the scholarship of the field. Although no brief summary can possibly cover the interdisciplinary discussions, some highlights of these essays may be helpful for readers.

A Long-waited Transition

This volume is divided into four parts. Part One starts with a re-evaluation of major features of the principal existing traditions of China as they were confronted by Western civilization in the 19th century; following is China's problems in adapting to the modern international system in the 20th century and challenges posed by recent reforms and modernization. China's unique experience in social transition has provided the Chinese a different understanding of modernization.

In the past two or three centuries, many countries have experienced the historical transition from traditional society to modern society. Generally speaking, modernization includes industrialization, urbanization, democratization, and globalization.[17] Although globalization in fact started at the very beginning of modern capitalism, it has just been widely accepted and made rapid progress in the recent decades. Globalization means that our world is gradually turned into a "global village," within the same capitalist system or a world economic network, by the modern technology of transportation and communication. The Chinese view of "globalization" is different from that of others. An ideal world order in Chinese eyes has long since been described by Confucius as "grand harmony" (*da tong*). The "grand harmony" emphasizes the "common good" and "good faith" with which people in the world would "not labor for their own profit" and "the source of all greed was stopped."[18] Obviously, such ideals are not capitalism. In the first article of Part One, China in comparison with Japan, LIU Guoli re-examines China's experience in the context of social, cultural, and political changes during the late 19th century. Given that there should be a significant link and necessary interactions between political culture and social changes, he concludes that "A successful socio-economic reform needs a new cultural, or a new political cultural, environment."[19]

China's problems in social transition result from its following difficulties in modernization. (1) In contrast with most modern countries, China has four major transitions at the same time. The other industrial countries had theirs separately or one at a time. Japan, for example, had its industrialization in the Meiji Restoration during the late 19th century and its democratization after World War II. (2) China then was not willing and now is forced to have these transitions in which other countries were willing, eager, and ready for social changes. After 1840, China reluctantly accepted the idea of industrialization but was not ready for other modern concepts like democratization. (3) After 1949 China rejected modernization and even criticized its basic principle and necessity. The long refusal to incorporate these principles cost China a great deal in terms of both human and economic losses.

In short, all of these situations cause problems in China's transition and make any change, if not impossible, extremely difficult. Even a small step forward may need a systematic change in the society. In the second article, XU Xiaohe employs quantitative methods and analyzes data collected from the cities of Chengdu and Baoding to explore the important determinants of historical changes in freedom of mate choice. The finding indicates that "shifts away from the familial modes of social organization," such as the proliferation and expansion of education and non-familial labor force participation, are "the significant contributing factors to the transformation from parentally arranged to free choice marriages" in urban Chinese society.[20]

The two contributors to Part One provide a solid interpretation of the changes in Chinese civilization and the persistence and inflexibility of its traditional culture and values. They also explain how forces intermesh to produce the reform and transition that have taken places in China today. Tu added a very important point to the cultural difference in his keynote speech, "The Conflict of Values: Confucian Ethics as Modern Discourse." Though the modernization in the West contradicts many traditional Chinese values and the existing system, the difference does not mean an inevitable confrontation between the West and China as widely perceived during the Cold War. He questions if the West is challenged by Chinese traditional culture and Confucian values as some scholars believe.[21] The different understanding of the world does not derive from policy or political conflicts which belong to the Cold War mentality, but from cultural resources which could be inclusive, diffusive, assimilative, and able to learn from each other. Having agreed with Tu's argument, TIAN Guoqiang looks at some similarities in principle between Confucianism and Western thoughts in his keynote speech.[22] Confucianism, for instance, emphasizes the moral conduct in social and economic activities. Interestingly, Tian continues, when morality confronts an individual's survival, Mencius says that survival is more important than morality.

There was little if any disagreement that orthodox Confucianism has proved to be "ineffective and incompatible" with modern ideas and that Stalinist ideology and state-models have turned out to be "incapable" of dealing with the urgent task of modernization. So our next questions should be, as one of the authors asks in his article, what kind of new ideas should China embrace? What old thinking to discard? How to manage the conflict between changes and continuity?[23] Jiang and the Chinese reformers may have to answer these questions when the conflicts of different schools of thinking are becoming more intense and more relevant for China's social transitions.

Major Changes and Achievements

The three articles in Part Two focus on the transitions in rural China which in the past twenty years initiated China's economic reform, and now is taking pioneer efforts in promoting China's democratization and decentralization through free elections and autonomous operation of the villager committees after 1987. Economic reform has generally demonstrated Beijing's strategy of "country first and city following." According to the authors' investigations in this part, the rural reforms such as the household responsibility system established in the late 1970s and the township and village enterprise in the early 1980s promoted urban economic reform in the middle of 1980s. Both also promoted the property rights reform of state-owned enterprise in the early 1990s. Currently, rural China is playing "another pioneer role of promoting China's political reform through the election and operation of the villager committee."[24]

As the author of the first article in Part Two, HONG Zhaohui made three research trips to China, visiting many villages, interviewing recently-elected committee members, researching local documents, and reviewing central governmental files including the data and information of the past ten years between 1987 and 1997 at the Ministry of Civil Affairs in Beijing. Hong begins with discussion of the periodization and driving forces of the villager committees. With emphasis on the "positive impact" of the committee, he examines the role of free elections, the elected officials' authority, legal system construction, organizational operation, internal structure, and political participation in rural stability. His finding shows that "the most democratic organizations with free elections and high levels of participation in China" today are the more than one million villager committees (*cunmin weiyuanhui*) representing 900 million villagers. The villager committees are a "positive force in maintaining social order during this critical transition stage from an agricultural society to an industrial society."[25] The village democracy and autonomy today may possibly lead to urban democracy tomorrow.

China's rural population constitutes more than 70% of the total population. Historically, the communist revolution succeeded largely because the CCP was able to build a revolutionary movement on peasant discontent through careful, painstaking organization, as CHEN Weixing explains in the second article. From the 1920s to 1949, the CCP was able to lead peasants where they wanted to go. "The successful handling of the peasant challenge" enabled the CCP to gain control of China. But from the late 1950s to 1979, the CCP was "forcing peasants to go where they did not want to go" by "binding peasants physically on land and politically under the people's commune system."[26] The policy failed because it built peasant discontent and resulted in great economic, ideological, and political losses. From 1979 to the present, the CCP has tried to lead peasants where they want to go by sponsoring economic and social reforms. The success of rural transformation, however, is "contingent upon the stability of rural China." Chen analyzes the roots of social instability with which the rural transition has been fraught, and discusses their implications and policy dilemmas, which have been created by the CCP itself. In order to promote economic growth, the CCP "has to reject its ideology in practice, relax its control over the peasantry, and discard one of its most familiar political vehicles--mobilization."[27] The CCP now has to face the consequences and deal with its dilemmas.

To explain the dynamism behind the economic growth of China, it is necessary to examine the weakening role of the state in the economy and the increased autonomy of individuals, enterprises, and local governments. The recent centralization efforts, however, intend to rebuild necessary state capacities to manage a developing country with a transitional economic system rather than to drag China's economy back to central planning. ZHANG Baohui in the third article studies the economic and political logic behind one of the most notable reforms--the 1994 fiscal reform. He notes that the recent reform has "reversed fiscal decentralization of the 1980s and sought to strengthen the fiscal capacity of the central government."[28] However, the purpose of the reform was to strengthen the government in macro-economic management. A market economy can provide varied roles for government in macro-economic management, ranging from the hands-off approach of the U.S. to the statist system of Japan to the essentially planned capitalism of South Korea. Zhang concludes that the experience with the fiscal reform "closely conforms" to DENG Xiaoping's idea of "crossing the river by feeling the stones."

All of the authors in Part Two stress that Deng's opening up and economic reform policy has saved the country from a total disaster and permitted great economic achievements in the past two decades. Deng knew what he was talking about when he said that "China has no future without a major reform," and "Reform must be insisted on for 100 years."[29] As part of economic reform, privatization of state-owned enterprises has created tremendous progress and success. CAO Siyuan summarized this important process in his keynote speech, "China's Economic Reform and Its Bankruptcy Law." At the beginning of the reform in 1979, the government owned 91.8% of the nation's industrial enterprises.[30] By the end of 1994, the government ownership was reduced to 69.1% across the country. Meanwhile, privately owned companies as 30% of the nation's enterprises manufactured more than 70% of the nation's total products. Cao believes that privatization has a very strong and positive impact on the society which tends toward a "social pluralism." Deng's era is pictured by WEI Jingsheng as "a transitional period from a black age to a better time." On his way to America as an exile in late November 1997, the dissident characterized the 92-year-old patriarch's death in early 1997 as "the departure of the old generation of idealistic communists."[31]

Unexpected Problems

The release of the human rights activist WEI Jingsheng in mid-November 1997 reflected JIANG Zemin's willingness to further China's reform and transition. In order to commence his new leadership and win endorsement from his own party, Jiang needs to step out of the shadow of his predecessor DENG Xiaoping. Deng did provide him opportunities or "challenges" as Jiang described in his report to the CCP Fifteenth National Congress held at Beijing in September 1997.

On one hand, Deng succeeded in his opening up and economic reforms at a high cost to both his country and to the next generation of leadership. In order to save China from the most self-defeating precepts of Marxism and Leninism and prevent China's economy from completely collapsing in his hands, Deng tried to ignore the consequences of his radical methods and postpone or avoid to face and solve serious problems during the seismic changes. He has passed them to his chosen successor Jiang, who must now face and struggle to solve the political and economic problems. The real challenge to the new leadership in Beijing is posed by Deng's legacy itself.

On the other hand, however, what are considered as Deng's problems is exactly Jiang's opportunity to step ahead of Deng and consolidate his "coronation" as China's supremo. The best example is Jiang's declaration at the CCP's Fifteenth National Congress that China will privatize most state industries. More than half of China's 125,000 state industries are "hamstrung by outmoded management." Though they employ 110 million workers, the factories can not pay them. Deng had always been "afraid of the social turmoil" that could be unleashed if millions of those workers were dismissed.[32] He rejected such suggestions of privatization made by former Premier ZHAO Ziyang in 1988-1989. Now, having been waiting for his turn for eight years (from 1989 when he was appointed as the CCP Chairman), Jiang makes his own major move as a new, strong reforming leader rather than a weak, transitional successor who can only take advantages as Deng's beneficiary as some people discredit his taking-over of Hong Kong in July 1997.

Jiang's economic move is not the only sign of his determination and willingness to continue what Deng has started and push it forward. He has also designed a new grand framework at the party's historical meeting for China's development at the turn of the century.[33] Mostly important, his ideas are to carry on Deng's reforming theory of constructing the "socialism with Chinese characteristics" and continue Deng's major policies toward opening up and reform; to recognize that China's socialist development is still at its low, primary level so as to restrain any radical and unrealistic policy or idea; and to make two slow and smooth transformations at the same time: from a planning economy to a market economy, and from an agricultural society to an industrial society.

As we can tell, his plan reveals extreme caution and obvious limitation of the new leadership. Realistic as he is, Jiang seeks the following policy goals in the near future: a balance among different political groups and policy options; a continuity of the transitional period for the two transformations rather than their completion or a new revolution; and a social order in which the two transformations should be safeguarded and some of the social problems should be solved. These policy goals should be achieved through new methods such as civil administrations, reasonable concessions, and the rule of law (not rule by law).

His limited and conservative goals also reflect the seriousness of China's social problems that sometimes can reach a crisis level. Their causes are discussed in Part Three, which begins with the article written by ZHANG Lening and DENG Xiaogang. The co-authors explore the association between crime in China and structural changes in community and work units. They depict the characteristics of community and work units and their "functions of social control" as two basic social establishments at the grass-roots level.[34] Further, the article discusses the possible influence of economic reform and the "open door" policy on structural changes in community and work units and the implication of these changes for social control of crime. To deal with China's increasing crime problem, the article proposes two kinds of theoretical models which provide valuable insights for "developing criminological understanding of social change and crime" across different social contexts.

More policy suggestions are proposed in the second article by CHEN Jiafang, who continues the discussion by analyzing the increase of crime in China. In 1982, according to Chen's research, there were 750,000 criminal cases reported. Six years later, in 1988, 830,000 crimes were reported nationwide, averaging more than seven cases per 100 thousand population. In 1994, after six more years, there were 1,660,000 cases, which doubled the number of 1988, with the average of 14.3 cases per 100 thousand population.[35] Chen also shows some new characteristics of China's crime such as the increase of young criminals, robbery and theft as the main component of juvenile crimes, and the increasing trend of violent crimes. His policy suggestions against crime include re-education of youth, a crackdown on all crimes by law enforcement officials, cooperation between the community and government, and early prevention.

Besides the increasing crime and other social problems, advanced technology in communication and computerization also challenge the new leadership. The last article, authored by YU Yanmin in Part Three, focuses on China's recent development of communication and information infrastructure through her research on computer popularization, e-mail and internet expansion, and government regulation.[36] The revolution of communication and information in China has shown a strong social and cultural impact on the reform and transition. Problems created by new electronic technology apparently put more pressure on Jiang, even though he has relatively conservative and limited domestic policy goals.

An Uncertain Future

Comparing Jiang with MAO Zedong as the first generation leader and Deng as the leader of the second generation, we may conclude that Jiang's policy goals deserve some credit since balance, transition, and order had long eluded China because of Mao's extremist idealism and revolutionary spirit and Deng's political pragmatism and practical ignorance. JIANG Shufeng told the author of this introduction that, though JIANG Zemin admires Mao's strategic thinking, he is critical to Mao's methodology.[37]
At the CCP Fifteenth National Congress, Jiang asked the party, especially its high-level leaders, to have a comprehensive and accurate understanding of Deng's reforming theory by separating Deng's thoughts from his mistakes. Apparently, with his own ideas, Jiang wants to make history as the chief of the third generation leadership rather than a transitional political "lightweight" as dismissed by some China experts in the West.
Today's world that Jiang lives in is totally different from where Mao lived forty years ago and different from where Deng lived twenty years ago. The end of the Cold War, collapse of the European communist nations, and tremendous changes in globalization and communication, all have created a historical opportunity as well as a biggest challenge to Beijing's leadership. Jiang intends to join the new world by leading China

beyond its revolutionary myths. He told his staff many times not to miss the historical opportunity and not be afraid of the new challenges in a changed social environment.[38]

Part Four, which is made up of three articles, focuses on China's changing attitude, new self-image, and changed views toward the outside world in general and toward America in particular. In the first article, Jessie Fan, XIAO Jing Jian, and XU Yinzhou discuss changes of attitudes among college students in China toward the free market. The authors collected their survey data at five universities in the Guangzhou area of South China in 1996. Their data are compared to the results of Hemesath and Pomponio's 1995 study, which reported the comparative survey results from college students in Shanghai, China, and Minnesota in 1992-1993. This article suggests that the attitudinal differences between Chinese and American students are "both situational and cultural."[39] The differences between the Guangzhou and Shanghai sample are "mainly geographical."

The second article written by LI Jian explores how the changes in address norms involving kinship terms, titles, and names reflect the tremendous social transformations in China through her research on the effects of the recent economic reform on the use of social, official, and occupational titles. Focusing on the social conditions, the article demonstrates how norms of address "maintain and re-create social solidarity and hierarchy" in China.[40]

In the third article of Part Four, XU Guangqiu examines changes of Chinese attitudes toward America during the period between 1979 and 1996. A "rapid anti-Americanism had gradually given way to cautious pro-Americanism" in the general Chinese media and specialized professional publications.[41] From 1979 to 1989, according to Xu's survey, a pro-Americanism image in the media emerged. After 1989, anti-Americanism has been rising. The latest survey conducted in 1996 shows that the majority of respondents found the U.S. unfriendly to China on many issues such as Taiwan, human rights, and GATT. Among the other reasons for a less friendly attitude are Beijing's critique of U.S. China policy, state-controlled media, and a new nationalism commensurate with China's growing economic power and China's outcry against U.S. attempts to maintain its power in the world.

During his U.S. state visit, Jiang told American people that his aim for his visit "is nothing less than to change the minds of Americans about what is going on in China and why they should care about it."[42] Certainly he tried almost everything so as to change the image of himself and his government because he knows that the American people as well as the entire world are worrying about China's future. Not surprisingly, the

American people reacted in different ways to his visit because they were confused by China's domestic policies and not sure what role China wants to play in the world. The difficulties in understanding China's social situations have made it harder for the American people to judge China and the Chinese government. The confusion about China itself leads to a confused relationship with America.

As he carefully planned, Jiang did not miss his opportunity to send his signal and break new ground in some areas. When he made a toast in the White House, the Chinese President declared that "China and the United States should strengthen cooperation and endeavor to build a constructive strategic partnership oriented toward the 21st century."[43] Nevertheless, "Differences that can not be resolved for the time being can be put aside while concentrating on seeking common ground," Jiang added.[44] Until we can have a better understanding of China's internal reform and transition, the differences and the common ground between the two countries remain "a very troubling question mark."[45]

Notes

1.   The writer of this introduction is indebted to the co-editor ZHANG Jie for offering many comments and suggestions on various aspects, but, of course, he is not responsible for any mistakes and flaws.
2.   David Shambaugh, "The United States and China: Cooperation or Confrontation?" *Current History*, vol. 96 (September 1997): 243-244.
3.   Shambaugh, *ibid.*, 244.
4.   Harry Harding said at a recent symposium in Washington, D.C. before the summit that Jiang is strategically and tactically capable of managing the China-U.S. relationship in the near future. He suggested that the U.S. should improve its relations with China according to its own interests.
5.   George Wehrfritz and Melinda Liu, "A Noise in Jiang's Ears," *Newsweek*, November 10, 1997, 44-46.
6.   Thomas Metzger and Ramon Myers eds., *Greater China and U.S. Foreign Policy; The Choice between Confrontation and Mutual Respect* (Stanford, CA: Hoover Institution Press, 1996), 2.
7.   Metzger and Myers eds., *ibid.*, 2-3.
8.   Andrew Nathan's opening remarks at the International Conference on "China after the CCP Fifteenth National Congress," New York City, November 7-9, 1997.
9.   John L. Gaddis, *The United States and the End of the Cold War; Implications, Reconsideration, Provocations* (Oxford, London: Oxford University Press, 1992), 194-195.
10.   Henry Kissinger's keynote address during the International Conference on "Preparing America's Foreign Policy for the 21st Century" at the University of Oklahoma, September 15, 1997, "Kissinger Urges Respect for Foreign Cultures," *The Daily Oklahoma*, September 16, 1997, 1-2.

11. Gaddis, *ibid.*, 185.

12. Charles Tilly, "Does Modernization Breed Revolution?" *Comparative litics*, vol. 5, no. 3 (1973): 425-447.

13. JIANG Zemin in an exclusive interview with *Time*'s editor, "U.S. and China: Ups and Downs," *Time*, October 27, 1997, 56-58.

14. For "China exception," see Andrew Nathan, "China's Path from Communism," *Journal of Democracy*, vol. 4, no. 2 (1993): 30.

15. Jiang, "U.S. and China: Ups and Downs," *Time*, October 27, 1997, 58.

16. A record of TU Weiming's remarks, "The Conflict of Values: Confucian Ethics as Modern Discourse," was made orally at the conference. All statements in the Introduction ascribed to him are taken from this record.

17. Scholars include different transitions in their definition of modernization. For instance, some of them include marketization (or market revolution) instead of democratization in the modernization.

18. The ancient ideal of the Grand Harmony is presented in *The Book of Rites*: "When the Great Way prevailed in the world, all mankind worked for the common good. Men of virtue and ability were elected to fill public offices. Good faith was universally observed and friendly relations cultivated. People's love was not confined to their own parents and their own children, so that all the aged ones were enabled to live out the natural span of their lives, ... This is called the Age of Grand Harmony." L. G. Thompson, *Ta T'ung Shu: The One-World Philosophy of K'ang Yu-wei* (London, England: Allen & Unwin, 1958), 66.

19. LIU Guoli, "Political Culture and Social Change: Rethinking China's Experience," 19-34.

20. XU Xiaohe, "The Social Origins of Historical Changes in Freedom of Mate Choice under State Socialism: the Case of Urban China," 35-60.

21. According to the record of Tu's remarks, among other scholars and schools was Samuel Huntington's "clash of the civilizations" mentioned.

22. As the immediate past president of ACPSS, TIAN Guoqiang made one of the keynote speeches at the conference, "China's Technology and Economic Reforms and Social Transition." A record of remarks made orally at the conference by Tian and all statements in the Introduction ascribed to him are taken from this record.

23. Liu, *ibid.*, 19-34.

24. HONG Zhaohui, "The Role of Villager Committees in Rural China's Stability," 63-85.

25. Hong, *ibid.*, 63-85.

26. CHEN Weixing, "Economic Reform and Social Instability in Rural China," 87-101.

27. Chen, *ibid.*, 87-101.

28. ZHANG Baohui, "Fiscal Reform and State Capacity Building," 103-129.

29. DENG Xiaoping, "Learning from Our Experience," *Deng Xiaoping Wenxuan* (Selected Works of Deng Xiaoping), vol. 3 (Beijing: People's Press, 1993), 368.

30. CAO Siyuan, "China's Economic Reform and Its Bankruptcy Law," the keynote speech at the ACPSS International Symposium on "Socio-economic Transition and Cultural Re-construction in China." A record of Cao's remarks was

made orally at the conference.

31. WEI Jingsheng's first interview by *Newsweek* on his flight to America on November 16, 1997. George Wehrfritz, "What Now for Wei?" *Newsweek,* December 1, 1997, 42-43.

32. Michael Serrill, "Socialism Dies, Again," *Time,* September 22, 1997, 44.

33. Jiang's party working report to the CCP Fifteenth National Congress in *Renmin Ribao (Haiwaiban)* (People's Daily, Overseas Edition), September 22, 1997, 1-4.

34. ZHANG Lening and DENG Xiaogang, "The Effects of Structural Changes in Community and Work Unit in China," 133-154.

35. CHEN Jiafang, "Crime in China's Modernization," 155-170.

36. YU Yanmin, "The Development of Communication Information Infrastructure: A Revolution in Networking," 171-175.

37. Personal interviews with JIANG Shufeng in Beijing in July 1992. As JIANG Zemin's uncle, JIANG Shufeng brought JIANG Zemin up as his own child since JIANG Zemin's father, JIANG Shangqing, died when JIANG Zemin was very young.

38. Personal interview with JIANG Shufeng, *ibid.*

39. Jessie Fan, XIAO Jing Jian, and XU Yinzhou, "Student Attitudes toward Free Markets: China and the United States Compared," 189-212.

40. LI Jian, "The Effect of Social Changes on Address Norms in China," 213-230.

41. XU Guangqiu, "The Resurgence of Chinese Anti-Americanism in the Post-Cold War Era," 231-252.

42. McGeary, "How You Can Judge Jiang's Visit," *Time,* November 3, 1997, 73.

43. Jiang's White House toast on October 29 is from Harvey Sicherman, "The Clinton-Jiang Summit: An Uninvited Guest," *Foreign Policy Research Institute Notes,* December 4, 1997, FPRI@AOL.COM

44. Jiang, *ibid.*

45. McGeary, "The Next China," *Time,* March 3, 1997.

PART ONE

TRADITION
VS.
CHANGES

Chapter 2

Political Culture and Social Change: Rethinking China's Experience

LIU Guoli

What are the relations between political cultural and social change? How does political culture influence the pattern of social change? What kind of political culture will precipitate revolution? What type of political culture will facilitate political reform? How have different types of social change helped to shape political culture in different societies? What are the major elements of political culture that contributed to the distinctive patterns of political change in China? This essay examines these questions by analyzing the experience of China in comparison with Japan.

Key historical turning points for China and Japan will be examined in the context of cultural and political changes. The two Asian countries faced serious challenge from Western culture in the late 19th century. Different attitudes and responses of China and Japan toward Western culture will be examined as factors for the failure of Chinese 1898 reform and the success of the Meiji Restoration. The Allied Occupation of Japan partially transformed Japanese political culture. The social revolution in China reflected a struggle between Chinese traditional culture and a new culture. Since 1978, China has entered a period of unprecedented socioeconomic reform and opening to the outside world. The reforms have created a new environment for Chinese culture to flourish.

Understanding Political Culture

The concept of political culture is often discussed but not adequately understood. Political scientist Archie Brown suggests that a political culture "consists of the subjective perception of history and politics, the fundamental beliefs and values, the foci of identification and loyalty, and the political knowledge and expectations which are the product of the specific historical experience of the nations and groups."[1] Robert Tucker defined political culture more comprehensively, "a culture is a society's customary way of life, comprising both accepted modes of thought and belief and accepted patterns of conduct. Political culture is everything in a culture that pertains to government and politics."[2] Understanding political culture is very important for explaining the patterns of political change.

Lucian Pye and Sidney Verba suggest that the concept of political culture provides a useful basis for examining the links between social and economic factors and political performance. In their view, the concept of political culture suggests that "the traditions of a society, the spirit of its public institutions, the passions and the collective reasoning of its citizenry, and the style and operating codes of its leaders are not just random products of historical experience but fit together as a part of a meaningful whole and constitute an intelligible web of relations. For the individual the political culture provides controlling guidelines for effective political behavior, and for the collectivity it gives a systematic structure of values and rational considerations." In essence, political culture "consists of the system of empirical beliefs, expressive symbols, and values which defines the situation in which political action takes place."[3]

Chinese culture and Japanese culture differ from each other in many ways. First, the whole process of Japanese borrowing from the Chinese civilization was quite selective. Japan never totally accepted Confucianism. Second, when facing the challenge of Western powers, Japan was able to learn many aspects of Western culture while keeping its own national identity. In China, the deeply rooted traditional culture, especially the Middle Kingdom mentality, became a big obstacle for learning from Western cultures. Third, Chinese culture was fundamentally transformed by the twentieth century revolutions. Japanese culture was dramatically changed because of the defeat in World War II and the Allied Occupation. Fourth, cultural differences contribute to the emergence of sharply contrasting socioeconomic systems in China and Japan. On the other hand, different socioeconomic systems re-strengthen the two distinctive cultural patterns.

Political power is extraordinarily sensitive to cultural nuances. Therefore, cultural variations are decisive in determining the course of sociopolitical development. The evolution of Confucianism in East Asia produced four distinct political cultures, each with a unique approach to the concept of power. The differences in political culture are important factors accounting for quite different patterns of social development. Pye tries to demonstrate the connections: "In China, the hierarchies of virtue and the idealization of the family made authority an end in itself; in Japan, paternalistic authority was steeled by the purposefulness of intense competition; in Korea, any claim to authority legitimized audacious risk-taking; and in Vietnam, authority became associated with excelling at foreign ways while asserting nationalistic pride."[4] The fundamental polarity of China's traditional culture was between the orthodoxy of Confucianism (the elite culture) and a heterodox blend of Taoism, Buddhism, and more localized belief systems (the rebel culture). The rebel culture, like the Maoism, had a passion for faith, while the Confucianists, like the Dengists, were more restrained in their ideological protestations.[5]

Cultural explanations are essentially explanations of differences. On the one hand, different patterns of social change can be explained to a certain extent by cultural difference. On the other hand, different patterns of social change also bring changes into political culture. One of the controversies within the discipline of comparative politics concerns the appropriateness of explaining political behavior in terms of culture as opposed to more "structural" considerations. The separation of cultural and structural factors may be justified for analytical purposes. If political institution is the structural aspect of political system, political culture is the psychological aspect of the same system. In the real life, it is always difficult to completely separate the two aspects of the political system.

Different Responses to the Western Challenge

Before the industrial revolution, China was one of the most advanced countries in the world with a glorious civilization. However, China failed to meet the direct challenge from the West starting with the Opium War of 1839-1841. In contrast, Japan was able to escape the fate of being forced into a semi-colonial status by the West by conducting a comprehensive reform. What factors contributed to Japan's quick and decisive response to the West and China's initial failures? Scholars have pointed out many different reasons. We would like to highlight some factors here.

Japan is a successful case of modernization in non-Western societies. Tokugawa Ieyasu created a strong, centralized administration that maintained domestic peace for more the two centuries before the Meiji Restoration. The major goals of the Meiji Restoration leaders was to "restore" authority to the emperor and to protect Japan from colonization by the West. The reformers created a powerful central government. They abolished all estate distinctions, doing away with warrior privileges and throwing office open to anyone with the education and ability to hold it. They instituted a system of compulsory military service, although commoners had previously been forbidden to possess arms. They also established a system of universal public education.

The Japanese modernization has unique characteristics. It was carried out under pressure from outside. In other words, it is a defensive modernization. The history of Japan from the 1850s to the 1880s stands out as an extraordinary experience. No other country responded more quickly and successfully than Japan to the challenge of superior Western economic and military technology. Japan is an island nation, which is relatively easy to defend. Japan's locality helped it to escape from conquest and colonial rule. At the same time, Japan was still exposed to a great enough danger to induce a pervasive sense of national crisis among both its leaders and people. Japanese modernization had a strong military feature. The main aim of the Restoration was to make the country strong in order to defend itself against aggression from outside. The homogeneous race facilitated the growth of a strong sense of nationalism. Japan enjoyed the advantage of timing in comparison with the rest of the non-Western world. The Japanese have a strong ability and willingness to learn from advanced countries. Japan's case demonstrates that many elements of the traditional society could be converted into positive factors for achieving modernization.

The Japanese shared the tradition of political unity with the other countries of East Asia, but four factors distinguished them from their near neighbors. In Edwin Reischauer's view, one was their self-conscious distinction from China. The second difference was that in Japan the ideal of uniform, centralized political rule conflicted sharply with the feudal realities of local autonomy and class divisions. The third distinguishing feature from the rest of East Asia was that the nineteenth-century Japanese could find adequate native justification for the great political, economic, and social revolution being forced on them by the menace of the West. Fourth, Japanese were willing to learn from the West even though their original objective was to repel the West and restore their own antique institutions. Still another important heritage of the nineteenth-century Japanese was the strong entrepreneurial spirit, which, though basically associated with economic development, also had political implications.[6]

Another characteristic that has been part of Japan since the period of feudalism is goal orientation rather than ideological orientation. Most Japanese are relatively neutral about religion and ideological politics. Each group competed with neighboring groups to excel in the production of some goods. When the target was articulated by the leadership, most members of the group worked for success on the goal. This characteristic served Japan well when challenged by the West in the mid-nineteenth century and it continues to be valuable today.

Japan responded to the challenge of the West with much greater speed and far more success than China. Obviously in the mid-nineteenth century, even though it had derived a large part of its culture from China, Japan was a very different country, capable of very different response to the Western challenge. The adaptability of Japanese political and social institutions to capitalist principles enabled Japan to avoid the costs of a revolutionary entrance onto the stage of modern history.

One clear and crucial difference between Chinese and Japanese leaders lay in their respective attitudes toward the outside world. The Chinese elites, long accustomed to the idea that China was the unique land of civilization, did not believe that there was much of value to be learned from "barbarians," and could not really see the seriousness of the challenge. Well aware of all that they had learned from the Chinese and even from Korea and India, the Japanese could readily see that there was much to be learned from the West too. Accustomed to thinking of China as far larger, much older, and more advanced than Japan, they had no sublime sense of cultural superiority but rather a fear of inferiority. Thus, when menaced by the West, they did not react with disdain but rather with that combination of fear, resentment, and pride that one associates with nationalism.[7]

The traditional social class divisions also had significant effect. While the samurai, with their feudal military power acted more quickly in meeting challenge from the West than did the Chinese civil bureaucracy, Japanese peasant entrepreneurs and city merchants, with their emphasis on personal economic goals, responded quickly to the new opportunities for foreign trade. The broad and functionally stratified samurai class, constituting around 6 per cent of the total population and including many men close to the details of the economy and administration, also produced a much wider spectrum of responses than did the relatively narrow higher bureaucracy and elite of gentry degree-holders in China. Whereas the samurai was the most highly esteemed class in Japan, the soldier ranked the lowest in the Chinese social scale. Therefore the new Chinese army and the navy of the 1880s and 1890s did not have a good change to develop. With the destruction of the Chinese navy in the Sino-Japanese war of 1894-1895, all the new industries--the ship-yard, the merchant marine, the government operated iron and steel industry--which were to feed the new war machine, generally suffered destruction.

The dynastic cycles characterized the Chinese political history for several thousand years up to the Qing. When a dynasty was on the rising, like the Tang dynasty, the Chinese were self-confident and open to the outside world. But when a dynasty was in decline, like the late Qing, the rulers tended to be afraid of opening to the outside world. By cutting off economic and cultural exchange with the Western world, China missed the chance to enriched itself through industrialization in the nineteenth century. After the Opium War of the 1840, China's door was forced to open by Great Britain and other Western powers. There are profound differences between a voluntary opening and a forced upon open door policy. The former had control of initiatives and conditions; the later had to accept unequal conditions set by the invaders.

The breakdown of the old way of life in China and the building of new ways is a very dramatic story. The major periods of change, considered as a single revolutionary process, may be grouped to form two main stages: a period of anti-dynastic rebellion along traditional lines which was suppressed in a rather traditional fashion, and a period of reform and Westernization which merged into revolution. The most outstanding event in the first phase is the Taiping Rebellion of 1851-1864. The religious leadership of this rebellion was anti-Confucian in ideology and failed to enlist the support of the Confucian literati, who instead supported a restoration of the traditional administration. The Reform Movement at the end of the nineteenth century was led by gentry-literati, who sought to retain Confucian values while strengthening the Chinese state by adopting Western methods. But these scholar reformers sought change through the emperor, from the top down, and had no thought of mobilizing peasant support.[8]

During the decades following the Qing restoration of the 1860s, leading personalities among the Manchu and Chinese officials worked to strengthen the Chinese position by imitating and adapting Western devices and institutions. This movement for "self-strengthening" was posited on the attractive though fallacious doctrine of "Chinese learning as the fundamental structure, Western learning for practical use"--as though Western arms, steamships, science, and technology could somehow be utilized to preserve Confucian values, instead of destroying them. Kang Yu-wei, the most famous reformer in the late Qing, argued that China must reform or perish. In reforming, he believed China should learn particularly form Japan, whose experience was closer in time and space than that of Western countries. In 1898, Kang's view gained the support of the emperor. The emperor issued a series of reform edicts aimed to carry out wide-range reforms. But the Manchu Empress Dowager, Cixi, was able to effect a coup d'etat, deposed the unfortunate emperor, declare herself regent, and rescind his edicts. The failure of the reform again tested the stubbornness of Chinese conservative forces. In comparison with the case of Japan, the elite in China faced far greater threats from below. The reformers were deeply aware and frequently wrote of peasant unrest and the danger it presented to national stability. There were peasant uprisings in the late Tokugawa, but by no means on the same scale and importance as in China. Hence the dissatisfied elite in Japan could support major change with less fear that it might cause a breakdown that would bring the whole system toppling around them. One conclusion emerging from the comparative study of the Meiji Restoration and 1898 reform is that the effective reformers and anti-imperialist forces in both countries came from opposition groups with a deep sense that successful action required strong moral links with the past.[9]

Why could Japan succeed in its military modernization while China did not? The differences in sociopolitical tradition can provide part of the answer. Both China and Japan have been influenced by Confucianism. But there were some difference between the two. In Japan, the social hierarchy was like this: warriors-administrators, peasants, artisans, and merchants. In China, the ranking was from the scholar-officials to peasants, artisans, merchants, and soldiers. When it was necessary to build a strong army to defend the country, Japan enjoyed obvious advantage with this tradition. In several decades after the Meiji Restoration, Japan built a strong army. In 1895, Japan won the Sino-Japanese war. In 1905, Japan defeated the Russian army. The victories in the two major war reduced the internal tensions in Japan, gave the Japanese a stronger sense of nationalism and self-confidence, enhanced Japan's stand in the international community. The large amount of war indemnity from China also provided new capital for Japanese military, economic, and educational development.

According to Richard Solomon, China's difficulties in responding to the changing world of the past century have been largely cultural and psychological in quality rather than institutional or economic. Social "harmony" and peace have long been considered basic and enduring political values in the Confucian tradition. However, these values have contrasted with the historical reality of periods of tranquillity and social order shattered by episodes of uncompromising political conflict and unrestrained violence. Historians of Chinese society have termed this alternating pattern of peace and conflict the "dynastic cycle." Solomon characterizes the individual social orientation in the Chinese tradition as one of dependency.[10] The Confucian political order was centered on the notion that the family was the matrix of society's political relations. The Confucianists sought no "war" with nature, only accommodation; and

China's scientific insights never became translated into attempts to control a threatening physical environment. Commercial activity remained bound within a state-controlled framework of monopoly enterprise, stunting the growth of entrepreneurship which in other societies developed through the stimulus of competition.

Revolutionary Change and Cultural Transformation

The 1911 revolution ended the Qing dynasty and opened the era of the republic. But the ideal of republic was brutally destroyed by the military dictatorship of Yuan Shih-kai. After Yuan died in 1916, Chinese politics degenerated into warlordism. Warlordism was in part an old-style political phenomenon, regionalism carried to the level of power struggle with the support of military forces. One major reason for the failure of the 1911 revolution is that the ideas of political organization through a constitutional parliament and cabinet, which the Republic of China had borrowed from the West, could not be linked up with the Chinese political tradition.

With the fall of the Qing dynasty, the hold of Confucian orthodoxy was gradually broken. The disgust with warlord politics, exposure to new ideas in the West, the growth of native Chinese bourgeois and proletarian classes during the temporary withdrawal of foreign interests during the First World War, and the accumulated anger at imperialist exploitation and betrayal combined to foster an intellectual revolution and the growth of virulent modern nationalism.

The May Fourth Movement of 1919 was not only an anti-imperialist protest but also an attempt to redefine China's culture as a valid part of the modern world. In the attempt, reformers followed different avenues of thought and conduct. Some thinkers concentrated on launching attacks against reactionary or irrelevant old ways such as Confucianism, the patriarchal family, arranged marriages, or traditional education. Some focused on reform of the Chinese writing style by using contemporary vernacular speech patterns in works of literature, thus putting an end to the inevitable elitism that accompanied the mastery of the intensely difficult classical Chinese. Some had a deep interest in Western culture. Most reformers shared a central patriotic ground: they wished for a rejuvenated, unified China that would have the means to cope with the problems of warlordism, an exploitative landlord system, and foreign imperialism. The respect of reformers for Western technological power blended with a yearning to retain some essence of Chinese culture.[11]

The traditional Chinese political culture, as is true of most traditional polities, was nonparticipant for the majority of the people. Involvement in public issues was discouraged by authority's appeals to those elements of personality-anxiety in the face of authority and a willingness to depend on the powerful-which had been developed through childhood socialization. Given the burden of passivity before power which was the legacy of China's traditional political culture, problems of mobilization predominated in the efforts of the Communist party to gain support. Yet maintaining discipline over those mobilized was also a problem, largely because tradition provided no cultural framework for the purposeful, politicized promotion of conflict or for limited ways of challenging established authority.[12]

The revolution overthrew the old regime in China and established a new system under the guidance of Marxism-Leninism and its Chinese version--Mao Zedong Thought. However, those people who adhered to the orthodox Bolshevism were removed from the party leadership in the late 1930s and the 1940s. After the Yenan rectification campaign in the early 1940s, Mao's thought became the dominant theory in Chinese Communist Party. Mao emphasized the revolutionary role of the peasantry and the importance of mass mobilization. The politics under Mao was characterized by the so-called class struggle. One political campaign followed another aimed at creating "new socialist men" and revolutionary culture only led China into a ultra-leftist feudal totalitarianism in the Cultural Revolution.

In contrast, the defeat of Japan and the Allied Occupation of Japan opened a new page in Japanese history. The most immediate task was that of dismantling the Japanese war machine. Military supplies and installations were destroyed and over two million men were demobilized at home. Another three million, plus as many civilians, were repatriated from overseas as a consequence of the allied decision to deprive Japan of all the territorial gains it had made since 1868. The Japanese economic reform was carried out in the following aspects. First, land reform. According to a plan put through in 1948, absentee landlords were required to sell all their land to the government, and even cultivating landlords had to sell any land above ten acres. Once the state acquired the land, it was resold cheap to the tenant farmers by whom it had been worked. Second, labor reform. Trade unions were formed and were given the rights of bargaining and strike. Third, business reform. This reform was aimed at weakening the economic power of the zaibatsu.[13]

The 1947 constitution not only stripped the emperor of all claim to political power but also made clear where actual power did lie-in the hands of the Diet, or parliament. The Allied Occupation was a successful peaceful revolution. Most of the reforms carried out under the occupation enjoyed wide popular support. The development in the last several decades has proven that the basic changes brought by the occupation are endurable. The acceptance of the structure of democracy--a constitutional order based on the sovereignty of the people, representative institutions, civil liberties, free and competitive elections, and the other aspects of political pluralism--is even more remarkable if we recall that this system was imposed on the Japanese by a foreign, occupying power.

Although many continuities undoubtedly can be observed between prewar and postwar political cultures in Japan, it is equally important to appreciate the degree of change in political life and socialization patterns in these two periods. The prewar period did indeed have its paradoxes and important sectorial differences where popular political attitudes are concerned, but that, overall, tendencies were toward authoritarian or "subject" attitudes about the relationship of the ordinary people to political life. The early postwar period witnessed a sharp break with known political tradition. The economic underpinnings of social and political hierarchy in the rural sector were removed by a far reaching land reform, while educational curricula, political institutions, economic organization and labor relations were all subjected to controlled change designed to favor the implementation of political democracy. The sum effect of these reforms, and the widespread and self-conscious concern for democratic behavior, was to disseminate the norms of popular government throughout Japanese society. The postwar Japan experienced an emphasis on democratization in both school curricula and political institutions that was unprecedented in the political development of Japan. Even though the long process of social and political change accompanying modernization in Japan undoubtedly created an especially receptive climate for the catalytic reforms of the postwar period, the postwar period is itself a major epoch in Japan's century of change, and can be seen as encompassing a separate set of causal influences where the attitudes of contemporary citizens are concerned.[14]

After the defeat in World War II, the Japanese devoted to building a rich country. The slogan "enrich the country, strengthen the army," which had summed up the nation's objectives at the time of the first opening of Japan by America's Black Ships, was amended. The second opening of Japan by the American Occupation struck out the second half of the slogan. The first half, "enriching the country," became even more centrally important. In other words, working for the new national goal, i.e., economic growth, has been a key feature of the development of Japan since the end of the Second World War.

Political Culture and Social Change

From above analysis, we have seen connections between political culture and social change. The Japanese experience represents a unique example of conversion from the traditional agrarian to the modern industrial style. A majority of Japanese labor force is now employed in the service sector. This sector generates a larger proportion of the GNP than do the agricultural and industrial sectors. Today, traditional Japanese organizations confront new problems as they face the costs of growth and new modes of citizen participation. Modern science and rationality consist of a key part of Japanese culture today. Japan's social development has been basically evolutionary rather than revolutionary. However, recent development suggests that tensions in Japanese culture and the sociopolitical institutions are growing. More and more Japanese citizens are demanding changes in the political and economic systems. Such demands are reflected in the downfall of the Liberal Democratic Party in 1993 and subsequent formation and reorganizations of several coalition governments. In addition to political instability and economic recession, Japan is also confronting with the issues of how to deal with its aggressive role in World War II, and how to manage its relations with other countries in the post-Cold War environment.

The total crisis in Chinese political and economic systems, and the combination of Marxism-Leninism and Chinese peasant rebel culture facilitated the revolutions in China. As a result, nationalism was strengthened with the creation of the unified independent People's Republic of China. Many traditional patterns of thinking and behavior were replaced by new ways. But the processes of socioeconomic modernization have been consistently creating new tensions. The Cultural Revolution, in one way, was the explosion of the internal tensions. Unfortunately, the Cultural Revolution did not created a new culture but resorted to the worst part of tradition--the feudal totalitarianism. According to Tang Tsou, the Chinese totalistic response contained two elements that turned it into a potentially totalitarian movement and regime. These two elements are the decisive and central role given to political power and the use of violence as a component of political power by a tightly organized elite that regards itself as the vanguard of a particular class. The CCP tried to overcome the total crisis by capturing total power and to re-establish effective political authority in order to bring about a fundamental transformation of the social structure, to establish a new economic system and a new society, and to inculcate new values and attitudes espoused by new men. This approach appealed to many Chinese because it made sense to them. For events in twentieth-century China proved to their satisfaction that education, science, industry, and a new culture could not be developed fast enough to preserve China as a national entity and that they could not be developed without first establishing an effective government. At the same time, an effective system of political authority could not be established without at the same time solving some of the most pressing social and economic problems. Because the approach seemed sensible, its inherent and submerged totalitarian tendency, as well as its many potentially devastating consequences, was overlooked or minimized and rationalized if they were recognized.[15]

Viewed from this perspective, political development since 1949 can be understood as a conflict between the inherent totalist tendency with rural orientation and the need to recognize the indispensable roles played by various functional groups in the urban sector in achieving economic growth and modernizing the society and the state. But in dealing with the intellectuals, who constitute one of the most important functional groups in any modern society, the party instituted a series of policies which finally led to disastrous results in the Cultural Revolution. In 1956 Mao called for a hundred flowers to bloom, a hundred schools to contend, soliciting criticism of the party from intellectuals, stimulating criticism from educated public opinion to build a fire under the party to cause it to turn away from "dogmatism, sectarianism, bureaucratism," its alienation from the people. The intellectuals were more outspokenly hostile than Mao had imagined. The reaction to the criticism in the party was a fierce and extended anti-rightist campaign, a purge of those who had spoken out and a tightening up of party control and ideological orthodoxy. The anti-rightist campaign set the atmosphere for and led into the ultraradical economic policies of the 1958 Great Leap Forward.

The anti-rightist movement in 1957 marked a turning point in the relationship between the state and society. From that time to 1966, no social groups outside the party would offer any active resistance to the party. The penetration of politics into other spheres of society broke through all non-party barriers. Only internal party restraints existed. By breaking most of the internal party restraints and suppressing with some success whatever institutional and political pluralism existed within the party, the Cultural Revolution of 1966-1976 marked the culmination of the totalitarian tendency that found expression in the program and actions of the ultraleftists. Political actions undertaken by the Red Guards or mobs mobilized or encouraged by a group of leaders or simply permitted and protected by them broke through almost all restraints, legal, political, civic, social, and traditional, in utter disregard of common decency in an attempt to change man and society. "Politics takes command" degenerated into "politics may assault or overwhelm everything." The cult of personality derived strong implicit support from the cult of the emperor although the new cult was attached to a charismatic, revolutionary leader and used to effect revolutionary changes, whereas the traditional cult was an institutionalized practice to preserve the political system.[16]

In traditional China, the political bureaucracy had always dominated the merchant and other classes and groups; its belief system achieved ideological hegemony. When the total crisis in the twentieth-century demanded total solutions, when a revolutionary party monopolizing power was determined to transform the whole society, and when modern means of communications and control and modern organizational forms and techniques were available, the tradition of politics in command easily and imperceptibly slid into the trend toward totalitarian control.

Thus after a protracted revolution of half a century to eliminate "feudal" ideas and practices, the CCP found that these very ideas again erupted at the very top of its political system and threatened to overwhelm everything it had fought for. No wonder "feudalism" is now considered by many to be the main source of errors committed in the past and the main obstacle to modernization at the present time. The 1981 Party Resolution on CCP history largely explained the Cultural Revolution on the basis of "feudal remnants" in Chinese authority relations. The post-Mao era of "opening to the world" revealed the fact that while China had changed, there is still much cultural continuity. The theory of culture opens the door to possibly one of the best ways of understanding and forecasting change. For it is culture that establishes both the parameters of likely change and the dynamics that drive and shape social and political change. In contrast to China's concentration in political conflicts before 1978, the postwar Japan has been concentrating on economic development. Some analysts attribute Japan's economic success to its unique pattern of government-business interaction. The essential characteristic of the Japanese government-business relationship is that the business community and the various government departments have been in close communication with each from the days of the Meiji Restoration. The result is a style of industrial development which has allowed Japanese business considerable initiative and independence even when subject to administrative guidance facilitated by a variety of government aid and incentives.

One decisive factor for Japan's fast economic growth is the quality and quantity of the skilled workers, engineers, managers, and civil servants produced by the educational system. The educational level in prewar Japan was already comparable or even higher than that of many Western countries. However, it was heavily influenced by the militarist indoctrination. The Allied Occupation carried a fundamental reform in education. Like the constitution and multiparty politics, the occupation-fostered education system proved destined to survive in Japan. In postwar times, education has been always a national priority of Japanese government.

A remarkable difference between the patterns of change in China and Japan is the distinction between reform and revolution. When facing the powerful challenge from the West, both Japan and China tried to carry out reform to adapt to the changing world. But Japan carried out more thorough reforms than China did and was able to proceed along an orderly way. The Manchu dynasty could not solve its deep sociopolitical crises. After the collapse of the Qing in 1911, China entered a long period of revolutionary movement which led to the establishment of the centralized Communist government in 1949. In Japan, the deepening of socioeconomic crisis in the 1920s and the 1930s led to the growth of militarism. The Allied Occupation gave Japan an opportunity to carry out fundamental reforms which laid the foundation for Japan's postwar development.

Some tentative conclusions can be drawn from the above analysis: First, difference in political culture does matter in deciding the pattern of political change. Japan's political change since the Meiji Restoration can be seen as a process of integrating the traditional Japanese culture with Western civilization. The Japanese have been successful in modernizing their social, political, and economic systems while keeping its distinctive national characteristics. In China, the orthodox Confucianism proved to be ineffective and incompatible with the modern Western values. After the revolution, the Chinese system built upon the Stalinist model turned out to be incapable of dealing with the urgent task of modernization.

Second, the modernization of technology must accompanied by building of new infrastructure including the appropriate sociopolitical system. The contrast between Japan's fast success and China's initial failure in their modernization drives demonstrated the vital importance of transforming the whole system rather than only part of the system. Modernization is not simply a mechanical application of new technology. It must be a coordinated growth of modern institutions, scientific ideas, and advanced technology.

Third, the role of the state is important in modernization. In Japan, the government initiated modernization by reforming the economic and political system, and by direct entrepreneurship at the beginning stage of industrialization. In the close interaction between government and business, Japanese government has been always very supportive to business, particularly to the big corporations. The China, the weak Qing regime failed to support the growth of national capitalist forces. The warlord politics brought chaos and violence that deprived the chances for peaceful economic development. Mao and other leaders of the People's Republic were eager to build a strong state and a modern economy. By building a central planned economy, however, individual entrepreneurship was restrained to the minimal. The strategy of self-reliance and autarky cut off the link between China and the world economy. In the age of opening to the world, the changing role of the state and the growth of the economy are the two sides of the same story.

Fourth, the history of the modernization Japan demonstrated in many ways not only the ability of modern institutions and orientations to coexist with traditional ones for very substantial period of time, but also the manner in which traditional attitudes and practices can be of great positive value to the modernization process. One example is the use of the emperor as a institution to attract the popular loyalty and support for the modernizing reforms. In the Chinese revolution, Mao successfully employed the tradition of peasant rebellion for revolutionary mobilization in the countryside.

Fifth, in the contemporary period, the link between political culture and social change is growing stronger than that of the old ages. The development of the communication and transportation technology has greatly enhanced the scope and speed of cultural exchanges. A trend of "internationalization" is becoming more influential in Japan, while nationalist sentiment is also growing in some sections of the society. If the former trend continues to gain support over the later, Japan will become a country that is easy for other countries to live with. In China, the conflict of different schools of thinking is becoming more intense and more relevant for socioeconomic and political development. China's reformers must answer the following questions: What kind of new ideas to embrace? What old thinking to discard? How to manage the conflict of between change and continuity?

The above analysis only solved a small portion of the questions posed at the beginning of this essay. Most old questions remain to be answered; new questions are emerging from time to time. This is a truly exciting time for theoretical inquiry. Research approach plays a critical role in making scientific progress. Experience shown that it was unproductive to conduct purely structural analysis of politics. On the other hand, political culture approach cannot provide a complete explanation of the dynamics of political change. It seems ideal to have a combination of cultural and structural approaches.

Notes

1. Archie Brown, "Introduction," in Archie Brown and Jack Gray ed., *Political Culture and Political Change in Communist States* (London: Macmillan, 1977), 1.
2. Robert C. Tucker, *Political Culture and Leadership in Soviet Russia: From Lenin to Gorbachev* (New York: W. W. Norton & Company, 1987), vii.
3. Lucian W. Pye and Sidney Verba ed. *Political Culture and Political Development* (New Jersey: Princeton University Press, 1965), 7.
4. Lucian W. Pye with Mary W. Pye, *Asian Power and Politics: The Cultural Dimensions of Authority* (Cambridge: Harvard University Press, 1985), 59.
5. Lucian W. Pye, *The Mandarin and the Cadre: China's Political Cultures* (The University of Michigan: Center for Chinese Studies, 1988).
6. Edwin O. Reischauer, *The Japanese Today: Change and Continuity* (Cambridge: Harvard University Press, 1988), 232-237.
7. Edwin O. Reischauer and Albert M. Craig, *Japan: Tradition & Transformation* (Boston: Houghton Mifflin Company, 1978), 122-123.
8. John King Fairbank, *The United States and China* (Cambridge: Harvard University Press, 1983), 176-178.
9. John E. Schrecker, "The Reform Movement of 1898 and the Meiji Restoration as Ch'ing-i Movements," in Akira Iriye ed. *The Chinese and the Japanese: Essays in Political and Cultural Interactions* (Princeton: Princeton University Press, 1980), 104.
10. Richard H. Solomon, *Mao's Revolution and the Chinese Political Culture* (Berkeley: University of California Press, 1971), 1, 5.
11. Jonathan D. Spence, *The Search for Modern China* (New York: W. W. Norton & Company, 1990), 313.
12. Solomon, *Mao's Revolution and the Chinese Political Culture*, 194, 210.
13. Guoli Liu, *States and Markets: Comparing Japan and Russia* (Boulder: Westview Press, 1994), 43-45.
14. Bradley M. Richardson, *The Political Culture of Japan* (Berkeley: University of California Press, 1974), 13-14, 241.
15. Tang Tsou, "Back from the Brink of Revolutionary-`Feudal' Totalitarianism," in Victor Nee and David Mozingo ed. *State and Society in Contemporary China* (Ithaca: Cornell University Press, 1983), 82-83.
16. *Ibid*, 86-87.

Chapter 3

The Social Origins of Historical Changes in Freedom of Mate Choice under State Socialism: The Case of Urban China

XU Xiaohe

Introduction

Research on historical transformation in freedom of mate choice in non-socialist or agrarian societies is not new.[1] However, studies on the social origins of historical changes in the marriage system under state socialism are not only scarce, but also isolated and tangential. With the earlier self-quarantine of the PRC (People's Republic of China) and the recent collapse of the former Soviet Union and the Eastern blocks, opportunities to conduct such research are limited. In the case of urban China, although the impacts of industrialization, urbanization, and Westernization on freedom of mate choice in the pre-1949 society have been well documented,[2] the extent to which the Chinese Revolution, the socialist party-state, and especially the recent economic reforms further transformed the historical marriage system is still a subject of debate.[3] This paper will employ recent survey data collected from urban China to scrutinize the debated issues and, therefore, shed further light on the social transformation of marriage arrangements under state socialism.

Freedom of Mate Choice:
Two Systems of Marriage Arrangements in China

In historical China, the extended family was normative and the society, by and large, was based on familial and kinship ties. In order for elders to maintain their control over family members and to keep families intact over generations, marriages were parentally arranged. Parents, along with the older family members, not only governed but also monopolized the process of mate selection. As a consequence, some couples did not even get to see each other until the wedding night. Marriages that were contracted under such extreme circumstances were known as "blind marriages".[4] Similarly, it was also the custom to betroth children at a very early age so that the bride could be brought up in the home of her future parents-in-law. In some areas of China, especially in the South, betrothing even an unborn child was favored.[5] In this paper, for the purpose of discussion, both blind marriages and betrothals arranged by parents or senior kin are defined as *historical marriage arrangements*, which are characterized by little or no freedom of mate choice. According to Yang, the goal of this historical marriage arrangement was to provide protection and security to the family unit at the expense of the intimacy and emotional well-being of the marrying children.[6] For centuries, this traditional institution of marriage has been a major source of personal frustration and unhappiness in China.[7] Numerous earlier studies reported that parentally arranged marriages often led to the ill-treatment of wives, and under certain circumstances, led to rape and even suicide.[8]

Contrary to parentally arranged marriages, marital unions initiated by couples themselves and based on mutual attraction and consent are referred to as *free choice marriages*, or simply, *love match marriages*.[9] These marriages are typically characterized by a good deal of freedom in mate selection and a high degree of premarital intimacy. Many China scholars contended that the emergence of this type of marriage can be dated back as early as the 1920s and 1930s.[10] It is important to note, however, that free choice marriage in urban China does not necessarily imply a Western style, love match marriage as Macfarlane described in *Marriage and Love in England*.[11] On the contrary, an intensified period of courtship and a sentimental romance, as it is often idealized and tinted in the West, may not exist, albeit the marriage may well be based on free choice and free will.[12] In sharp contrast to parentally arranged marriages, it has been reported that free choice marriages demonstrate a much stronger tendency toward companionship and yield far more satisfaction with marital relationship.[13]

So, to what extent has freedom of mate choice that underlies the two different systems of marriage arrangements in urban China been transformed? What are the changing forces at work? The answers to these questions are the objectives of this paper.

The Goode Model

To answer these questions, *the Goode model* of family change is considered. Since the 1960s, Goode's emphasis on the diminution of the extended family as a consequence of industrialization has remained the prototype for comparative family studies.[14] In simple terms, the Goode model can be stated as follows. With growing industrialization and urbanization in agrarian societies, there is a worldwide transformation from the extended family system toward the conjugal family system. Because industrialization demands a mobile population, there is an attenuation of familial control over the adult offspring. Thus, there is a greater emphasis on the marital relationship with mate selection the prerogative of the prospective spouses rather than of their kin groups. This, in turn, gives rise to a transformation in the marriage system toward freer marriages.

Applying the Goode model to Chinese society, Whyte and Parish found that in the late Mao era there was a widespread disapproval of traditional marriages in urban China and, "the norm of freedom of mate choice has been fairly widely diffused and accepted among the general population."[15]

In addition to the support for the Goode model, they also asserted that the absence of a Western style dating culture in urban Chinese society (in the earlier 1980s) was largely "due to CCP (Chinese Communist Party) organizational and political resources that are not present among other industrializing agrarian societies."[16] However, according to them, the role of the Chinese government's change efforts in transforming historical marriage arrangements is only secondary. The socialist transformations of the Chinese economy and society, which took place swiftly and often violently in the 1950s, are identified as the primary causes of changes in the marriage and family systems.[17]

Bring the State Back in: The Modes of Social Organization Approach

Despite the pervasiveness of the Goode model, several challenges and critiques have emerged over the past decade. Davis and Harrell bluntly but correctly commented:

[The] Goode model, which drew heavily on the experience of Western Europe and North America and could not have used material on China after 1960, never dealt with a state as intrusive and coercive as the Chinese. In Goode's overview, state regulation of family life was a consequence of industrialization and urbanization. Clearly, in the People's Republic of China state power and policies have been the creators, not the creations, of a transformed society.[18]

This is to argue that the party-state, as an important change agent under state socialism, was never adequately discussed and addressed by Goode. Therefore, the possibility of complex pathways of changes in marriage arrangements, due to the party-state's intervention, was left out of the Goode model.[19]

In order to overcome theoretical limitations in the Goode model, particularly its inability to deal with the pivotal role played by the party-state, the current research also uses the modes of social organization approach, which has been substantiated by Thornton and Fricke and Thornton and Lin.[20] In the context of Chinese society, this approach suggests that in the family mode of organization (e.g., in historical China), people experience all their activities, associates, information, means of subsistence, cosmology and authority within a family frame of reference or within a matrix of kinship relations.[21] As the family mode of social organization shifts to the nonfamilial institutions such as schools, factories, government and the mass media, departures from the traditional familial authority and control uniformly take place. Consequently, marriage decisions are transformed from the parental generation to autonomous youth themselves. This arrangement, in turn, shifts the center of marital unions from familial obligations to individual welfare.

By framing the change in these terms, the party-state that is capable of transforming authority patterns and the locus of control can be incorporated. Guided by these two theoretical perspectives, the following change mechanisms are identified.

Theoretical Mechanisms and Hypotheses

The Historical Context, the Party-State, and the Locus of Control

Historically, the strong state was an intimate part of Chinese society. According to the Confucian value system, the state and the family should be in harmony and mutually supportive. At times when conflict arose between family and state, the state often emerged victorious.[22] This tradition was largely inherited by the Communist Party when it came to power in 1949 with a proclaimed mandate to reform the family and to destroy the "feudal" marriage system. Because the state in contemporary China is so closely tied to personal lives, teasing out the relationship between how the state implements its programs and the individual's freedom of marriage is critical. The position of the CCP has been consistently in favor of free choice marriages. The Marriage Regulations of 1931, published as a formal document of the Chinese Soviet Republic, stated that freedom of marriage involved much more than simply the free will of the parties. It included absence of coercion from any third party, and connoted the absence of any material considerations or obstacles when marriage was concluded.[23] The Marriage Law of 1934 of the Chinese Soviet Republic and the marriage regulations in the border areas from 1939 to the middle of the 1940s contained comparable stipulations. Not surprisingly, similar regulations were twice codified in the 1950 and 1980 Marriage Laws.

Regardless of whether or not the socialist state has fully achieved it goals by advocating freedom of marriages, its efforts may have, at least in part, transformed the locus of authority and control from parents to the state, both directly and indirectly. The direct efforts made by the state were, by and large, realized through the enactment of marriage laws and related policies. In addition, campaigns launched by the party-state, as a part of the marriage and family reform programs, also effectively prevented the occurrence of arranged marriages, most especially during the period of nation building and socialist transformation in the 1950s. Moreover, throughout the PRC history, state policies, including those related to freedom of marriages, are effectively implemented through grass roots organizations. The Communist Party, the Communist Youth League (CYL), and the worker's and the woman's organizations all become the gatekeepers of the state's regulations. Even in the reform era, sanction can still be taken to penalize individuals who violate state policies.[24] This rudimentary control of Chinese state socialism over the individual's behavior with regard to freedom of mate selection led to paradoxical policies. On the one hand, the party-state promotes freedom of marriage by outlawing the arranged marriage system; on the other hand, the party-state strictly regulates and even monitors the individual's premarital interactions, making sure that Western "free love" and dating culture will not threaten the "spiritual civilization" of Chinese state socialism. Added to these direct controls by the party-state is the fact that many Chinese urbanites have become socially and economically dependent on their work units (employers) for their life chances, especially before the economic reforms.[25] Therefore, the freedom that they obtained from their parents and families might have been lost, in part, to the party-state.[26]

The indirect influences of the party-state on freedom of marriages can be further classified into two kinds. First, the influence can come from changes in the structural arrangements of society that people then react to, perhaps inducing changes in mate choice behavior, such as the expansion of education, urbanization and industrialization. Second, throughout the PRC history, the CCP has made constant efforts to directly get people to change their attitudes toward marriage choice by politicizing marriages.[27] Thus, the notion of freedom of mate choice in contemporary China has been sporadically shaped and reshaped by a variety of political campaigns inaugurated by the state. This is particularly noticeable in the Mao era when politics dominated all aspects of social life. For instance, during the Culture Revolution, while arranged marriage was attacked as a feudalist evil element from the old society, romantic love was also denounced as a bourgeois sentiment. Despite this irony, the party was able to successfully reach out and exercise control over individuals ideologically through the manipulation of thought reform and other political movements. Given the state's ability to intervene in civil lives in urban China, it is hypothesized that those who were CCP or CYL members, employed by the state-owned firms, agencies or organizations, and grew up with "good" class origins while marrying, may enjoy more freedom of mate choice than their counterparts. And this relationship is also hypothesized to depend on the historical contexts in which the marriage took place.

Formal Education and the Locus of Control

With respect to freedom of mate choice, formal education has powerful and profound impacts on young people in terms of shaping and reshaping the opportunity structure, human capital and gender role outlooks, therefore, leading to revolutionary changes.[28] In historical China, marriage arrangement was a matter of parental control and familial authority. As the responsibility of socialization was taken over by public schools and carried away from parents and the home, the locus of parental control and familial authority was shifted. With the communists coming to power after 1949, the expansion of public and ideological education took the power and influences farther away from parents and the family.

School provides youngsters with opportunities. These opportunities are not only structural, but cultural as well. The former may refer to the opportunity to mingle with the opposite sex and to learn basic skills for a future career. The latter may include the opportunity to develop new gender role beliefs, to have access to new ideas, and especially to be exposed to different cultures. In fact, the school system in China is an extremely important source of getting information about Western culture, particularly the ideology of romantic love. Though exposure to Marxism (the hegemonic ideology in all Chinese schools since 1949) is different from exposure to other Western ideas, with regard to freedom of mate choice, the message from both sources is surprisingly similar. Since various opportunities provided by the expansion of education can weaken parental and familial authority and enable youth to acquire new gender role outlooks, it is hypothesized that individuals who received more formal education will be more likely to reject traditional marriage arrangements in favor of free choice marriages than those who had little or no formal education.

Non-Family Employment, Wage Income, and Economic Independence

It has long been argued that in non-industrialized societies, young people have to depend upon their parents and the family unit for economic considerations such as land and property inheritance. While societies industrialize, they are able to leave their parents to seek alternative employment opportunities outside the family (e.g., to work in factories). As a result, the family is no longer organized around economic production and subsistence, and parental control stemmed from property relationships is undermined. Industrial development in post-revolutionary China can be used to exemplify this process. In 1956, the Chinese government completed nationalization of private business. During the massive push (known as the Great Leap Forward) to collectivize the urban economy in 1958, every woman under the age of forty-five was required to work full-time outside the family. Thus, full-time housewives under the age of fifty virtually disappeared.[29] More significantly, after the 1960s, the wage income, in essence, became the sole income source for each individual and family unit in urban China. These drastic industrial and economic changes that occurred uniformly across urban China gave young men and women an enormous amount of economic independence.

However, freedom in selecting marriage partners based on nonfamilial employment and wage income is expected to vary. If the parents have used their connections to arrange the job for their child, and if the child sends much of his or her wages home to the family as remittances, then freedom in finding a mate may be minimal.

A twist, however, exists, restricting seemingly autonomous youth. Though urban Chinese youth may be increasingly free from parental and familial control, they may be, however, subject to a different type of control forced upon by the socialist state. It is true that the vast majority of young urban Chinese are employed and do have wage income but, given the nature of the redistributive economic system under state socialism, they become involuntarily dependent upon the government of the Chinese socialist state through their work units.[30] Due to a great degree of social, economic and political dependency of young people on their superiors and work units for necessary resources, any further increase in freedom of mate choice might be constrained.[31] Nevertheless, industrial development and nonfamilial labor force participation, especially by young women, are hypothesized to foster the emergence and development of the new system of marriage arrangements in urban China.

Age at First Marriage and Freedom of Marriage

In historical China, individuals in traditional marriages were likely to marry at very young age.[32] Parents arranged marriages for their children at relatively young ages for a variety of reasons: wanting grandchildren as soon as possible to continue family line and to increase the family labor force, getting the daughter-in-law's domestic help, and controlling children at younger ages. As the average age at first marriage is steadily increasing for both males and females throughout the post-1949 period in urban China, one should expect that the number of arranged marriages will decline.[33] However, the direct effect of the increased average age at first marriage on shifts in freedom of mate choice may hinge on other change mechanisms, such as the government's intervention through marriage age regulations, an increase in educational attainment and a higher rate of nonfamilial labor force participation. Therefore, it is argued that the expansion of education, industrial development and the state's regulations on marriage age might have collectively delayed young people's marriages. Thus, it becomes increasingly difficult for parents to arrange their children's marriages. In this paper, age at first marriage will be primarily used as an intervening mechanism to explain historical transformation in freedom of mate choice in urban China.

Rural-Urban Migration

As most agrarian societies have experienced, free choice marriages are prevalent only in the urban population, whereas in the countryside arranged marriages remain popular. Because educational and economic opportunities are not widely available in the rural areas, previous studies consistently found that exposure to and experiences in the urban environment foster the shift toward a new system of marriage arrangements.[34] In other words, rural to urban migration in the general population can provoke a large-scale shift from parentally arranged to free choice marriages. However, due to a peculiar pattern of rural to urban migration under Chinese state socialism, this urbanization effect is cohort specific. During the first decade of the PRC, there was a large wave of migration of young people moving from the countryside into cities as a result of the communist victory. But the population flow was quickly cut off by the government and a strict migration policy was implemented. In 1955, the Chinese government established a household registration system nationwide as a part of a plan to control rural to urban migration. Therefore, under this and other related regulations, opportunities for migration from rural to urban areas were extremely rare after the first decade of the communist government. This leads to a hypothesis that individuals who have strong rural backgrounds will be more likely to experience historical marriage arrangements than their urban counterparts. This should hold true especially for those who were married during the socialist transformation period.

DATA AND METHODS

Data

In order to empirically test these theoretical mechanisms and hypotheses, two sets of survey data collected from urban China, the People's Republic, were used. The first survey was conducted in Chengdu, the capital of Sichuan Province in 1987 and the second was carried out in Baoding, a major industrial city of Hebei Province in 1991. The two surveys can be used to account for a possible regional variation in urban China: the North represented by Baoding and the South represented by Chengdu.[35] It is important to understand that both cities may not be typical of urban areas in China. They do, however, in their own rights, represent a new research trend that probes into the inland cities of China. The decision to use combined surveys was based on the consistent outcomes of a systematic comparison of the changing trends in freedom of marriages in Baoding and Chengdu with those reported by previous studies (e.g., the Five City Study).[36] Moreover, the decision to merge the two samples is also due to the fact that a significant proportion of the questionnaire items are identical across the two surveys. In addition, both surveys utilized a similar random, multistage sampling technique and a pretested questionnaire. While the Chengdu survey interviewed 586 ever-married Chinese women between the ages of 20 and 70, the Baoding Survey interviewed 671 married women and their husbands with similar age intervals. In order to match the Chengdu data, only wives' responses in the Baoding survey were considered.

Measures

Dependent variable. The dependent variable in this study is freedom of mate choice of ever-married urban Chinese women at their first marriages. Multiple indicators were used to operationalize and indicate this latent and theoretical concept. As shown in Table 1, the questionnaire items from one to five were employed to capture different aspects of freedom of mate choice in terms of who had the final say about selecting a marriage prospect and how much autonomy was granted by parents to their children, whereas the items from six to eight were taken to measure the degree of premarital intimacy shared by the respondents and their grooms. To facilitate data analysis, except for items four and five, all six items were chosen to be synthesized so that a composite variable can be constructed and used to model the social origins of historical changes in freedom of mate choice. Because of the unequal measurement scales, these six items were first z-scored to achieve a common metric, and then summated and averaged. The resulting index variable, the freedom of mate choice index, ranges from -1.63 (indicating historical marriage arrangements with little or no freedom of mate choice) to +1.41 (indicating love match marriages with a great deal of freedom of mate choice). The reliability coefficient was .63, an acceptable value.

Contextual variables. To depict changing trends in freedom of mate choice, multiple indicators of the dependent variable were cross-classified by five macro-contextual variables: five marriage cohorts, each representing a turning point and drastic policy shift in the political history of the PRC. This marriage cohort approach traces ever-married urban Chinese women over time in order to assess the effects of the common sociopolitical experiences on the extent of freedom of mate choice. By doing so, it is assumed that there is an intra-cohort stability and persistence of attitudes and behavior related to marriage decisions.[37] The first marriage cohort included those who were married prior to the victory of the Chinese revolution from 1933 to 1948.[38] The second marriage cohort consisted of those who were married in the early Mao period; the massive socialist transformation of the Chinese economy and society from 1949 to 1957. The third marriage cohort was formed by including those who were wed in a "high-Mao" period from 1958 to 1965. The fourth marriage cohort was created by grouping those who contracted their first marriages during the ten-year period of the Cultural Revolution from 1966 to 1976. Finally, the last marriage cohort included those who married in the post-Mao or reform era, from 1977 to the survey years, 1987 for Chengdu and 1991 for Baoding respectively. Based on the observed trends in freedom of mate choice in Baoding and Chengdu, the

Table 1. Historical Changes in Freedom of Mate Choice in Urban China, 1933-1991 (in percentages)

Questionnaire Items	1933-48	N	1949-57	N	1958-65	N	1966-76	N	1977-91	N
1. Type of Marriage Arrangement										
Arranged	68.3	82	27.4	51	3.4	6	.8	2	1.2	6
Intermediate	20.8	25	41.4	77	57.1	100	58.8	144	61.9	306
Free Choice	10.8	13	31.2	58	39.4	69	40.4	99	36.8	182
Total	100	120	100	186	100	175	100	245	100	494
2. How Couples Knew Each Other										
Via Introduction	92.4	110	81.8	153	66.3	116	66.5	163	70.4	348
Self Initiation	7.6	9	18.2	34	33.7	59	33.5	82	29.6	146
Total	100	119	100	187	100	175	100	245	100	494
3. Who Provided Introduction										
Friends and Relative	29.0	31	42.1	64	65.9	83	66.1	113	72.4	252
Parents and Relative	43.9	47	30.3	46	19.8	25	16.4	28	14.9	52
Match Makers	16.8	18	10.5	16	4.0	5	5.3	9	4.3	15
All Others	10.3	11	17.1	26	10.3	13	12.3	21	8.3	29
Total	100	107	100	152	100	126	100	171	100	384
4. Where Couples Met										
At Work	22.7	5	30.0	18	45.9	39	40.9	47	39.6	93
At School	4.5	1	8.3	5	21.2	18	17.4	20	11.5	27
All Others	72.7	16	61.7	37	32.9	28	41.7	48	48.9	115
Total	100	22	100	60	100	85	100	115	100	235
5. Who Played an Important Role in Mate Selection										
Parents & Others	75.0	90	61.3	114	55.7	97	53.1	130	58.3	287
Self	25.0	30	38.7	72	44.3	77	46.9	115	41.7	205
Total	100	120	100	186	100	174	100	245	100	492
6. Number of Romances Including the Husband										
No Romance	79.0	94	37.3	69	18.5	32	9.0	22	3.7	18
One	19.3	23	57.3	106	65.9	114	65.6	160	66.1	325
Two	1.7	2	3.8	7	12.7	22	16.0	39	17.5	86
Three & More	0.0	0	1.6	3	2.9	5	9.4	23	12.8	63
Total	100	119	100	185	100	173	100	244	100	492
7. Frequency of Dating Husband										
Never	69.0	80	48.4	90	24.0	42	20.0	49	6.7	33
Rarely	19.0	22	20.4	38	32.0	56	29.4	72	19.9	98
Sometimes	5.2	6	17.7	33	21.7	38	21.6	53	26.0	128
Often	6.9	8	13.4	25	22.3	39	29.0	71	47.4	233
Total	100	116	100	186	100	175	100	245	100	492
8. How Much in Love When Married										
Not in Love	24.8	29	10.9	20	2.3	4	0.8	2	0.8	4
.	8.5	10	3.8	7	3.4	6	1.6	4	1.6	8
.	29.9	35	21.7	40	16.7	29	18.1	44	8.3	41
.	23.1	27	27.2	50	23.0	40	24.3	59	25.6	126
Very Much in Love	13.7	16	36.4	67	54.6	95	55.1	134	63.6	313
Total	100	117	100	184	100	174	100	243	100	492

first three marriage cohorts were later consolidated to form one larger marriage cohort, which, along with cohorts four and five, were eventually used in the multivariate analysis.

Predictor variables. In modeling the social origins of historical changes in freedom of mate choice, numerous predictor variables were considered.

First, the family class origins of the wife and the husband were classified into five categories with 1 = capitalist and landlord, 2 = peasant, 3 = urban poor, petty merchant and craftsmen, 4 = worker, and 5 = cadre, professional and intellectual. It should be emphasized that the ranking order of this variable is not important to the analysis, but the political connotation is. Second, party membership at marriage was recoded into 1 for no party affiliation or others, 2 for Communist Youth League, and 3 for Chinese Communist Party. Notice that the party membership variable is the best individual-level measure of the party-state available in the two data sets. Therefore, it is somewhat risky to make cross-level inferences. Third, educational attainment of the wife and the husband at first marriage was recoded into five levels with 1 = illiterate, 2 = elementary school, 3 = middle school, 4 = high school, and 5 = university or more. Fourth, since property rights of work units determine the degree of autonomy, prestige, and resources in urban China,[39] the respondent's employment status at first marriage was combined with the kinds of work units in which they were employed. There were four categories for wives and three for husbands: 1 = government agency, public organization and state firm, 2 = collective firm, 3 = others including joint venture and private business, and 4 = not employed (for wives only).[40] It is crucial to understand that the work unit variable underlies two related theoretical concepts, namely employment status and the level of state control. Finally, age at first marriage and the rural origin index (for wives only) were included as covariates. The rural origin index is a summary measure of the respondent's rural residence and ruralness. In addition, two dichotomized variables, city (1 for Baoding and 2 for Chengdu), and post-marital residence (1 for other residential arrangement and 2 for neolocal residence) were included for the purpose of statistical control.[41]

Statistical Methods

Multiple Classification Analysis was used to examine the social origins of historical changes in freedom of mate choice.[42] The MCA procedure under ANOVA in SPSS was used to estimate the observed and adjusted means of the dependent variable for categories of the predictor variables.[43] The eta coefficient for the unadjusted means and the beta coefficient for the adjusted means were also reported along with the mean values to assess the relative importance of each predictor variable.[44] In MCA multivariate analyses, the adjusted means were not only adjusted for other categorical predictors already in the model, but for covariates as well. For the MCA covariates, the "raw" regression coefficients were reported.[45]

Multivariate MCA analyses of historical changes in freedom of mate choice were carried out separately for the wife and husband predictors. Because a marriage is a union of two, it makes sense to examine in what ways the husband's socioeconomic characteristics are linked to the changes in marriage arrangements. Moreover, three multivariate models were fit for both the wife and the husband predictors. Each of these three models corresponded to the contextual or marriage cohort variables discussed above. Technically, these models, across marriage cohorts, assume complex interaction effects between the predictor variables and the marriage cohort variables on freedom of mate choice. This analytic strategy allows an investigation of how shifts in state policies may affect shifts in freedom of mate choice at the macro-societal level.

RESULTS

Historical Changes in Freedom of Mate Choice in Urban China

Over the past several decades, marriages and marriage relationships in urban China have undergone momentous changes.[46] What has been changing - and changing dramatically - is the shift in freedom of mate choice. Table 1 summarizes this historical change across five marriage cohorts from wives' point of view. Shown in the table are two simultaneous shifts in the twin spheres of parental arrangements of marriages and children's premarital intimacy. Collectively, the questionnaire items one through five in the table indicate that, across marriage cohorts, there was a sharp decline in parental control over or parental involvement into whom the young should marry. For instance, arranged marriages virtually disappeared after the second marriage generation (item one). More and more young women in urban China started on their own love journeys (item two), met their sweet hearts at work or schools (item four), and made their own marriage choices (item five). In a similar fashion, the questionnaire items six through eight in the table show that there is also a great increase in premarital intimacy shared by the bride and the groom. More urban Chinese women developed romantic feelings toward their marrying husbands (item six), regularly dated them (item seven), and fell in love with them while putting on the wedding dresses (item eight). Compared to historical marriages, these are indeed revolutionary changes.

The foregoing presentation indicates there is a general support for the conclusion that a fundamental shift from parentally arranged toward free choice marriages has taken place in urban China. Historical marriages that were once firmly controlled by parents, kinsmen or other senior relatives have largely been left behind. In the course to pursue love and personal happiness, today's women in urban China have shown more self-determination in making a marriage decision than the previous generations. While a Western style dating culture has yet to emerge (very few women had ever had more than two romances), the majority of young women in urban China are no longer marrying primarily for familial obligations. Instead, they are marrying for their own welfare, including love.

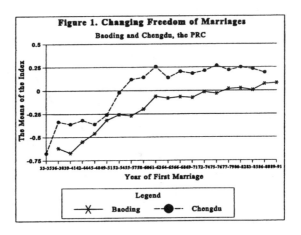

Figure 1. Changing Freedom of Marriages
Baoding and Chengdu, the PRC

The "Stalled" Transformation

To further visualize the trends, Figure 1 displays the freedom of mate choice index variable (a summary measure of items 1, 2, 5, 6, 7 and 8 in Table 1) across numerous smaller marriage cohorts for both Baoding and Chengdu. As can be seen from the figure, the two curvilinear lines are essentially parallel to each other with the Chengdu women reporting a higher level of freedom of marriages. Leaving this notable regional variation aside, a common pattern of changes in freedom of mate choice across cities emerges: the fundamental shift in freedom of mate choice presented in the figure appears to be "stalled."[47] That is, the transformation in freedom of marriages in urban China has decelerated and even leveled off after the earlier 1960's marriage cohorts. This pattern of change differs notably from the changes observed in other Asian societies, particularly in Japan and Taiwan.[48] In both cases, the changes in freedom of mate choice are gradual and accompanied by a well developed Western style dating culture.[49]

Then, what factors have determined such a unique pathway to the greater degree of freedom in mate choice under Chinese state socialism? Why did not China follow either Japan or Taiwan's path? For what reason has the transformation in freedom of marriages in urban China become "stalled?" These are the questions to which we will turn next.

The Social Origins of Historical Changes in Freedom of Mate Choice

Given the "stalled" transformation, the two-city combined data were divided into three subsamples in order to address cohort-specific questions. These three subsamples are characterized by three marriage cohorts used to reflect large-scale socioeconomic changes and shifts in state polices: 1933-65, 1966-76, and 1977-91. The following multivariate analyses are, therefore, conducted accordingly.

The socialist transformation period, 1933-65. To establish the theoretical linkages between the hypothesized mechanisms and freedom of mate choice, the multivariate MCA models for the first marriage cohort are estimated and displayed in Table 2 and Table 3. Considering the wife predictors (Table 2), everything else being equal, educational attainment, work unit and employment status, and age at first marriage have large and significant impacts on freedom of mate choice. More specifically, prior to first marriages, those who had formal education above the middle school level are 20 to 30 times more likely than illiterates to have the freedom to select their own future husbands, with the university graduates possessing the greatest autonomy in decision making. With regard to employment outside the home and wage income, the categorical means show that those who were not employed at first marriage are two times more likely than those who were employed by the state to experience arranged marriages (-0.5 vs. -0.15). As expected, the older the brides, the better the chances are for them to think and decide for themselves. For the husband predictors (see Table 3), the stories become more telling. While the effect of age at first marriage diminishes, family class origin and party membership become important, along with educational attainment and employment status. That is, after controlling for other factors, if the marrying husbands were born into a cadre family (vs. a peasant family), college educated (vs. illiterates), associated with the CCP (vs. none) and employed by the state (vs. other), their marriages are more likely to be based on free choice. The evidence from the wife and husband models jointly provides support for the research hypotheses, with exception to the rural background variable (which is statistically insignificant, although the direction agrees with the theoretical expectation, -0.01).

Table 2. Multivariate Analysis of Freedom of Mate Choice in Urban China (the Wife Predictors)

	Marriage Cohort: 1933-65			Marriage Cohort: 1966-76			Marriage Cohort: 1977-91		
	N	Means[1]	Means[2]	N	Means[1]	Means[2]	N	Means[1]	Means[2]
City									
Baoding	215	-.52	-.51	127	-.10	-.04	261	.07	.11
Chengdu	235	-.15	-.17	112	.42	.37	207	.47	.42
Eta/Beta		.27***	.24***		.58***	.45***		.49***	.38***
Family Class Origin									
Capitalist and Landlord	34	.15	-.33	10	.25	.11	1	.99	.88
Peasant	276	-.51	-.35	106	-.07	.12	177	.07	.19
Urban Poor	77	-.13	-.35	41	.32	.17	37	.33	.23
Worker	34	-.23	-.27	48	.23	.17	173	.35	.28
Cadre	29	.25	-.15	34	.44	.19	80	.40	.31
Eta/Beta		.37***	.07		.44***	.07		.37***	.14_
Educational Attainment									
Illiterate	137	-.89	-.68	1	-.45	-.24	3	-.30	-.13
Elementary School	152	-.32	-.27	59	.03	-.14	56	.21	.30
Middle School	65	.08	-.06	93	.14	.16	202	.24	.25
High School	62	.08	-.16	46	.14	-.14	169	.29	.24
University or More	34	.42	.02	40	.36	.17	38	.25	.23
Eta/Beta		.62***	.36***		.25**	.06		.13**	.09
Party Membership									
No or Others	353	-.44	-.33	165	.04	.12	316	.18	.22
CYL	45	.27	-.30	52	.47	.21	133	.41	.31
CCP	52	-.11	-.34	22	.14	.23	19	.35	.37
Eta/Beta		.33***	.02		.39***	.09		.26***	.12*
Work Unit and Employment Status									
State	191	.00	-.15	172	.19	.16	317	.25	.25
Collective	40	-.52	-.36	44	-.01	.15	132	.24	.25
Other	22	-.19	-.31	6	.05	.08	7	.21	.33
Not Employed	197	-.62	-.50	17	.15	.04	12	.27	.34
Eta/Beta		.42***	.23***		.17	.07		.03	.04
Postmarital Residence									
Other Arrangements	225	-.60	-.44	96	.00	.07	223	.23	.22
Neolocal	225	-.06	-.22	143	.24	.12	245	.27	.28
Eta/Beta		.39***	.17***		.26***	.14**		.06	.07_
Age at First Marriage (covariate)[3]			.04***			.002			-.002
Rural Origin Index (covariate)[3]			-.01			.012			.003
R-Square			.526			.390			.278

[1] The unadjusted means are the observed means on the dependent variable within categories of the predictors; [2] The adjusted means are estimated from a M(ultiple) C(lassification) A(nalysis) ; [3] Unstandardized regression coefficient; _p<.10; *p<.05; **p<.01; ***p<.001.

The results, thus far, demonstrate that the modes of social organization approach is quite plausible. Namely, when the modes of social organization shifted from familial to nonfamilial institutions during the dramatic socialist transformation, the locus of control changed. As schools and the labor force participation were expanded by the People's

Table 3. Multivariate Analysis of Freedom of Mate Choice in Urban China (the Husband Predictors)

	Marriage Cohort: 1933-65			Marriage Cohort: 1966-76			Marriage Cohort: 1977-91		
	N	Means[1]	Means[2]	N	Means[1]	Means[2]	N	Means[1]	Means[2]
City									
Baoding	160	-.49	-.46	111	-.09	-.05	225	.08	.10
Chengdu	203	-.02	-.05	106	.44	.40	202	.47	.46
Eta/Beta		.34***	.31***		.59***	.51***		.49***	.45***
Family Class Origin									
Capitalist and Landlord	15	.30	-.12	14	.37	.10	6	.29	.21
Peasant	241	-.37	-.28	106	.00	.15	168	.10	.23
Urban Poor	61	.04	-.20	28	.32	.18	33	.44	.37
Worker	40	-.07	-.09	51	.31	.23	143	.32	.27
Cadre	6	.45	.35	18	.36	.17	77	.43	.33
Eta/Beta		.32***	.14*		.37***	.09		.35***	.12
Educational Attainment									
Illiterate	33	-.61	-.45	NA	NA	NA	1	-.58	-.04
Elementary School	132	-.41	-.34	38	.07	.10	35	.28	.28
Middle School	77	-.13	-.11	69	.05	.10	201	.25	.27
High School	63	-.20	-.25	46	.29	.25	123	.26	.25
University or More	58	.26	.01	64	.27	.23	67	.33	.33
Eta/Beta		.38***	.21***		.25***	.15_		.13	.08
Party Membership									
No or Others	199	-.34	-.32	115	.19	.22	254	.23	.28
CYL	35	.20	-.21	33	.01	.19	98	.43	.30
CCP	129	-.16	-.10	69	-.01	.08	75	.16	.19
Eta/Beta		.24***	.15**		.35***	.15*		.24***	.09
Work Unit and Employment Status									
State	272	-.12	-.15	189	.19	.17	332	.26	.27
Collective	26	-.60	-.37	13	-.01	.17	69	.28	.27
Other	65	-.51	-.53	15	-.03	.11	26	.28	.31
Eta/Beta		.26***	.22***		.15	.04		.02	.03
Postmarital Residence									
Other Arrangements	168	-.47	-.36	84	.03	.09	203	.24	.24
Neolocal	195	-.02	-.12	133	.25	.22	224	.29	.30
Eta/Beta		.33***	.18***		.25***	.14**		.07	.08_
Age at First Marriage (covariate)[3]			.012			-.009			-.008
R-Square			.375			.421			.281

[1] The unadjusted means are the observed means on the dependent variable within categories of the predictors; [2] The adjusted means are estimated from a M(ultiple) C(lassification) A(nalysis) ; [3] Unstandardized regression coefficient; _p<.10; *p<.05; **p<.01; ***p<.001.

Republic, parental power was weakened. Consequently, freedom in mate selection increased. If the effects of education and nonfamilial employment can be comprehended with ease, the effects of the "good" family origin, party membership, and state employment may require some pondering. Why would the increased political control by the party-state foster freedom of mate choice? Why should state employment and Party membership promote such behavioral change? The answers to these questions probably lie in the historical contexts of the changes. Throughout the 1950s, the young People's Republic saw an unprecedented reform in the marriage system: the new Marriage Law was enacted in 1950 and a large-scale campaign to implement the law was launched and sustained. The major theme of the campaign, of course, was to eliminate "feudal" arranged marriages (child bride and forced marriages) and to advocate free choice marriages. According to a government directive dated January 17, 1953, the People's Government of all levels was to take the lead and conduct an organized and systematic movement to implement the new marriage law:

> Discussion meetings on the Marriage Law in all factories, villages, organizations, government agencies, army units, schools, and street committees were held. Mistakes would be given definite punishment in order to educate the people themselves as well as others; cruelty cases were to be handled by the courts, after sufficient preparation, in public trials.[50]

Under such tremendous pressure from the party-state, individuals who were party members and who worked in the state-owned enterprises were expected and even forced to adopt a new way of life, including getting married via free choice. As the party cadres were looked up to as vanguards, it is not too difficult to understand why they would prefer autonomy to parental arrangements for their own and their children's marriages. In short, as the empirical evidence shows, during the national building and socialist transformation period, the party-state was a major source that induced changes in marriage arrangements in urban China.

The Cultural Revolution period, 1966-76. The results derived from multivariate MCA analyses presented in Table 2 and Table 3 for the Cultural Revolution cohort are almost shocking in contrast with those from the socialist transformation cohort. For the wife predictors, the effects as hypothesized and observed thus far have uniformly vanished, except for control variables. The mean levels of freedom in mate choice are surprisingly similar, cutting across all categories of family class origin, educational attainment, party membership, work unit and employment status, and age at first marriage. For the husband predictors, the pattern is similar. Net of control factors, the educational effect is weak, therefore, marginal; only party membership remains statistically significant, albeit with a reversed direction. Unlike the first marriage cohort, the mean levels of freedom in mate choice for party members are lower than for

CYL members and substantially lower than for nonparty members (0.08 vs. 0.19 and 0.22). This finding makes some sense only if it is argued that party members might be subject to more stringent controls by the party-state as compared to other social groups. This is not to say the party-state reversed its policy during the Cultural Revolution, thus advocating parentally arranged marriages. As marrying for love was condemned as bourgeois,[51] who would risk life to become an antirevolutionary? The fact is that during the Cultural Revolution, the dominant sociopolitical discourse was radical and extreme, which often deliberately connected the institution of marriage with the ultimate course of the revolution. In order to replace parental control with state control, the party branches were granted authority to check on the prospects, ensuring that they were indeed politically appropriate mates for their members.[52] As such, it can be argued that it is entirely conceivable that the party member's freedom of marriage was seriously circumscribed.

In addition to the effect of the husband's party membership, the systematic weakening power of the predictor variables is extremely intriguing. This could be due to "the homogenizing effect" that can be explained as follows. By examining the adjusted means of freedom in mate choice for all predictors across the first and the second marriage cohorts (see Table 2 and Table 3), there appears to be an uneven increase, meaning that social groups that enjoyed less selection freedom in the earlier marriage cohort improved faster than those groups that previously enjoy more freedom in mate choice, given that they all improved. In turn, the variation among social groups (categories) decreased. Substantively, this means that, under the extreme circumstances during the Cultural Revolution, no particular social groups were either advantaged or disadvantaged in comparison with other social groups, with reference to mate choice freedom. Put differently, ideological or behavioral control was not only homogeneously enforced by the party-state, but homogeneously approved and accepted by the general population as well. The unisex, blue, green or gray-colored uniforms that were once extremely fashionable during the Cultural Revolution can serve as the best examples. Moreover, with the interrupted educational and occupational systems, social inequality which stemmed from educational achievement and occupational prestige was significantly reduced. Therefore, personal characteristics included in the analysis are no longer important factors.

The reform era, 1977-91. The Deng reform era brought yet another reversal in state policies. As the door of Chinese society is opened to the West, and as Hollywood movies, rock and roll, and Western youth culture "invaded" urban China, another dramatic shift in freedom of mate choice is expected. However, this has yet to occur. The multivariate MCA models reported in Table 2 and Table 3 are almost a mirror image of the results derived from the Cultural Revolution cohort. Neither the wife variables nor the husband variables explain freedom of mate choice well (the R-square values are much smaller than those in the previous two marriage cohorts). The only significant effect is the wife's party membership, after all other effects are removed. Once again, family class background, educational attainment, employment status and the work unit provided neither advantages nor disadvantages for those who were marrying. Even though the brides who were party members continued to be more autonomous than their counterparts, this result should be interpreted with caution due to a small number (19) of cases. It is, nevertheless, speculated that the reason for most of the hypotheses to be rejected is because free choice marriages in urban China may have already become a strong social norm, regardless of variations in individuals' socioeconomic characteristics. In other words, if a threshold on the continuum of freedom in mate choice can be identified, the vast majority of individuals will be located around the threshold. Therefore, not much variation is left to be explained (the variance in the freedom of mate choice index is indeed smaller than its counterparts in the previous two marriage cohorts). In order to capture more variation, freedom of mate choice, as a theoretical concept, should be expanded to encompass dimensions such as premarital sexual relationship, premarital pregnancy, and abortion. This can certainly be served as a topic for future research.

DISCUSSION AND CONCLUSIONS

In China, historically, the extended corporate families wanted to exercise parental control over mate choice and arranged marriages before children became too old and headstrong. Since marriages amounted to the continuation of the family line more than anything else, they were seriously negotiated and arranged either through go-betweens or elderly relatives who were trusted members of the family. Therefore, a lack of affection between the bride and groom was irrelevant or even desirable because the son's loyalty was supposed to remain primarily toward his parents, not his wife. Like the long-survived "feudal" social structure, this historical Chinese marriage system was relatively stable over centuries. However, the process of rapid urban and industrial development that started around the turn of the century began to alter the Chinese social structure and the family system. Consequently, China embarked on a course that eventually undermined parental authority stemmed from a combination of chronological and generational age hierarchy, the lineage system, and the norm of filial piety. The evidence provided by the

Chengdu and Baoding data shows that the two intertwined aspects of freedom in mate choice - parental control over children's marriages and children's premarital intimacy - have all steadily changed since the 1930s. This paper finds evidence of three forms of marriage arrangements that deviate considerably from the historical form of parentally arranged marriages: 1) parents arranged the marriage but asked their children's consent; 2) the young people selected their own mates but asked their parent's approval; and 3) the young people married without asking parental consent. It is also evident from this research that the increase in freedom of marriages was drastic under the young People's Republic. By the time a large-scale socialist transformation and nation building was completed prior to the Cultural Revolution, Chinese state socialism had essentially eradicated arranged marriages in the urban areas.

Through statistical modeling, it is found that among many social origins, the expansion of education, increased labor force participation outside the home, cadre family origin, party membership, state employment and increased age at first marriage are the roots of changes in freedom of marriages. Results further indicate that the party-state is one of the major forces influencing freedom of mate choice in urban China. The Chinese party-state is not only organizationally instrumental, but also ideologically pugnacious in promoting free choice marriages. This, in turn, seems to suggest that the socialist transformation of Chinese urban society and marriage reform have been at the heart of structural changes.

With respect to the "stalled" transformation in freedom of mate choice after the period of the socialist transformation and nation building, there are two tentative explanations. First, it has been argued that after the massive socialist transformation, the sociopolitical structure of urban Chinese society has remained virtually unaltered. During the Cultural Revolution, the party-state's intervention in regulating youth through powerful organizational controls was so far reaching and ubiquitous that the variation in freedom of marriage across the spectrum of sociopolitical status diminished (except for the husband's party membership). Similarly, it has been argued that in the economic reform era, free choice marriages have become a prevailing norm that cuts across all social groups, therefore personal characteristics along with weakened state controls become relatively unimportant. Meanwhile, although a Western style dating culture might be welcomed by urban Chinese youth, it is clearly incongruent with the party's ideology.

In summary, the above findings and discussions point to a complex and nonlinear pathway of changes in freedom of mate choice under Chinese state socialism. This finding not only suggests a need to re-theorize our conceptual frameworks of family change but also exhorts comparative family scholars to re-think the Goode model of family change, which may have indeed glossed over the crucial role played by the party-state in the case of socialist China. Finally, this research suggests that, in addition to the Goode model, the modes of social organization approach should be utilized. It has been argued that, to study changes in freedom of mate choice under state socialism, the important change agent, the party-state, must be brought back in.

Notes

1. For Taiwan, see Arland Thornton and Hui-Sheng Lin, *Social Change and the Family in Taiwan* (Chicago: the University of Chicago Press, 1994). For Southeast Asia, see Noriko. O. Tsuya and Minja Kim Choe, "Nupitiality Change in Asia: Patterns, Causes, and Prospects." Unpublished paper, 1994. For Japan, see Orpett Susan Long, "Japanese Family Change." Unpublished paper prepared for the Annual Meeting of the American Sociological Association, Chicago, Illinois, August 21, 1987; Takashi Mochizuki, "Changing Pattern of Mate Selection." *Journal of Comparative Family Studies* 12 (Summer 1981): 317-328; and Robert Blood, *Love Match and Arranged Marriage*, (New York: The Free Press, 1967). For India, see Giri Raj Gupta, "Love, Arranged Marriage and the Indian Social Structure." *Journal of Comparative Family Studies* 1 (Spring 1976): 75-85. For Turkey, see G. Litton Fox, "Love Match and Arranged Marriage in a Modernizing Nation: Mate Selection in Ankara,Turkey." *Journal of Marriage and the Family* 37 (2 1975): 180-193. For other societies, see William Goode, *World Revolution and Family Patterns* (New York: The Free Press, 1963).

2. Goode, *World Revolution and Family Patterns.* Olga Lang, *Chinese Family and Society* (New Haven: Yale University Press, 1946). Marion J. Levy, *The Family Revolution in Modern China* (New York: Octagon Books, Inc., 1963). C. K. Yang, *The Chinese Family in the Communist Revolution* (Cambridge: MIT Press, 1959).

3. Deborah Davis and Stevan Harrell (ed.), *Chines Families in the Post-Mao Era* (Berkeley: University of California Press, 1993). M. J. Meijer, *Marriage Law and Policy in the Chinese People's Republic* (Hong Kong: Hong Kong University Press, 1971). Judith Stacey, *Patriarchy and Socialist Revolution in China* (Berkeley and Los Angeles: University of California Press, 1983). Isabelle Thireau, "The Power of the State and the Power of Traditions. The Evolution of Peasant Marriage in China from 1949 to 1982." *Archives Europeennes de Sociologie* 27(2 1986): 260-293. Martin K. Whyte and William Parish, *Urban Life in Contemporary China* (Chicago: University of Chicago Press, 1984). Arthur Wolf, "The Preeminent Role of Government Intervention in china's Family Revolution." *Population and Development Review* 12(March 1986): 101-116. Margery Wolf, "Marriage, Family, and the State in Contemporary China." *Pacific Affairs* 57(Summer 1984): 213-236.

4. Whyte and Parish, *Urban Life in Contemporary China.*

5. Meijer, *Marriage Law and Policy in the Chinese People's Republic.*

6. Yang, *The Chinese Family in the Communist Revolution.*

7. Ellen Efron Pimentel, *The Determinants of Marriage Quality in Urban China* (Doctoral Dissertation, the University of Michigan, 1994). Xiaohe Xu, *The Determinants and Consequences of the Transformation from Arranged Marriages to Free Choice Marriages in Chengdu, China* (Doctoral Dissertation, the University of Michigan, 1994). Xiaohe Xu. "Measuring the Concept of Marital Quality as Social Indicators in Urban China." *Social Indicators Research* 37(1996): 189-206. Xiaohe Xu, "The Cross-Cultural Differences and Similarities in Conceptualizing and Predicting Marital Quality of Ever Married Women in Urban America and China: Detroit and Chengdu." *International Journal of Sociology of the Family* 26 (Autumn 1996): 55-78. Xiaohe Xu and Martin K. Whyte, "Love Matches and Arranged Marriages: a Chinese Replication." *Journal of Marriage and the Family* 52(8 1990):709-722.

8. Goode, *World Revolution and Family Patterns.* Lang, *Chinese Family and Society.* Levy, *The Family Revolution in Modern China.* Meijer, *Marriage Law and Policy in the Chinese People's Republic.*

9. Alan Macfarlane, *Marriage and Love in England* (New York: Basil Blackwell, 1986). Blood, *Love Match and Arranged Marriage.*

10. Hugh Baker, Chinese Family and Kinship (New York: Columbia University Press, 1979).

11. Macfarlane, *Marriage and Love in England.*

12. A. Wolf, "The Preeminent Role of Government Intervention in china's Family Revolution."

13. Xu, *The Determinants and Consequences of the Transformation from Arranged Marriages to Free Choice Marriages in Chengdu, China.* Xu. "Measuring the Concept of Marital Quality as Social Indicators in Urban China." Xu, "The Cross-Cultural Differences and Similarities in Conceptualizing and Predicting Marital Quality of Ever Married Women in Urban America and China: Detroit and Chengdu." Xu and Whyte, "Love Matches and Arranged Marriages: a Chinese Replication."

14. See Goode, *World Revolution and Family Patterns,* and *The Family,* 2nd. ed. (Englewood Cliffs, N.J.: Prentice-Hall, 1982).

15. Whyte and Parish, *Urban Life in Contemporary China,* p.135.

16. Ibid., p.147-151.

17. Also see Martin K. Whyte, "Changes in Mate Choice in Chengdu." Pp. 181-213 in Deborah Davis and Ezra F. Vogel (ed) *Chinese Society on the Eve of Tianmen* (The Council on East Asian Studies, Harvard University, 1990)

18. Davis and Harrell, *Chines Families in the Post-Mao Era,* p. 5.

19. For similar critiques, see Stacey, *Patriarchy and Socialist Revolution in China;* A. Wolf, "The Preeminent Role of Government Intervention in china's Family Revolution", and M. Wolf, "Marriage, Family, and the State in Contemporary China."

20. See Arland Thornton and Thomas Fricke, "Social Change and the Family: Comparative Perspective from the West, China, and South Asia." *Sociological Forum* 2 (4 1987): 746-779, and Thornton and Lin, *Social Change and the Family in Taiwan.*

21. Thornton and Lin, *Social Change and the Family in Taiwan,* p. 9.

22. M. Wolf, "Marriage, Family, and the State in Contemporary China."

23. Meijer, *Marriage Law and Policy in the Chinese People's Republic.*

24. The "totalitarian" model is often used to analyze Chinese politics, implying a total control of state over society. While the model captures important characteristics of state socialism, it also tends to miss other autonomous sociopolitical processes. Deviating from the model, it is argued that social institutions and individuals under Chinese state socialism can and still maintain varying degrees of autonomy. There is no doubt that at times state control may be absolute (e.g., during the Cultural Revolution), it is also true that at times individuals may be able to find just enough room to negotiate.

25. Xueguang Zhou, Nancy Brandon Tuma, and Phyllis Moen, "Stratification Dynamics under State Socialism: The Case of Urban China, 1949-1993." *Social Forces* 74(3 1996):759-796.

26. See Martin K. Whyte, "Wedding Behavior and Family Strategies in Chengdu" Pp. 189-216 in Davis, Deborah and Stevan Harrell (ed) *Chines Families in the Post-Mao Era* (Berkeley: University of California Press, 1993).

27. Elisabeth Croll, *The Politics of Marriage in Contemporary China* (Cambridge: Cambridge University Press, 1981). Lucy Jen Huang, "Mate Selection and Marital Happiness in the Mainland Chinese Family." *International Journal of Sociology of the Family* 2(9 1972):121-138.

28. Thornton and Fricke, "Social Change and the Family: Comparative Perspective from the West, China, and South Asia."

29. Davis and Harrell, *Chines Families in the Post-Mao Era.*

30. See Andrew Walder, *Communist Neo-traditionalism: Work and Authority in Chinese Industry* (Berkeley: University of California Press, 1986). Zhou, Tuma, and Moen, "Stratification Dynamics under State Socialism: The Case of Urban China, 1949-1993."

31. Whyte, "Wedding Behavior and Family Strategies in Chengdu."

32. See Goode, *World Revolution and Family Patterns,* and Yang, *The Chinese Family in the Communist Revolution.*

33. Whyte and Parish, *Urban Life in Contemporary China.*

34. Fox, "Love Match and Arranged Marriage in a Modernizing Nation: Mate Selection in Ankara,Turkey." Goode, *World Revolution and Family Patterns,* and Yang, *The Chinese Family in the Communist Revolution.*

35. The Chengdu survey is a collaborative project between the University of Michigan and Sichuan University. This project is jointly directed by Martin K. Whyte, Yuan Yayu and the author. The research is supported by grants from the U.S.-China Cooperative Science Program of the National Science Foundation, the United Board for Christian Higher Education in Asia, Sichuan University, and China's State Educational Commission. The Baoding survey is also a collaborative project between the University of Michigan and Beijing University.

36. See Jonathan Unger, "Urban Families in the Eighties: An Analysis of Chinese Surveys." Pp. 25-49 in Davis, Deborah and Stevan Harrell (ed) *Chines Families in the Post-Mao Era* (Berkeley: University of California Press, 1993). Xiaowei Zang, "Household Structure and Marriage in Urban China: 1900-1982. *Journal of Comparative Family Studies* 1 (Spring 1993): 35-44.

37. Norman B. Ryder, "The Cohort in the study of Social Change." *American Sociological Review* 30 (6 1965): 843-861.

38. Note that age truncation bias may be present in this marriage cohort due

to the fact that this cohort includes the oldest respondents in the data. Because they married young, their marriages are likely to be parentally arranged. See Thornton in Thornton and Lin (1994) for further discussion.

39. Nan Lin and Wen Xie, "Occupational Prestige in Urban China." *American Journal of Sociology* 93(1988):793-832. Zhou, Tuma, and Moen, "Stratification Dynamics under State Socialism: The Case of Urban China, 1949-1993."

40. For the Baoding Survey, in many cases, educational attainment, party membership and work unit of the wife and the husband at first marriage had to be imputed from current status due to a large number of missing records. This may cause some bias in earlier marriage cohorts as a result of upward mobility.

41. Post-marital residence may imply a reversed causal relationship with freedom of mate choice. However, given the difficult housing situation in urban China, whose who can manage to live away from the parents after marriage must have a sufficient amount of social resources or already employed by the state and lived independently prior to the marriage. Hence, the variable may limply the respondent's family structure before the marriage, which we failed to obtain good measures. It is also entirely possible, but unlikely, that the parents made both arrangements: marriage and post-marital residence. Nevertheless, post-marital residence was treated only as a control variable. Its implications will not be discussed.

42. Frank M. Andrews, James N. Morgan, John A. Sonquist, and Laura Klem, *Multiple Classification Analysis.* 2nd. ed. (Ann Arbor: The University of Michigan, 1973).

43. SPSS, *SPSS Reference Guide* (SPSS Inc., 1990).

44. The squared eta coefficients for the unadjusted means and the squared beta coefficients for the adjusted means can be interpreted as the proportion of variance in the dependent variable explained by a particular predictor variable..

45. SPSS, *SPSS Reference Guide.*

46. Emily Honig and Gail Hershatter, *Personal Voice* (Stanford: Stanford University Press, 1988). Xiaohe Xu, "Changes in Marriage Relations in Urban China: 1933-1991." in Phylis Lan Lin and David Decker, (ed.). *China (The Mainland and Taiwan) in Transition: Selected Essays* (Indianapolis, Indiana: University of Indianapolis Press, 1997). Xiaohe Xu, "The Prevalence and Determinants of Wife Abuse in Urban China." *Journal of Comparative Family Studies* 3(Autumn 1997):280-303. Xiaohe Xu, "Divergence or Convergence: The Transformation of Marriage Relationships in Urban America and China." *Journal of Asian and African Studies* (Forthcoming, 1998).

47. Also see Xu and Whyte, "Love Matches and Arranged Marriages: a Chinese Replication."

48. Xu, *The Determinants and Consequences of the Transformation from Arranged Marriages to Free Choice Marriages in Chengdu, China.*

49. See Takie Sugiyama Lebra, *Japanese Women: Constraint and Fulfillment* (Honolulu: University of Hawaii Press, 1984); Long, "Japanese Family Change" and Thornton and Lin, *Social Change and the Family in Taiwan.*

50. Meijer, *Marriage Law and Policy in the Chinese People's Republic,* p. 131.

51. Huang, "Mate Selection and Marital Happiness in the Mainland Chinese Family." Thireau, "The Power of the State and the Power of Traditions. The Evolution of Peasant Marriage in China from 1949 to 1982."

52. Croll, *The Politics of Marriage in Contemporary China.*

Part Two

Rural Challenge

Chapter 4

The Role of Villager Committees in Rural China's Stability

HONG Zhaohui

Introduction

The relationship between democracy and stability is a controversial issue. As Richard Bernstein and Ross Munro argue in their popular book, *The Coming Conflict with China*, "China's leaders are probably sincere in their equation of democratic reform with social chaos."[1] Samuel Huntington also claims that democratic elections are not necessarily positive for social stability. In Huntington's view, "In many, if not most, modernizing countries elections serve only to enhance the power of disruptive and often reactionary social forces and to tear down the structure of public authority." Therefore, Huntington believes, "the problem is not to hold elections, but to create organization."[2] In other words, as a meaningful tool for the objective of social stability, an election must create an effective political organization with a high degree of popular participation. Thus, a political organization is a key factor in ensuring stability after the election.

This perception provides a useful approach to observe and understand China's rural organization and rural stability in the past twenty years. At present, the most democratic organizations with free elections and high levels of participation in China are the more than one million villager committees (VCs) (*cunmin weiyuanhui*) representing 900 million villagers. This paper will focus on the positive impact of VCs on rural stability from the 1980s to the 1990s through intensive discussion of VCs emergence, development, election processes, organizational operation, and internal structure. To be sure, in a country of more than one million villages, one should be cautious before generalizing from the small number of cases that I investigated and studied. Nevertheless, I have studied every stage of VCs operation, and I conclude that China's VCs are a positive force in maintaining social order during this critical transition stage from an agricultural society to an industrial society.

The Driving Forces and Development of VCs

In general, similar to the Household Responsibility System (HRS) and the Township and Village Enterprise (TVE), the VC was also initiated and promoted by Chinese farmers and its development was characterized by three principles: "from bottom up," "doing prior to reporting," and "heated inside but cooled outside." Its general direction was initiative from bottom first, legalizing it by government following, and finally promoting it nationwide.

To a large measure, there were four basic stages for VCs development over the past twenty years. The first one (1980-1981) was a period of spontaneous autonomy. Chongwai Village in Luocheng County, Guangxi Province, established its first VC in February of 1980 which initially was designed to solve field irrigation problems. To protect the village from theft and robbery, the Village of Xin in Yishan County, Guangxi, also set up its VC in December, 1980.[3] Basically, this stage of VCs was stimulated and promoted by the collapse of the people's commune after the Cultural Revolution. Farmers, consequently, lost their traditional protection from the collective and had to create a new organization to protect themselves. Although VCs in this phase were quite premature, this great initiative provided a political and organizational condition for a successful transition of rural economic reform.

The second stage (1982-1984) was characterized by vague governmental legislation. In response to extensive demands for villager autonomy, the central government issued some general reports and acts to offer vague regulations for VCs without specific and distinct clarifications. The new constitution of 1982 says "the urban resident committee or the villager committee is a local autonomous organization." In early 1983, the number one document of the Central Committee of the Chinese Communist Party (CCP) officially initiated a project which established township to replace the former communes and set up villages to substitute for the former brigade. It directly promoted a massive emergence of VCs. From 1984, the CCP began to consider an Organic Law on Villager Committee.

However, VCs at this stage were "new bottle with old wine" because they just changed a name of rural organization without substantial democratic elections and popular participation. Essentially, VCs were still subject to their higher authority and the CCP without effective autonomy.[4]

The third phase of VCs development (1985-1990) was processing of both government legislation and local election simultaneously. On November 24, 1987, China's congress officially issued the Organic Law on Villager Committees of the People's Republic of China (for trial implementation), which would be effective on June 1, 1988. This significant law established the framework for conducting direct elections by secret ballot with multiple candidates for the VC. Under this law, each VC includes three to seven members headed by a director and an associate director. All the members are elected to a three-year term. Designed by the Law, the VC is able to manage the village's finances and, in some cases, its enterprises, and organizes projects to develop the infrastructure.

The CCP in 1990 also implemented an exemplary program of villager autonomy.[5] At the same time, six provinces, including Fujian, Zhejiang, Gansu, Hubei, Guizhou, and Hunan, took a pioneer effort of issuing specific and detailed regulations and guidelines for the villager elections based upon the principles of the Organic Law. By the end of 1989, VC officials in 14 provinces had been elected.[6] However, the necessity of VCs was still an arguable issue and the elections were also far from professional in this period.

The last stage (1991-present) was to enjoy nationwide promotion and effective implementation of local elections and villager autonomy. By December, 1992, all provinces, including Tibet, completed at least the first run of VC elections. Meanwhile, twenty provinces finished their second run of elections in which 1,004,349 VCs and 4,308,878 village officials were involved. By early 1997, VCs in eighteen provinces conducted the third term of direct elections.[7] Some provinces like Fujian, Hebei, and Heilongjiang will conduct the fourth term of VC elections which will improve mutuality of local elections.[8] By July, 1995, twenty-four provinces issued their implemented regulation of villager elections and reached more than 90% of voter turnout rate.[9]

In particular, the quality of elections in this fourth period has been significantly improved by an VC Election Regulation of the central government aimed at standardizing all specific processes and technical requirements of election. To a large measure, almost all elections during this stage followed the principles of secret ballot, direct election, multiple candidates for each position, transparent count, and 3-year fixed term.

General speaking, many scholars at present are underestimating and even discrediting these unprecedented democratic elections because few, if any, believe that the Chinese communist regime, which essentially favors dictatorship and authority, will allow any real and substantial democracy in favor of self-government at the local level.[10] In fact, the CCP in the past twenty years of economic reform always violated the fundamental principles of the communist ideal by means of promoting market economy, stock market, privatization, land speculation, shareholding system, layoff of workers, and bankruptcy of the state-owned enterprises. Skepticism about China's village democracy today is similar to a popular suspicion of China's market economy twenty years ago. This kind of reasonable doubt cannot be modified unless we review the historical driving forces of local elections which will indicate that local election and villager autonomy, similar to the former HRS and TVS, were essentially forced by new economic development and were only choices without better alternatives for the CCP in the 1980s.

According to Huntington's theory, "social and economic changes necessarily disrupt traditional social and political groupings and undermine loyalty to traditional authorities."[11] Huntington believes that a purely traditional society would be ignorant, poor and stable. "If poor countries appear to be unstable," in Huntington's view, "it is not because they are poor, but because they are trying to become rich."[12] This theory was verified by the nationwide famine from 1960 to 1962 when more than twenty million Chinese people died of starvation, but without any substantial peasant rebellions during this period of extensive poverty. However, in the 1980s, when farmers were getting rich, the revolution of rising expectations has seized the minds of many people. Subsequently, they began to be dissatisfied with what they have and to challenge traditional authority. A serious organizational crisis became evident in rural society.

Three organizational crises, to a larger measure, provided main driving forces to advance the autonomous VCs and free elections. First of all, local authorities gradually lost control of villagers when villagers began to enjoy their rights to use land. In the late 1970s, the communal system in the countryside broke down, and farmers began to produce for their families in what would become known as the HRS. After regaining their control of land operation, product distribution, and social mobility, villagers began to be reliant on their own family resources rather than collective support. Peasants in 1978, for instance, benefited their 66.3% of income (88.53 yuan) from collective resource and only 26.8% of their earnings (35.29 yuan) from their household performance. By contrast, by 1988 each family provided 83.2% (453.40 yuan) of their total income and only 9.1% (49.72 yuan) from collective economy.[13]

As production was decentralized from commune to household, the administrative system in the villages broke down. Given economic independence of each family, the villagers began to say no to local officials who were the so-called "three want cadres"--want grain, money and life (abortion with force).[14] The villagers were urging a balance of economic independence and political autonomy through free elections and political participation aimed at protecting their economic rights.

Aside from losing control of villagers, village officials also became more independent from the higher level government. After dissolving of people's commune and the collapse of the collective economy, village officials lost their advantages to abuse collective resources. Consequently, the positions of local officials at the village level were not attractive at all.

As a result, higher lever officials in township and county had to ask some influential villagers to be a head of village. Village leaders, in turn, would be able to do what they wanted without supervision of their power. They forced villagers to contribute "taxes" and "donations" without any legal process and regulations. Perhaps corruption is most prevalent in places which lack effective political organizations.[15] Therefore, majority of farmers strongly requested free elections to replace those government "agents."[16]

Additionally, the authoritarian decay of village organizations contributed other critical forces to advance the growth of self-government at the village level. To be sure, the HRS destroyed the former dictator commune without producing any new organization as a substitute. Given this vacuum of political authority, each individual family became an influential unit in rural communities which were characterized by individualism, independence, diversity, and complexity. In Liaoning province, for instance, 90% of the villages in 1991 were decay without any collective economic capacity and organizational function.[17]

Confronting this organizational and administrative decay, the CCP had only three alternatives. The worst choice was to resume the former commune in order to maintain authoritarian control again which, of course, would definitely terminate rural economic reform. The second best option was to ignore this negative situation without any active actions. However, as a dictatorial communist regime, it fully understood the critical importance of a local organization which was a necessary means of maintaining communist legitimacy. The best choice or only proper choice was to set up a self-government which was between authoritarian organization and decayed organization.

According to Wang Zhenyao, the new format of organization must match the new economic structure in order to reorganize villagers at village level. Fundamentally, this reorganization was designed to fully respect farmers' rights, consider farmers' demands, and accept farmers' supervision. "This is the essential principle of self-government," In Wang's view, "to reorganize farmers politically."[18] The new economic reality called for new political organization.

Therefore, the fact that the CCP permitted, even encouraged village autonomy was essentially forced by massive uncontrollable pressures. Aimed at maintaining social stability, transferring rural social crises, and improving relations between villagers and village cadres, the central government had to promote village elections and local autonomy. This kind of self-government, the CCP believed, would permit villagers to approach self-management, self-organization, self-education, and self-service while villagers enjoyed democratic elections. After understanding of those historical reasons and political crises, we will notice that the establishment of VCs with democratic and autonomous orientations was not a political show and ridiculous drama only directed by the CCP.

The Villager Elections and Social Stability

A common assumption believes that it is negative for social stability when uneducated people get involved in free elections due to their lack of rational judgement and political responsibility. However, Huntington argues that political participation by illiterates should be less dangerous to democratic political institutions than participation by literates because "the latter typically have higher aspirations and make more demands on government." Political participation by illiterates, Huntington further indicates, "is likely to remain limited, while participation by literates is more likely to snowball with potentially disastrous effects on political stability."[19] The practice of villager elections in China proved Huntington's perception because local elections with illiterate villagers did not result in enormous social chaos in rural China. Instead, the elected administrations provided a positive driving force against the previous disfunctional organization and political decay.

As designed by Sun Yat-sen, founding father of the Republic of China, Chinese democracy should follow three basic steps: military politics (*junzheng*), training politics (*xunzheng*), and constitutional politics (*xianzheng*). In other words, before China implements its constitutional politics which is the final destination of Chinese democracy, according to Sun, it is necessary to have a process of training politics aimed at educating majority of Chinese people with democratic principles and discipline in opposition to a possible instability caused by a transition from military politics to constitutional politics. To this end, villager elections are actually implementing training politics to educate more than 900 million Chinese villagers. "VCs, in fact, are democratic training workshops" to teach Chinese farmers behaviors in approaching a healthy, smooth, effective, and stable democracy in the future.[20]

It should be noted that the election officials in the Ministry of Civil Affairs deserve credit for their intensive efforts in the implementation of tedious but necessary technical processes of local elections. In general, the electorial process in a village is divided into nine specific stages, including election organization installation, election official training, election mobilization, registration, nomination, campaigning, voting, tabulating votes, and the election machinery. What I would like to emphasize is the relationships between the vote and social stability at the village level because the vote is a very procedural and technical process which affects villagers' behaviors considerably.

Basically, election through voting for VCs has three major procedures which directly influence the quality of elections and the stability of elections as well. The first one is to check voters' identification card, sign the voters' list, and distribute ballots. This process seems very simple, but the key obstacle is how to persuade villagers to line up for a ballot. Initially, many villagers refused to line up for their ballots and rushed to pick them up as soon as possible. As explained by Wang Zhenyao, currently, the majority of urban residents are not used to getting in a line to go shopping and taking the bus in the cities. How can you ask villagers to behave better than the urban residents?[21] However, keeping enough distance for those who are picking up ballots is terribly important not only for the necessary order of election, but for elimination of cheating in ballots. Through several runs of election, fortunately, this disorderly situation has been significantly changed. At present, the Ministry of Civil Affairs has standardized a nationwide regulation that "the distribution of ballots must be supervised by three election officials who are responsible for checking identification cards, signing the voters' list, and distributing ballots to voters respectively."[22]

The second key procedure of the vote is to ensure voting independence and confidentiality. Technically, there are three challenges for village voters. One is that villagers do not have a habit of marking their choices on ballots individually. Instead, villagers are usually chatting and discussing while they are filling out ballots in booths. It definitely violates the election principle of freedom and secrecy, and, inevitably, offers much room for cheating and manipulation. The second obstacle to independent voting comes from illiterates who need some official "representatives" to check their ballots. For this proxy vote, the problem is that, technically, nobody is able to discover immediately whether or not the "representative" votes as illiterates want. In Hua Yu Village in Airen County, Hunan Province, for example, one representative of illiterates manipulated two third of the ballots that failed three of six candidates.[23] The third problem is that many villagers tired of the secret ballot which they consider to be too complicated. Instead, they favor raising their hands as the way for voting. In Taihe County, Qinghai Province, voters even used beans as ballots, dropping their beans into specific bowl which represent each candidate.[24]

For those problems, the Ministry of Civil Affairs at present requires that all voters must check their ballots in voting booth individually and confidentially. And the representative of illiterates must be selected by illiterates themselves rather than appointed by local officials.[25]

The last critical step of the vote is to drop ballots into ballot box without any cheating. For this simple process, the villager elections have encountered two major obstacles. The first one related to the location of polling stations. Currently, a few villager elections took place in the one place after the election meeting.[26] Instead, majority of villages set up several polling stations in addition to a headquarter.[27] Many provinces are providing roving ballot boxes aimed at collecting ballots door by door and person by person. For instance, in some pastoral areas of Gansu province, the ballot box on horse back is a very common and effective way to collect ballots. In Xiaoshan County, Zhejiang province, many villagers always work for urban construction out of their hometowns. To attract them to vote, the election committees usually send their roving ballot boxes to where the voters are working. This enabled Xiaoshan County to reach voter turn out rates as high as 95.5%.[28] However, establishment of those roving ballot boxes did not have any regulations about their locations and numbers.

The supervision of roving ballot boxes is another obstacle to fairness and justice in local elections. In practice, many election officials usually are candidates' relatives because China's villages are often dominated by one clan. Therefore, when the staffs are delivering the roving ballot boxes door by door, they will inevitably indicate which candidates they favor, and even promise bribes or threats to the voters. This demonstrates that while roving ballot boxes do ensure high voter participation, they definitely lead to power abuse and election fraud. In this regard, several provinces began to prohibit roving ballot boxes. For instance, Shanxi, Aihui, Neimengu, and Qinghai decided that locations of the vote must be either in election headquarters or in polling stations. And Shandong province, in its second run of election, definitely banned any roving ballot boxes.[29] Here, standardization of the electoral procedures between villages in a county and eventually in a province is imperative because it will permit more effective and uniform civic education and training programs.[30]

Democracy is not a slogan. Instead, democracy is a process which enables the common people to operate and practice self government. According to a report from the Carter Center, which investigated villager elections in Fujian and Hebei provinces in March, 1997, the technical dimension of an election "is a very complicated administrative exercise that is very difficult for a poor, developing country to do without considerable practice, assistance, and experience." The elections the Carter Center observed were the fourth run in which the process proved extremely efficient and well organized. For instance, in the Village of Fuo Ying Zi, 786 people voted in 35 minutes, and in Qui Wo Village, 1,555 people voted in 50 minutes.[31]

Therefore, villager elections demonstrate a remarkably high level of technical proficiency. It is a significant training politics which enable 900 million villagers to practice democratic rule and follow democratic regulations. Elections are not synonymous with democracy, but democracy is impossible without them. Successful elections can provide a framework for peaceful, stable political change; flawed elections can provoke instability. In particular, elections ensure political participation and autonomous organization which make possible "the return of a genuine sense of community that was lost during decades of turmoil."[32]

The Authority of VCs and Social Stability

Huntington argues that in theory an organization can be autonomous without being coherent and coherent without being autonomous. However, "in actuality," in Huntington's view, "the two are often closely linked together. Autonomy becomes a means to coherence, enabling the organization to develop an esprit and style that become distinctive marks of its behavior. Autonomy also prevents the intrusion of disruptive external forces."[33] The VC, as an autonomous organization, maintained internal coherence against external intrusion through its elected leaders' legitimacy and authority which are positive factors for social stability.

The new authority of the elected officials, first of all, came from new qualified and capable leaders after extensive elections. Traditionally, village officials were appointed by a higher level government. Without surveillance by villagers, the cadres were inevitably and absolutely corrupt. According to a news report, the Village of Xinghe in Suqian County, Jiangsu province, was a very poor village, but its leaders used 60,000 yuan of public funds for their private banquets from 1985 to 1991. In particular, to collect enough public funds for their corruption, they forced every villager to offer an extra 120 yuan to them every year.[34] As a result, those leaders did not have any prestige to win people's respect and trust.

At present, the ordinary villagers are able to elect their leaders who are usually characterized by ability, youth, literacy, wealth and strength. Statistics from the Zhumadian Prefecture of Hebei Province show the average age of newly elected leaders as 32.1 years old and that 82% of them finished middle school.[35] In Donggu Village in Ruchen County, Hunan Province, villagers independently elected a new director of the VC who had sound ability but poor morality because he had a bad record of gambling. Similarly, in the Village of Ximen in Tong County, Qinghai Province, an owner of a private restaurant was elected as a director of the VC. A survey conducted by the Ministry of Civil Affair indicates that almost 70% of villagers believed that a qualified village official is not necessarily a good man, but must be a strong man.[36]

Under leadership of those new capable and legitimate officials, the elected VCs enjoyed much better reputation, popularity, prestige, and authority as well. For instance, a famous farmers' uprising, which took place in Renshou County, Sichuan Province in 1992, was aimed at protesting extra financial obligations for support of public road construction. To maintain their power of demonstration, farmers in

Renshou County tried to persuade their neighbors, villagers in Pengshan County, to join their protest. However, the villagers in Pengshan declined this request because the extra donation for the road construction was approved by their VCs in Pengshan which were elected by all villagers. Thus they did not object to the decision nor were they willing to embarrass their own elected leaders. The interesting difference was that the villages in Renshou County did not experience free elections yet in 1992, but in Pengshan County, by contrast, VCs were elected by all villagers.[37] This was a typical case verifying Huntington's theory that an autonomous organization is possible to preserve a coherent force either maintaining internal unity or opposing external intrusion.

An elected VC was also capable of dealing with various troubles that could not be solved for a long time. For instance, Caijia Village in Zaoyuan County, Shandong Province, was bothered for long time by a lack of public grain which, as a necessary obligation, should be offered by villagers. Through extensive free discussion, the VC in 1990 decided that everybody must submit grain to the government except for a few extremely poor villagers. And a tough punishment would be imposed if somebody refused to follow this decision. As a result, taking only one day, villagers submitted 6,550 kilograms of wheat to government.[38]

Similarly, in Dongwei Village and Zhenggezhuang Village, Jilin Province, all villagers contributed their extra obligations without any complaints as soon as their VCs made a decision on collection of money aimed at cultivating 700 mu of wasteland and construction of 8 rooms for a local school.[39] Some villagers said "If we do not follow what these elected officials say, we will feel guilty and unfair to our leaders."[40]

These cases demonstrate a political miracle created by villager elections. Given the same village, same villagers, and even same officials, the elected officials improved their authority and prestige dramatically as soon as these leaders got involved in free elections. And a number of the previous troubles disappeared under this new leadership and new organization.

Besides, free elections also promoted the common interests of both officials and villagers. Given the credibility and reputation the elected leaders enjoyed, many villagers began trusting their officials to represent them against unfair treatments imposed by higher level government. This positive cooperation thus reduced many individual villagers' protests, demonstrations, and appeals which had been very negative factors for social stability.

For instance, the villagers' interest in Beiguan Village in Yangyuan County, Hebei Province, was damaged by the Dachen Railroad which occupied 1,200 mu of land and affected 260 households. To protest this unfair occupation, villagers kept appealing to local government and the State Council for a long time, but without any positive response. After electing a new VC, the elected officials made this affair a top priority and fought for villagers' benefits. As a result, the higher level government had to yield and offer a reasonable subsidy to those who suffered from this railroad construction. And after that, villagers there never organized any collective demonstration and appeal.[41]

This case indicates that the VC is a representative institute which is designed to represent and protect villagers' interests. To be sure, the top priority of an elected representative of this institute is reelection in the next term. In this regard, as the elected VCs, they must try their best to offer some valuable services to villagers on the one side, and strive for villagers' interests on the other. This kind of service would be able to internalize villagers' complaints and protests to maintain community stability.

The Construction of Legal System and Social Stability

The elected VCs likewise provided a connection between the legal system and rural stability. Democracy and law, obviously, should be interactive and intertwined. Essentially, autonomy is a combination of both freedom with self-government and law with self-regulation. Without freedom, autonomy is meaningless; but without law, autonomy will be anarchism which eventually will destroy autonomy.

In approaching villager autonomy, the key format of village laws is the Regulations of Villager Autonomy which functions as "a local or little constitution" issued and implemented by VCs. By 1995, about one third of VCs in China issued their regulations aimed at social stability and economic prosperity.[42]

In practice, these local regulations promote rural stability in three fields. First of all, the regulations clarify villagers' responsibility and obligation which, on the one hand, offer legal protection for villagers against any extra and uncertain "assignments" from the higher level government, and on the other, provide mandatory and apparent duties for villagers in order to reduce villagers' unnecessary and unlimited protests.

Zhangqiu County in Shandong Province is a good model to design and implement the villager regulation. In terms of a difficult issue related to the amount of money each villager should offer to the village, first of all, its regulation rules that those who cultivate the collective land must pay 10% of their yields to the collective based upon average output of the last three years. Additionally, each villager must contribute 30 days of free labor service for the collective projects. As a result, 635 villages in Zhuangqiu County successfully collected 14,276,000 yuan of the land contract fee, received 7,089,000 days of free labor, completed more than 3,000 irrigation projects, and constructed 1,046 kilometers of new roads in 1990.

Meanwhile, significant input by villagers, of course, reinforced the collective resources which, in turn, are able to provide better service to villagers. In Zhuangqiu County, each village established the station of farming service which hired 5,329 service agents in total. Furthermore, 407 villages (64% of the total) were able to provide special services of farming for villagers, and 228 villages (36% of the total) combined their comprehensive service of ploughing, sowing, storing, and watering together.[43]

In addition, the villager regulation improved the villager morality and community harmony. To be sure, considerable rural chaos is not necessarily caused by illegal crime but immoral actions. To this end, the Villager Regulations in Zhuangqiu Country made mandatary guidelines for those adults who must fulfil their obligation to support their aged parents. For instance, it says every person must offer 200 kilogram of wheat, two sets of clothes, 500 kilogram of coal, and 150 yuan of cash to their father or mother every year. If somebody refuses to pay it, the VC has full authority to deduct equivalent value from their income. Mrs. Jin Huanan, 76 years old, did not get any support from her children for seven years. However, the next day after the Regulations was issued, her three sons actively fulfilled their obligations required by the Regulations.[44] In Buxi Village, Zhuangqiu County, its Regulation rules that if a sheep eats wheat, its owner should pay 5 yuan as penalty. When 100 sheep, owned by villager Guo Qingchang, damaged the wheat field, he had to pay 500 yuan without delay.[45]

As a complement to the villager regulations, VCs are good at conducting moral and public pressure against illegal and immoral behaviors. In rural China, as always, "the moral court" is much more effective and popular than legal court because, to many Chinese, face and reputation are much more important than money and life. Thus, encouraged and organized by VCs, many villages established some mass and public associations related to the villager wedding, funeral, moral evaluation, and family planning.[46]

As a result, the construction of the legal system improved rural security and public order effectively. Civil and criminal cases in Zhuangqiu County, for example, were reduced 11.8% and 24.8% respectively from 1989 to 1990.[47] In Chenjia Village in Zaoyuan County, Shandong Province, there were many thefts and robberies which damaged 3,000 mu of the wooded mountain land prior to the villager autonomy. After the VC was elected, the VC set up its own security organization, consisting of the elected villagers, to supervise and punish the illegal actions.[48] This is a strategy of using villagers against villagers.

The above cases indicate that the way of the villager autonomy has been gradually changed from administrative and economic penalties to legal regulations. But, to be sure, the current VCs are in favor of the legal system rather than rule of law. The essential difference between the two is that the legal system takes law as a temporary and pragmatic tool aimed at subjective and changeable purposes; rule of law, by contrast, regards law as the top priority and fundamental principle against rule of man.

The Channels of Political Participation and Social Stability

Historically, one of the reasons for many peasant rebellions in China was lack of a channel for the uneducated peasants to express their hostile and resentful feelings. Given the limited choices, peasants did not have enough alternatives but violence. VCs, by contract, are providing many unprecedented opportunities and channels to release villagers' tensions, promote communications of between officials and villagers, and adjust the relations between villagers through free election and democratic management.[49]

As suggested by Huntington, a political organization or procedure "is an arrangement for maintaining order, resolving disputes, selecting authoritative leaders, and thus promoting community among two or more social forces," including different ethnic, religious, territorial, economic, or status groups.[50] In particular, the key driving force of villager self-government derives from the needs of their own economic interests which ensure that autonomous behaviors are rational, responsible, and, consequently, peaceful and non-violence.

In practice, free elections, autonomous management, and the VCs regulations offered the ordinary villagers effective means of supervising officials against corruption and rule by man. For instance, the villagers in the Village of Yuanli in Zhuangqiu County, Shandong Province were angry at local officials who tried to buy an unnecessary

Jeep through a little collective fund. As a result, villagers showed their democratic power by rejecting this Jeep purchase.[51]

Also, in Xincheng Village in Guiyan County, Hunan Province, the names of three female candidates disappeared from official ballots because of election cheating. The voters now learned how to use their legal rights to protect their candidates through a legal process in opposition to election scandal. On this occasion, the county government also learned how to respect villagers' rights and how to avoid demonstrations. As a result, the county government immediately declared the election void and null.[52] Similarly, a village official in Anren County, Hunan Province, illegally added his nephew to the official ballot. The Civil Affairs Department of the county had to take disciplinary action against this official after a peaceful protest by villagers.[53] The above legal protests through internal and organizational channels not only expressed the villagers' objections, but avoided violence outside legal channels.

Additionally, the numerous channels of political participation promoted visibility and transparency of the VCs decision making. The villagers in Chongqing, for example, basically supervised their elected officials through public bulletins, regular business announcements, and treasury records updates. Villagers also passed a mandatary resolution that required VCs to open sensitive and important issues regularly. At the same time, villagers designed various regulations to identify the elected officials' duties, objectives, and obligations. In particular, officials must deliver their working reports regularly; these then became very important references for villagers' evaluation and voting in the next election.[54]

Besides, the villagers' participation imposed an effective pressure on the elected officials who had to keep their camping promises; otherwise, their reelection would be in trouble. For instance, the former VC director in Gaobao Village in Zhulu County, Hebei Province, broke his promise to operate democratic management in the VC. As a result, the majority of voters of this village elected a new one as a way of expressing their dissatisfaction in the next election. The voters pointed out, "we do not want any 'warlord' to control us after more than 40 years of the CCP leadership."[55]

To please the voters, therefore, many candidates had to offer substantial promises as simple as one sentence slogans: "construction of a good road."[56] Involved in this campaign and election process, villagers gradually protected and improved their interests.

Theoretically, political participation provides two functions in maintaining social stability. The first one is release of the villagers' complaints; the second one is relaxation of various tensions in opposition to any radical and extreme actions. VCs offer a base to practice the two functions of maintaining social order.

Conclusion

The election, operation, and effect of VCs in the past ten years sheds light on Chinese democracy in the future. However, at least five potential crises caused by VCs at present are jeopardizing rural stability: exaggeration of high voter participation (90%), inbalance of the voters' incentive, general regulations without mandatary punishment of the Organic Law on Villager Autonomy, frequent illegal actions without effective control mechanism, and the role of the CCP is still above the elected VCs. Despite the problems, our understanding of Chinese rural democracy might be improved through these pioneer practices of rural autonomous organizations.

First, the elected organization and popular political participation, in fact, function as a double sword which empowers 900 million villagers to supervise the elected officials on the one hand, and ensures that officials can control villagers on the other. However, there is at least one common role of this autonomous organization: the mutual balance and check between voters and the elected officials against both power abuse and corruption. As Huntington points out, "broadened participation in politics may enhance control of the people by the government, as in totalitarian states, or it may enhance control of the government by the people, as in some democratic ones."[57] Since rural China at present is making a transition from a totalitarian system to democratic politics, their premature political participation and deficient self-government might have dual capacities of either the government over the people or the people over the government.

In reality, more and more local officials have tasted positive results of free elections because this responsible democracy enables officials to operate a strategy of using villagers against villagers which ensures that numerous difficult assignments from the higher level government can be fulfilled without jeopardy. The local governments now realize that democracy and elections are very effective means to control villagers against social chaos. On the other, however, villagers also learn how to use democracy as an instrument to protect their own political economic interests against dictators. Therefore, this villager committee actually provides a perfect connection and combination of both interests of government and villagers.[58] In particular, the operation of VCs indicated that an economic reform must be followed by a political reform through free elections and self-government. "The village elections," a report from the Carter Center says, "demonstrate one way to manage the economic change in a peaceful, stable manner that permits people to assume responsibility for their community. Those who feared instability in the rural areas now can see how economic reforms and the village elections have reinforced each other and helped ensure progress and stability."[59]

Secondly, the function of VCs confirms that all effective organizations should be positive in maintaining social order, no matter in a democratic or a dictatorial society. As discussed by Huntington in 1968, the democratic United States, Great Britain, and the dictatorial Soviet Union "have strong, adaptable, coherent political institutions: effective bureaucracies, well-organized political parties, a high degree of popular participation in public affairs, working system of civilian control over the military, extensive activity by the government in the economy, and reasonably effective procedures for regulating succession and controlling political conflict." Therefore, according to Huntington, "organization is the road to political power, but it is also the foundation of political stability and thus the precondition of political liberty."[60]

This reminds us that the diversified rural communities caused by the rural economic reform does not make all organizations unnecessary. Instead, the new economy requests new organization to provide qualified, comprehensive and effective services to each individual family. The key issue here is how to adjust the structure and function of each organization to adapt to changing circumstances in order to maximize organizational function of promoting social stability. Tracing the changing rural organizations in the past fifty years, a dialectical theory, which divides historical process into three stages: the thesis, antithesis, and synthesis, can offer a better explanation. In a larger sense, rural organizations experienced three phases from 1949 to 1997. The first one, dominated by Mao Zedong's China (1949-1976), was characterized by an unified, centralized, and collective organization, such as the people's commune. The second one, created by Deng Xiaoping (1978-1997), began to dissolve the consolidated organization and consequently set up separated, decentralized and household organization, such as the HRS. At present, VCs in post-Deng China demonstrate a new pattern of rural organization during this third stage. VCs, to some extent, are designed to reorganize villagers through establishment of a new version of unified organization, which not only ensures autonomous operation of each household, but maintains collective capacity of economy and service. Thus, VCs, as a synthesis, are a dialectical development of the previous thesis (the people's commune) and antithesis (the HRS). To be sure, the VC is definitely not duplication of the people's commune. Instead, it is a synthetical effort to combine both collective and household economy.

Thirdly, villager autonomy also resumed congruence between the villagers' rights and responsibility, and on the other hand, ensured a modern government to match its power and duty. In Mao's China, peasants' rights and obligations were quite congruous because while peasants enjoyed free service and welfare from the commune and they had to contribute their grain, labor, and money to the collective. Similarly, the commune, as the most important rural government, was responsible for all needs of peasants; on the other hand, it was able to force all peasants to follow what it required. It thus created a very simple and understandable relationship between peasants and the commune.

Deng's China, by contrast, deviated from the principle of congruence of the villagers' duty and rights because after the collapse of the commune, villagers had to take care of themselves, including supply, production, and sale, with little support and service from the government. But, while losing rights of enjoying collective service, villagers still had to keep their traditional obligations to the collective. As a result, more and more villagers said no to the government which now lost its traditional legitimacy to collect free grain, labor and money from villagers.

The inconsistency of right and obligation for villagers and the inbalance of power and responsibility for government will necessarily make rural organization disfunctional. Huntington argues that the higher rates of social mobilization and expansion of political participation and the low rates of political organization and institutionalization will cause "political instability and disorder." The primary problem of politics, in Huntington's opinion, "is the lag in the development of political institutions behind social and economic change."[61]

To this end, VCs actually are an attempt to reconcile villagers' obligation and rights by means of offering political rights to villagers in exchange of the villagers' economic obligation. Again, it is not a repetition of Mao's China. It is a revised relationship between government and villagers. Given this new relationship, government must sacrifice some political rights to ensure economic prosperity to villagers. And villagers now have begun to enjoy their rights of free elections, political participation, and democratic supervision, but in turn, they must fulfil their economic obligations. It is a valuable win-win deal in promoting social stability.

Finally, the coexistence of both responsibility and obligation in a political organization essentially reflects the principle of social contract theory. Through a free election and self-government as an invisible contract, the elected officials, the voters, and the higher level government are effectively bound and restrained by a contract in three ways. The elected officials, first of all, are obligated by their campaign promises. The candidates sign a contract as soon as they are elected by the voters. If the elected officials violate the contract with villagers, the latter have an opportunity to cancel the original contract through impeachment and appeal against their former representative.

Furthermore, this contract has an equivalent effect of forcing villagers to behave themselves. The elected officials should have full representative power to impose necessary regulations and disciplinary actions after a majority vote. If any villagers violate the regulations, they must be punished. Villagers might claim "no taxation without representation" as an excuse for rejecting their obligation prior to election and self-government. But, villagers must pay their necessary "taxation" such as labor service, grain, and money as soon as they have selected their "representation."

This contract, finally, means power constraints on the higher lever government. Given an elected power, both the elected officials and villagers possess much more legitimacy to decline all unfair demands and orders from the higher level government. Meanwhile, the higher official governments must respect the contract signed by villagers, and cannot feel free to fire or select local officials.

Needless to say, the above three functions of the contract effectively control the elected officials, villagers and the higher level governments. As a result, this not only ensures possible social stability, but provides a fundamental base for Chinese democracy in the future.

China's economic reform over the past 20 years, in sum, has demonstrated a common strategy of "country first and city following," which has been verified by the reforms of the HRS in the late 1970s and TVE in early 1980s. Both HRS and TVE in rural China promoted urban economic reform in the middle of the 1980s and the property rights reform of the State-Owned Enterprise (SOE) in early 1990s respectively. Currently, rural China is playing another pioneer role of promoting China's political reform through the election and operation of the villager committee.

Obviously, these autonomous organizations at present are still confronting many deficiencies, but, as the Carter Center argues, "if one judges by the standards of experienced, industrialized democracies, then China's village elections cannot measure. If one bases the assessment on China's 5,000 years of history, which lacks a tradition of competitive elections, then China's new experiment merits a more positive assessment."[62] I strongly believe, therefore, that compared to Mao's China, that today's self-government is superior to the former dictatorial government, the current false democracy is better than the previous no democracy, and the present inflated elections are valuable than no elections of the past. The village democracy and autonomy today will possibly lead to urban democracy horizontally first, and then township, county, province level democracy vertically following. The most fundamental aspect of political modernization, according to Huntington, "is the participation in politics beyond the village or town level by social groups throughout the society and the development of new political institutions, such as political parties, to organize that participation."[63] History may prove that election and operation of VCs are a quiet, but fundamental political revolution in China.

Notes

1.   Richard Bernstein and Ross Munro, *The Coming Conflict with China* (New York: Alfred A. Knopf, 1997), p. 16.

2.   Samuel Huntington, *Political Order in Changing Societies* (New Haven and London: Yale University Press, 1968), p. 7.

3.   Zheng Shuping, eds., *Zhonggong nianbao, 1996* (Yearbook on Chinese Communism, 1996) (Taipei: Institute for the Study of Chinese Communist Problems, 1996), p, V-50.

4.   Ibid., pp. V-50, V-51.

5.   Ibid., pp. V-51, V-52.

6.   Wang Zhenyao, "quanguo cunmin zizhi jiben fazhan qushi ji jinyibu zhengce xuanze," (The General Direction and Policy Alternatives of Villager Autonomy in China). In *Shijian yu sikao* (Practices and Ideas). Edited by zhongguo jiceng zhengquan jianshe yanjiuhui (China Research Society of Basic-Level Governance). (Beijing: zhongguo shehui chubanshe, 1992), p. 17; Zhongguo jiceng zhengquan jianshe yanjiuhui (2), *Zhongguo nongcun cunmin weiyuanhui huanjie xuanju zhidu* (Study on the Election of Villager Committees in Rural China). (Beijing: zhongguo shehui chubanshe, 1994), p. 1.

7.   *Shijie ribao* (World Journal), April 20, 1997.

8.   Interviewed with Wang Zhenyao, Vice Director of the Department of Basic-Level Government, Ministry of Civil Affairs, State Council. Beijing, China, July 31. Wang Zhenyao has been honored as one of main engineers of the villager election in China.

9.   Zheng Shuping, etl., eds., *Zhonggong Nianbao, 1996*, p. V-52.

10.   Bernstein and Munro, *The Coming Conflict with China*, pp. 15-19.

11. Huntington, *Political Order in Changing Societies*, p. 36.

12. Ibid., p. 41.

13. Pang Enguo and Li Xiujian, "Lun cunmin zizhi de xianshi jichu," (Review on Practical Bases of Villager Autonomy), *Shijian yu sikao*, p. 39.

14. Huang Bailian, "Dui Kaizhan cunmin zizhi shifan huodong de sikao," (Review on Conducting Exemplary Activities of Villager Autonomy), *Shijian yu sikao*, p. 51.

15. Huntington, *Political Order in Changing Societies*, p. 71.

16. Xia Leshun, "Shiying cunmin zizhi shi huanjie nongcun ganqun maodun de zhongyao tujin," (The Positive Role of Villager Autonomy in Releasing the Tensions between Villagers and Officials in Rural China), *Shijian yu sikao*, p. 189.

17. Dong Zhulin, "Cunmin zizhi de zhanluue sikao," (Strategic Consideration of Villager Autonomy), *Shijian yu sikao*, p. 51.

18. Wang Zhenyao, *Shijian yu sikao*, pp. 23-24.

19. Huntington, *Political Order in Changing Societies*, p. 49.

20. Jia Zhihua, ect., "Xiaochu Ganbu, qunzhong de sixiang yiluu si cunmin zizhi de zhongyao qianti" (Villager Autonomy and Dispelling Misgivings of Rural Cadres and Villagers), *Shijian yu sikao*, p. 89.

21. Interviewed with Wang Zhenyao, Beijing, July 31, 1996.

22. Minzhengbu jiceng zhengquan jianshesi (Department of Basic-level Government, Ministry of Civil Affairs), *Zhonghua renmin gongheguo cunmin weiyuanhui xuanju guicheng* (Regulations of the Villager Committee Election in the People's Republic of China), (Beijing: Zhongguo shehui chubanshe, 1995), p. 54.

23. Zhongguo jiceng zhengquan jianshe weiyuanhui (2), *Zhongguo nongcun cunmin weiyuanhui huanjie xuanju zhidu*, p. 39.

24. Ibid., p. 38.

25. Minzhengbu jiceng zhengquan jianshesi, *Zhonghua renmin gongheguo cunmin weiyuanhui xuanju guicheng*, pp. 54-55.

26. Several counties in Hebei Province are conducting this effective way. See The Cater Center, "The Carter Center Delegation to Observe Village Elections in China," (Unpublished Report), March 4-16, 1997, p. 7.

27. Heilongjiang, Tianjin, Sichuan, Jiangsu, Zhejiang, Guizhou, Hunan, Gansu, Xinjiang, and Fujian are conducting this format. The Carter Center, "The Cater Center Delegation to Observe Village Elections in China," p. 7.

28. Zhongguo jiceng zhengquan jianshe weiyuanhui (2), *Zhongguo nongcun cunmin weiyuanhui huanjie xuanju zhidu*, pp. 55-56.

29. Ibid., pp. 55-56.

30. The Carter Center, "The Carter Center Delegation to Observe Village Elections in China," p. 14.

31. Ibid., p. 7.

32. Ibid., p. 5, p. 12.

33. Huntington, *Political Order in Changing Societies*, p. 22.

34. *Nongmin ribao* (Farmer's Daily), May 14, 1991.

35. Ouyan Zhongkuai, "Zhumadian diqu guice cunweihui zhuzhifa zhuangkuan fenxi," (Analysis on Carrying out the Organic Law on Villager Committees in Zhumadian), *Shijian yu sikao*, p. 289.

36. Zhongguo jiceng zhengquan jianshe yanjiuhui (2), *Zhongguo nongcun cunmin weiyuanhui huanjie xuanju zhidu*, p. 91.

37. Interviewed with Wang Zhenyao, Beijing, China, July 31, 1996.

38. Zhang Huating, "Zaoyuanxian shixing cunmin daibiao huiyi zhidu de diaocha," (Survey of Conducting the Villager Representative Assemblies in Zaoyuan County), *Shijian yu sikao*, p. 233.

39. Cao Guoying, "Lun cunmin zizhi de nandian jiqi jiechu," (Review on Difficulties and Resolutions of the Villager's Self-Government), *Shijian yu sikao*, p. 299.

40. Liu Zhenqi, "Cunmin zhijie minzhu de you yici shijian," (Another Practice of the Villager Direct Democracy), *Shijian yu sikao*, p. 273.

41. Liu Zhenqi, "Cunmin zhijie minzhu de you yici shijian," *Shijian yu sikao*, p. 273.

42. Zheng Shuping, eds., *Zhonggong nianbao, 1996*, p. V-52.

43. Luue Zongzhi, "Yifa jianzhang, shixian cunmin ziwo guanli," (The Legal Regulations and the Villager Self-Government), *Shijian yu sikao*, pp. 207-11.

44. Ibid., p. 211.

45. Zhang Huoai, "Cong Zhuangqiu jingyan kan nongcun shenhua gange xin de qidongdian," (The Experience in Zhuangqiu County and New Promotion of Rural Reform Development), *Shijian yu sikao*, p. 223.

46. Liu Zhenwei, "Guanyu cunmin zizhi de liangge guanxi wenti," (The Villager Autonomy and Its Two Issues), *Shijian yu sikao*, p. 146.

47. Liu Zongzhi, "Yifa jianzhang, shixian cunmin ziwo guanli," *Shijian yu sikao*, p. 213.

48. Zhang Huating, "zaoyuanxiang shixing cunmin daibiao huiyi zhidu de diaocha," *Shijian yu sikao*, p. 234.

49. Zhongguo jiceng zhengquan jianshe yanjiuhui (China Research Society of Basic-Level Governance) (3), *Zhongguo nongcun cunmin danbiao huiyi zhidu* (The Report on the Villager Representative Assemblies in China). (Beijing: Zhongguo shehui chubanshe, 1995), p. I-IV.

50. Huntington, *Political Order in Changing Societies*, pp. 8-9.

51. Zhang Huoan, "Cong Zhuangqiu Jingyan kan congcun shenhua gange xin de qidongdian," *Shijian yu sikao*, p. 25.

52. Zhongguo jiceng zhengquan jianshe yanjiuhu (2), *Zhongguo nongcun cunmin weiyuanhui huanjie xuanju zhidu*, p. 93.

53. Ibid., p. 93.

54. Zou Chunju, "Jianli minzhu jizhi shi guanche cunweihui zuzhifa de hexin," (The Construction of Democratic Mechanism and the Core of Conducting the Organic Law on the Villager Committees), *Shijian yu sikao*, p. 294.

55. Liu Zhenqi, "Cunmin zhijie xuanju de you yici shijian," *Shijian yu shikao*, p. 269.

56. Interviewed with Wang Zhenyao, Beijing, July 31, 1996.

57. Huntington, *Political Order in Changing Societies*, pp. 34-35.

58. Interviewed by Wang Zhenyao, Beijing, July 31, 1996.

59. The Carter Center, "The Carter Center Delegation to Observe Village Elections in China," p. 16.

60. Huntington, *Political Order in Changing Societies*, pp. 1, 461.

61. Huntington, *Political Order in Changing Societies*, p. 5.

62. The Cater Center, "The Cater Center Delegation to Observe Village Elections in China," p.12.

63. Huntington, *Political Order in Changing Societies*, p. 36.

Chapter 5

Economic Reform and Social Instability in Rural China

CHEN Weixing

Since the mid-1980s, fundamental changes have taken place in China. Politically, the Communist Party of China (CPC), though still at the helm of China's economic reform, is no longer the monolithic and pervasive party that it used to be. It has changed from a Party of politics to a Party of economics.[1] Economically, a planned economy has been replaced by a semi-planned, semi-market economy. China's ownership structure has undergone changes, and will undergo fundamental changes with the reform of state-owned enterprises after the CPC's 15th National Congress in 1997. Socially, Chinese society has become more mobile since the mid-1980s, and more space has been created for social activities. The transformation of Chinese society of such magnitude has naturally carried within itself seeds of social instability. As China is preparing to enter the new millennium, China is well aware of the latent dangers ahead. This chapter identifies and discusses the latent dangers from rural China.

China's rural population constitutes about 70% of China's total population. Historically, Chinese revolution succeeded largely because the CPC was able to build a revolutionary movement on peasant discontent through careful, pains-taking organization. Today, the success of China's modernization program largely depends on the transformation of rural China, while the success of rural China's transformation is contingent upon the stability of rural China. But rural China's transition has been fraught with sources of social instability. This chapter identifies the sources of social instability, analyze the roots of these sources, and discuss the policy dilemma that China faces in addressing these problems.

Sources of Social Instability

After nineteen years of economic reform, the rural scene in China has changed. On the positive side, China has become the fastest growing economy in the world in the 1980s, and peasants have contributed enormously to China's economic growth. About 30% of China's general social output value increase, 35% of national industrial output value increase and 45% of China's total export have been contributed by rural enterprise alone for the last fifteen years.[2] On the negative side, rural economic growth in China has its social and political consequences that may threaten China's social order and political stability. The consequences are: first, the collapse of village-level Party and government organizations has made it difficult to enforce government policies and resulted in the increase in crime rate; second, the wealthy and developed regions and villages have developed a tendency toward localism, while poor and underdeveloped regions and villages have become demoralized; third, large numbers of temporary rural-urban migrants from poor and undeveloped areas have emerged; fourth, and new patterns of human relations that bypass institutions have emerged.

The collapse of village-level organizations

It has been endlessly reported that many villages have been paralyzed in China since the mid-1980s. In a survey conducted by the Ministry of Civil Affairs, thirty-nine per cent of villages that local government had come to a standstill.[3] The consequences of the collapse of village-level organizations are twofold. First, the collapse of village-level organizations has made it extremely difficult for the state to enforce state policies such as environmental protection, compulsory grain procurement, taxes and birth control. Second, the break-down of village-level organizations has resulted in a surge of rural lawlessness.

One consequence of the failure on the part of the state due to the collapse of village-level organizations in enforcing measures of environmental protection and birth control is that China is heading for an ecological nightmare. China's cultivated land per head is about 800 square meters, well below the world average. China has to manage to feed about 24% of the world's population from about 7% of the world's arable land. China has continuously been losing agricultural land, about one third of its cropland over the past 40 years to soil erosion, desertification, energy projects, and, at an accelerating rate since the mid-1980s, to deforestation and industrial and housing developing. Despite the fact that the importance of agriculture has been repeatedly emphasized by the Central and provincial governments since the mid-1990s, regulations that prohibit the use of arable land for purposes other than agriculture have not been well and effectively enforced. The open space for industrial and housing developing is in the rural area. Peasants with money also preferred to build new houses, or to look for a higher return by investing in the development of rural industry. Peasants' effort and activity have never been well coordinated since the mid-1980s. At the same time, population control in rural China has been made more difficult since the mid-1980s. The growth of a predominantly young population with an increasing life expectancy will not be throttled down for decades to come. China is projected to add at least 490 million people in the four decades from 1990 to 2030, swelling the population to close to 1.7 billion. A soaring population would become ever growing strains on the ability of the Chinese to feed themselves unless population could be controlled and the continuing loss of agricultural land could be curbed. China today is already one of the very few countries in the world that has been using agricultural land so intensively. The pursuit of ever larger harvests has made China the world's biggest producer of fertilizer, but the use of fertilizer is subject to diminishing returns. Unsupervised use of chemicals and industrial effluents is polluting the water, while use of unwashed soft coal for energy is polluting the air. What are the implications for China and the world if China will have to raise substantially its reliance on imported food? According to *The Economist*, a China with the same fish consumption per head as Japan, for instance, would alone consume more fish than are at present caught in the world's oceans, and a China of the early 21st century with the eating habits of South Korea today would need 600 million tons of grain - implying, if China's harvest remained at its current level, a demand for imported grain roughly equivalent to all the world's grain shipments of 1994.[4] An ecological nightmare has significant social and political implications.

Murder, robbery, abduction and sale of women and children, illicit gambling, drugs, secret societies and extravagant ceremonies have all been flourishing in rural China since the mid-1980s. LIU Jiang, Minister of Agriculture, summed up the situation in 1995 by saying "the vicious power of local bullies, village tyrants, and other hoodlums is running amok in the countryside."[5] Drug taking and gambling have once again become common in rural China, which has led to the breaking-up of families, disputes, fighting, and various crimes. Various extravagant ceremonies such as marriage, funeral, etc. have resulted in great waste of resources and rupture of normal social activities. These activities and the dramatic increase in crime rate (murder, robbery, and abduction and sale of women of children) have already had the effect of overturning order and stability.

Localism and the wealth gap

China's policy of "let some people get rich first" has resulted in great uneven development in rural China. Since the mid-1980s, the gap between the poor and the rich and between the developed and undeveloped villages has widened. The rich and developed villages have developed a tendency toward localism, while the poor and underdeveloped villages have been demoralized.

Since the mid-1980s, many wealthy villages have become village conglomerates (hereafter VC), a comprehensive economic organization under unified leadership whose membership is restricted to a specific village.[6] It is a direct descendent of the collective economic activities of the brigade level of the commune system but operates in a transformed economic environment. The VC's economic success has been closely associated with market localism, the attempt to secure private advantage in an increasingly interdependent and unrestricted context. Market localism does not necessarily imply a war of all against all but does imply connection-building, deal-making, haggling and shielding of all with and against all at every level of society.[7] Their economic success thus has inclined them to develop a tendency toward localism. In addition, VC leaders rose to leadership positions in their native areas as natives, which made them even more inclined toward local interests.[8] The economic consequence of the development of localism is the "formation of 'dukedom' economies" (zhuhou jingji) which are extremely self-interest oriented,[9] while the political consequence of the development of localism is the establishment of various "local empires" that are independent of local, municipal, as well as provincial governments and bully and oppress their neighbor villages. They are able to establish their own "empires," both because of their wealth and economic strength, established ties and connections, and their monopoly of the local market and economy and because of their political influence. In some extreme cases, they developed their own security forces. The new rural elites that have emerged with the rise of the VC are both party secretaries and entrepreneurs who represent both the state and the society. They are not only "red and expert" but also wealthy. One case in point is the well-publicized Daqiu VC in suburban Tianjin. Daqiu VC has become one of the wealthiest villages in China since the reform. In 1992, its agricultural and industrial output value reached 4 billion *yuan*, and its per capita output value was about one million *yuan*. Under it were hundreds of factories and enterprises and 28 joint ventures. It hired thousands of employees, many of whom were professionals from urban areas throughout the nation. There were more than six hundreds of private cars in Daqiu VC, about thirty of which were Mercedes Benz. All villagers are now living in contemporary spacious houses. YU Zuomin, president and party secretary of the Daqiu VC, won the title of national peasant entrepreneur and became a national model worker in 1989. He was also a deputy to the National People's Congress. With the accumulation of economic wealth and political influence, Yu began to build his own empire, developed his own security force, and became the "king" of his kingdom. Neither the local government nor the local public security bureau could penetrate his empire. This case was first exposed because of homicide committed by the executive board of Daqiu VC. WEI Fuhe, a non-resident of Daqiu, was hired by Daqiu VC in 1990. As an outsider, Wei was suspected of graft and embezzlement and was brought to trial by the Daqiu executive board. When Wei denied the charges, he was tortured to death. When public security officers from Tianjin public security bureau came to investigate this case, they were held in custody by the Daqiu security force. These officers were not released until the direct intervention by the Tianjin Municipal government. The Tianjin Municipal government then organized a special committee to investigate this case and sent four hundred armed police to blockade Daqiu village. YU Zuomin and many others were eventually arrested and sentenced for murder, but only after frustrated pressure from national media, party and government. Yu was sentenced to 20 years' imprisonment.[10] Daqiu VC is an exception only in that it was exposed and reported. There are many other empires like Daqiu throughout China today. To a certain degree, Daqiu can be seen as a microcosm of a national pattern.

The gap between the poor and the rich has created a sense of social injustice among many Chinese peasants as the ideas of equality are still at the bottom of many Chinese peasants despite the nineteen years of economic reform.

Peasant mobility

The great success story of the richer areas has been the growth of enterprises. About 120 million peasants are now employed by various rural enterprises. But the overall picture of rural China is not as encouraging. Peasants' incomes in the poor areas have been stagnant for the past decade while inflation has been in double digit. The income correlation shows that the more dependent a province or an area is on farming, the poorer its people. As a result, investment in agriculture has been at a low ebb, having fallen from 6% of all national investment in 1981 to 1% in 1993. At the same time, rising farm productivity has left perhaps more than 110 million peasants without regular work. Under these circumstances and thanks to the freedom and autonomy that peasants have gained, a large "floating" population of temporary rural-urban migrants has emerged. The number of temporary rural-urban migrants has increased dramatically in recent years. Approximately 130 million rural Chinese have migrated to cities in search of better lives, and in the next decade, millions more are expected to leave the countryside.[11] In China, temporary migration is not defined in terms of its duration but in terms of the official household registration at the time of the move. Large numbers of temporary rural-urban migrants have been a mixed blessing for China. On the positive side, these migrants have contributed to China's economic growth in general by providing needed cheap labor for the urban area, and to rural development in particular by bringing capital, information, technology and know-how from the developed coastal urban areas such as Guangzhou and Fujian to rural areas. But on the negative side, these migrants have created serious social, political and policy problems. The problems produced by this large "floating" population include but are not limited to crimes, pressure on infrastructure, tensions between migrants and urban residents, birth control, pollution, education, and potential political instability. As temporary rural-urban migrants are a "floating" population that is under nobody's jurisdiction, they have become a tough problem for the CPC to tackle. The dramatic increase in crime rate for the last ten years can be attributed partly to this "floating" population. Crimes such as drug-dealings, prostitution, robbery, trade in human beings and stealing, are largely associated with these temporary rural-urban migrants.[12] In an environment of "money worship," many of the temporary migrants would do whatever necessary to make money. Illegal activities turned out to be one of the quickest ways to make big money for many of them. Majority of the prostitutes in Guangzhou, Shenzhen, and other major cities today belong to this population. Most drug-related crimes, robbery and trading in human beings are also associated with this large "floating" population. Given the limited resources and lack of space in the already crowded cities, this "floating" population has also created enormous pressure on communication, transportation and service facilities in urban areas. Numerous villages such as Sichuan village, Anhui village, etc. (migrant "slums" for peasants from the same province) have emerged in the inner corners of big cities in recent years throughout China. These "city villages" have caused serious environmental problems such as pollution and epidemics. All these have created tensions between urban residents and these temporary migrants, which may result in riots any time. This large "floating" population has also brought about many policy problems such as education and birth control. Thousands upon thousands of migrants' children would not have opportunities to go to school both due to the limited school facilities in already crowded cities and high tuition for these non-urban residents and due to their illegal status and discriminating admission policies. Given the fact that this population is under nobody's jurisdiction, it seems impossible to control the births of this population. Politically, such large a "floating" population is itself a source of instability. The real nightmare to the central government is that if this large "floating" population, no matter for whatever purpose or reason, is allied with radicalized urban groups or students, order would be out of control.

New patterns of human relations

There has been a popular saying in China: nothing could be accomplished without *guanxi* (connections). *Guanxi* politics takes two forms: patron-client relations and connections based on transactions of goods and money and on human feelings, which often involves behind-scene deals, transactions and politics. Connection-building, deal-making, haggling and shielding of all with and against all at every level of society have become a way of life in China today. The sources of *guanxi* include but are not limited to kinship, social and cultural ties, exchange relationships, connections with the party and government apparatus, and connections based on the transaction of goods, service and money. *Guanxi* politics can be attributed to several factors. Traditionally, Chinese society has always been a group-oriented society where the economic reform of the last eighteen years has not been able to change. Living so closely involved with family members, neighbors and other people has accustomed the Chinese people to group-oriented collective life that gives high priority to interpersonal connections and community life. Politically, if the relationship between peasants and the state in the context of an official ideology and a command economy is impersonal,

guanxi politics, which is based on interpersonal relations and
connections, is naturally becoming more important after the general
failure of communist ideology, the rejection of political campaigns, and
the transformation of the command economy. The institutional and
organizational linkage between the state and the peasant has always been
weaker, even under the people's commune in Mao's era. Vivienne Shue
discussed this weak linkage by describing the village communal
solidarity and the impotence of the center at the village level in Mao's
era.[13] The weak organizational and institutional linkages between the
state and the peasants have collapsed in the countryside since 1984.
According to a *Renmin Ribao* report, the more than 800,000 basic-level
organizations in the countryside throughout China must be rebuilt soon,[14]
because they are not functioning. Socially and economically, under the
current framework of "socialism with competitive capitalism," *guanxi*
politics has proven to be indispensable to the function and operation of
the economy and society due to its role in adjusting the circulation of
resources in the society and the demand-supply relationship on the
market. Since *guanxi* politics often involves behind-scene dealings and
transactions on an individual basis that involve the use of power and state
and collective resources for personal gains, *guanxi* politics and corruption
are two sides of one coin. More importantly, *guanxi* politics would make
"rule by law" and institutionalization of democratic processes more
difficult, if not impossible. It should be pointed out here that *guanxi*
politics based on patron-client relations is different from clientelist
politics in a corporate state. Clientelist politics emphasizes organized
interest and representation in the policy-making process, whereas *guanxi*
politics in the context of rural China focuses on interpersonal connections
and relations.

Mixed Blessing

The roots of the sources of instability lie in the process of
decentralization of policies in China since the economic reform in 1978.
Before the economic reform of 1978, peasants had been mobilized
through organizational means to serve primarily the CPC's political
purpose, often at the expense of economic development. Ideological
purity and economic development were always the two facets of the same
coin of development. Maoists believed that continuous socio-economic
and political changes would enable them to fulfill these purposes. The
development strategy developed for this purpose was embodied in the
"three red banners" of (1) the General Line for Socialist Construction"

(namely, go all out, aim high, and achieve greater, faster, better, and more economical results in building socialism), (2) the Great Leap Forward and (3) the People's Commune. Mao believed that communization with the integration of *xiang* (township today) with the commune was the embryonic form of future society.[15]

The People's Communes were to combine industry and agriculture, civilian and military affairs, and political leadership and economic management. It was believed that communization through control over economic activity and the ownership of the means of production to higher levels in the structural hierarchy would enable a structural change in the form of collectivity and integrate vertically the rural organization, merge production teams and transfer control over supply and marketing cooperatives from individual peasants to the commune. Collectivization would not only bridge a backward agrarian China to a modern China, but also set the stage for the transition from socialism to communism by destroying the peasants' tie to private property and making them rural proletarians. The people's commune and the Great Leap thus became the Maoist instrument for carrying out the socially revolutionary measures of the transitional period in China.

The collective directly managed the land and labor of the producers living on that land within the parameters of tight state control. Individual peasants must participate in collective production and activities. The collective produced what the state specified, purchased quantities of agricultural producer goods at state prices, and sold designed quantities of its produce to the state at low official prices.

According to the household registration and control system (implemented in 1955), collective members were bound to the village of their birth not only in the sense that they were barred from migrating elsewhere but also in that they were legally obligated to labor for, and on terms set by, the collective. State and collective closely restricted the movement of rural residents not only between town and countryside but also among different rural areas. As Mark Selden correctly stated, "the integration of peasants and land was so tight that one is almost tempted to say that the land owned the people."[16]

The framework of the people's commune and the household registration and control thus bound the peasant legally and substantively to the land. Under such circumstances, peasants' power was, at most, residual.[17] Maoist effort produced two undesirable outcomes: the permanent sacrifice of the peasants to the state and the consequent economic stagnation in rural China and deep grievances against the political chaos and economic losses that alienated peasants and large segments of the society from the CPC.

The economic reform that was started in the late 1970s represented the CPC's new effort to promote economic development. The direct consequence of this effort was that Chinese peasants were given more freedom and social space. The implementation of the household responsibility systems characterized by the assignment of land to individual peasants, division of village collective properties, and lease of the village enterprise by individual peasants and the dismantlement of the people's commune in 1984 have greatly weakened the organizational and institutional linkage between the state and the peasantry. The result of this is that the CPC has lost its material and organizational basis for political leadership in the countryside.

The former village brigade[18] was under the influence and control of a centralized command planning. The village's income and benefits were directly tied to their economic performance but the village had little freedom for its own production and economic activity. Production teams and brigades could not sell, transfer, or rent their land, except as directed by the state. Nor could they autonomously decide what to grow. Peasants had no right to sell, rent, or leave the land and were even heavily restricted in the use of their private plots. Peasants were forced to depend on the collective economy for the satisfaction of their various needs.[19] The economic model under the people's commune placed extreme emphasis on maximizing grain production throughout China.

It is true that Chinese peasantry are still under the influence of the state's guidance planning but they are more autonomous in their production and economic activity. They have the freedom to determine their own economic activity and to develop their own strength of production in response to the market. They also have control over their own labor and products. The state's power and control today are largely imposed indirectly on peasants through its guidance planning, finance, price and tax policy, and its control over resource allocation. More importantly, Chinese peasants can move freely. They were unable to move freely before the economic reform, because the strict residential registration system coupled with strict rationing system in an environment of scarcity made it impossible for peasants to make a living in areas other than their own registered residential area. Since the land on which they were bound was publicly owned and managed, peasants were virtually reduced to the slave of the land in the locality. With the dismantlement of the people's commune, the change of public ownership and management of land to public ownership and private management, the relaxation of ration system and the abolishment of the ration coupon system, peasants are no longer bound on the land. Thanks to these changes, the household registration system, though still intact, was no longer binding on peasants. Peasants are free to leave their land as they wish and go wherever they want to.

For centuries, Chinese peasants have been engaged in a fight against nature for subsistence. Agricultural production, though constrained by the rigid central policy before 1978, had managed to grow over the years. By 1980, two decades of effort by peasants had paid off, and most peasants were no longer troubled by subsistence. Blessed by the new policy environment and countered by large surplus of labor, Chinese peasants, freed to leave agriculture and eager to seek better economic opportunities, turned to handicrafts, transportation, service trades, rural enterprise, and commercial activities and were starting to explore all kinds of possibilities and opportunities for profit. The mid-1980s thus witnessed the beginning of the third wave of rural development in China.[20] With more freedom and better opportunities for individual peasants and with the rise of the rural enterprise and the development of cross-region, cross-province and multinational corporations, peasants today are able to and are better equipped to rebel against local governments and escape from various government constraints. They have more resources at their disposal to protect their own interest. They could also openly rebel against local authorities. According to Chinese press reports, at least 830 incidents of rural rebellion involving more than 500 people each were recorded in 1993, including 21 cases involving crowds of more than 5,000.[21] As a result, Chinese peasants can no longer be easily channeled into organizational action for the CPC's purpose in an environment of decentralizing policy.

In sum, to promote rural development and industrialization in the rural area, the CPC not only must conscientiously protect peasants' interest and encourage and endorse peasants' initiatives in rural development but also must conscientiously empower peasants by all means. The empowerment of the peasants is, after all, the key to the success of rural development. Peasants constitute about 70% of China's population. Rural development is essentially important in China, because unlike other developing and post-communist countries, China could not possibly absorb its large rural population into its urban areas. In its drive for modernization, China has to develop rural areas and turn rural areas into urban areas through industrialization.

Policy Dilemma

Some problems highlighted in part one of this paper are common problems of development that developing countries are often confronted with in their modernization process, while others are associated with China's current system of "socialism with capitalism." The limitation of policy responses under the current system is that policy response to one problem may have negative implications for others. China's economic success can largely be attributed to the relaxation of control by the central government, while solutions to many of the problems would require the tightening of government control. Could China effectively address these problems without reversing the modernization process? There is not an easy answer, especially in a country as huge as China.

Jean C. Oi, in her study of rural industrialization in China, used "local state corporatism" to refer to the workings of a local government that coordinates economic enterprises in its territory as if it were a diversified business corporation.[22] According to Oi, "local state corporatism" explains why local officials in China, unlike those in the Soviet Union, have embraced rather than resisted economic reforms and have succeeded in promoting economic growth in their localities. A case in point is the development and success of the VC. The VC has contributed enormously to rural development, and its impact on China's modernization process has been largely positive. For instance, since the late 1980s, many VCs have become the economic, financial and cultural centers of their localities. With the emergence of these centers appeared mini-cities in rural China. The VC's development, to a great extent, represents the direction of development in China. It has also provided one solution, if not the solution, to the "floating population." A large surplus of labor has emerged since the early 1980s. VCs and rural enterprises have employed millions upon millions of peasants that would otherwise have joined the "flight" to cities. VCs and rural enterprises have also attracted and employed large numbers of professionals from urban areas, which has affected the direction of population "flight." But at the same time, the VC's tendency toward localism has been strengthened in the same process. One possible prospect of the development of localism is the deconstruction of China.[23] A different prospect, as suggested by Oi, is that while local state corporatism has provided China with a relatively non-threatening alternative economic system that allows for strong local state intervention, the success of local state corporatism may in the long run force the emergence of something akin to a federal system that more clearly recognizes the rights and power of localities. Even a federal system (which is very unlikely for foreseeable future) is not a guarantee of social stability, as other sources of social instability as discussed above, may find a better environment to grow.

Guanxi politics has provided new channels of communication, new access to the political process, and new political linkages between different levels of authorities in a politically closed society but at the same time, it has contributed to the rampancy of corruption under the current "socialism with capitalism." If *guanxi* politics is an organic part of the current system, corruption is structural by nature. Without systemic change, the CPC's attempt to fight corruption by enforcing discipline would be of no effect.

The prevalence of commercialism in the wake of the death of Communist ideology is destroying the moral fabric of the Chinese society, while the ideological excesses from 1957 to 1978 had created an aversion and resistance to the creation of any new ideology among the Chinese. Many problems that China is confronted with today could be understood in light of the ideological vacuum, but ideological solutions are not available. Power is not shared through institutional arrangement, and institutional checks have always been weak in China. Power wielding is largely subject to individual government officials' consciousness. But with the death of Communist ideology and in an environment of "money worship," CPC members and government officials are not exempt from materialistic appeals. Using power for personal gains has thus become a norm instead of an exception. The rise of crimes is also related to "money worship." Having failed to build "the spirit of socialism" and create "socialist new men" from the late 1950s to the late 1970s under the people's commune system, the CPC would find it extremely difficult to fight corruption in society in general and curb the revival of old practice in rural China in particular. Punishment alone would not be able to solve the problems derived from the deterioration of moral values.

Conclusion

From 1978 to the present, the CPC has tried to lead peasants where they wanted to go by sponsoring a modernization program and relaxing its control over the peasantry, but the CPC has created a dilemma for itself. To promote economic growth, the CPC has to reject its ideology in practice, relax its control over the peasantry, and discard one of the CPC's most familiar political vehicles - mobilization. But now the CPC has to face the consequences that the CPC was not prepared for - sources of instability. What alternatives does the CPC have to respond these sources of instability? This is an open question that demands more research from China scholars.

Notes

1.   See Weixing Chen, "Transition and Transition Problems in China," *The Journal of East Asian Affairs* Vol. X, No. 2 (Summer/Fall 1996), pp.309-336.

2.   *Renmin Ribao (People's Daily)* overseas edition (December 27, 1994), p.1.

3.   Zheng Quan, "Quanguo cun ji zuzhi zhuangkuang de diaocha (national survey of the state of village-level organization*)"   Zhongguo Minzheng (Chinese Civil Administration)* (September 1989), p.16.

4.   "A Survey of China," *The Economist* (March 18, 1995), p.21.

5.   Daniel Kelliher, "The Chinese Debate over Village Self-Government," *The China Journal* issue 37 (January 1997), p.66.

6.   See Weixing Chen, "The Political Economy of Rural Industrialization: the Village Conglomerate in Shandong Province," *Modern China* Vol. 24, No. 1 (January 1998), pp.73-96.

7.   See Brantly Womack and Guangzhi Zhao, "The Many Worlds of China's Provinces" in David goodman and Gerald Segal, eds. *China Deconstructs* (London and New York: Routledge, 1994),p.170.

8.   This was discussed by Cheng Li and David Bachman. See Li and Bachman, "Localism, Elitism, and Immobilism: Elite Formation and Social Change in Post-Mao China," *World Politics* vol.XLII no.1 (October 1989), pp.85-87.

9.   See Shen Liren and Dai Yuanchen, "Formation of 'Dukedom' Economics' and Their Causes and Defects," *Chinese Economic Studies* Vol.25 No.4 (Summer 1992), pp.6-24.

10.   For a detailed description of this case, see *Renmin Ribao*, overseas edition (August 28, 1993), p.1 and p.3.

11.   Joseph R. Gregory, "China, Taiwan, and Hong Kong: U.S. Challenges," *Great Decisions 1995* (Foreign Policy Association, 1995), p.61.

12.   Official data for these "negative things" are not available.

13.   See Vivienne Shue, *The Reach of the State: Sketches of the Chinese Body Politic* (Stanford: Stanford University Press, 1988).

14.   *Renmin Ribao* overseas edition (October 31, 1994), p.1.

15.   Li Rui, *A True Account of Lushan Meeting* (Wuhan: Chunqiu Press and Hunan Education Press, 1988), p.363.

16.   Mark Selden, *The Political Economy of Chinese Development* (Armonk, New York: M.E. Sharpe, 1993), p.190.

17.   See Weixing Chen, "Peasant challenge in Post-Communist China," *Journal of Contemporary China* Vol.6, No.14 (March 1997), pp.101-115.

18.   The natural village became the village brigade in the people's commune,

which was the intermediate level between the commune (township today) and the production team within the village.

19. Detailed discussions of peasant situation under the people's commune were provided in Sulamith H. Potter/Jack M. Potter, *China's Peasant* (Cambridge: Cambridge University Press, 1990) and Mark Selden, *The Political Economy of Chinese Development* (Armonk, New York: M.E. Sharpe, 1993).

20. Rural China has undergone three waves of development, namely, communization from 1957 to 1978, the implementation of the household responsibility system from 1978 to 1984, and the rise of rural enterprise and commercial activities from 1985 to the present.

21. Given the nature of controlled media and press in China, there should be more incidents of this kind that were not reported. The figures presented here are from "A Survey of China," *The Economist* (March 18, 1995), p.19.

22. Jean C. Oi, "Fiscal Reform and the Economic Foundations of Local State Corporatism in China," *World Politics* Vol.45 No.1 (October 1992), pp.100-101.

23. See David S.G. Goodman and Gerald Segal, eds., *China Deconstructs* (London and New York: Routledge, 1994).

Chapter 6

Fiscal reform and State Capacity Building

ZHANG Baohui

The Chinese economic reform is often characterized as a miracle. It is one of the very few cases of reform that not only successfully transformed the economic system but also generated spectacular sustained economic growth. The weakening role of the state in the economy and increased autonomy of individuals, enterprises, and local governments explained the dynamism behind the economic growth of China. However, a recent trend has been the attempts by China to rebuild its state capacity of economic management. The most notable policy was the 1994 fiscal reform that reversed fiscal decentralization of the 1980s and sought to strengthen the fiscal capacity of the central government. This chapter studies the economic and political logic behind this important new policy.

State Capacity and Economic Reforms

State capacity of economic management has been an important subject in the study of East Asian economic miracles. As some argue, what differentiate East Asian economic experience from the rest of the world is the strong capacity of the state. In fact, the statist school is the most influential approach in studying the economic miracles of Japan, South Korea, and Taiwan. In those countries, strategic management of the economy is accomplished through a combination of powerful and autonomous planning agencies, industrial policies that target selective sectors, and government control over resource allocation.

Although economic reform requires increased role for the market, maintaining appropriate state capacity during the transition process is also important. As Rana and Paz point out, "The task of transforming a former state socialist economy is significantly more complicated than the development issues facing a typical developing country."[2] To manage this highly complicated process, recent studies of economic reform argue that certain state capacities need to be strengthened or rebuilt. As Linz and Stephan observe, economic reform entails less state scope but greater state capacity.[3] In the post-communist transitions in Eastern Europe and the former Soviet Union, many states "with rapidly eroding capacity" simply failed to manage their economic transitions and the result has been collapse of the economy. In contrast, new democracies in Southern Europe all strengthened their states and improved their economies after the democratic transition. They accomplished this primarily through increased state capacity in revenue mobilization which in turn allowed the state to "increase significantly social welfare spending and state employment."[4]

Armijo, Bierseker, and Lowenthal also argue that adequate state capacity is central to successful economic transitions. Since state capacity tends to decline dramatically during democratization, they maintain that simultaneous political and economic transitions should be avoided.[5] Economic reform, as the experiences of Chile and China demonstrate, has a better chance of success under authoritarian regimes. These regimes tend to have stronger state capacity in organizing and implementing highly complicated and crisis-ridden transitions to market economy.

Moises Naim, in his study of the problems of economic reforms in Latin America, argues that the goal of the second stage of reform in continent should be rebuilding state capacity. Having played an important role in drafting Venezuela's economic reforms as the Minister of Industry, Naim observes that although it was essential to dismantle inefficient state institutions during the first phase of reform, it had the unintended consequence of undermining state capacity and functions that are indispensable for economic development. To pull Latin American countries out of their economic decline requires a reorganization of state institutions and enhancement of state capacities. This process is called "renovating the state."[6]

In China, since the late 1980s there has been a trend to rebuild state capacity of macro-economic management. Even before the reform, China's central management institutions, compared with those in the

Soviet Union, were never powerful as result of Mao's economic decentralization during the Great Leap Forward and the Cultural Revolution. The economic reform in the 1980s further weakened China's state capacity of macro-economic management. This caused several prominent problems for the Chinese economy during the reform years, including the cycles of boom and bust, irrational industrial structures, and increasing regional disparity. In the period of late 1980s to early 1990s Chinese leaders came to the conclusion that stronger macro-economic management required rebuilding of state capacity. As a 1989 resolution by the Central Committee of CCP pointed out: "In our reform of the old over-controlled economic system, we overlooked necessary centralization. In our emphasis on increasing dynamics at the micro-level, we overlooked macro-level management."[8]

The World Bank also supported the efforts to rebuild China's state capacity in macro-economic management. According to a bank report: "One of the most problematic aspects of the current regime is the lack of institutions to formulate and implement appropriate policies.... It appears that some form of recentralization also is needed to achieve future market reform."[9] Another World Bank study points out that effective macro-economic management "will be crucial to the success of future reform efforts." Therefore, "Further institutional change might be needed to enhance the capacity of central agencies to implement policies."[10]

China's efforts to rebuild its macro-economic management capacity included efforts in several fronts. One was to strengthen strategic planning through a renovated State Planning Commission. The SPC was never powerful under Mao's efforts to weaken the central bureaucracy. Moreover, according to economist Zhou Shu-lian, in the old days the SPC "gave priority to annual plans to guide the economy and paid little attention to medium and long term planning."[11] In 1988 China abolished the old SPC and created a new SPC with new missions. The new SPC no longer manages the economy through specific production plans, as the old SPC did. Rather, it focuses on long-range strategic planning. To accomplish this, a new Department of Long Range Planning and a Department of Industrial Policy were added to the SPC. They were designed to strengthen SPC's institutional capacity to macro-manage the economic development of China.[12]

As the experiences of other East Asian economies demonstrate, for the planning agencies to be effective it must be institutionally insulated and stand above other economic bureaucracies. According to Wade, the pilot planning agency must occupy a position capable of controlling and coordinating other ministries.[13] To achieve this, the new SPC is led by a committee. Its members, beside the Chairman and Vice Chairman of SPC, include heads of the Finance Ministry, the Central Bank, the State Price Bureau, and the State Statistical Bureau. This increases the political power base of SPC and enhances its ability to formulate and implement macro-economic policies.[14]

China also tried to strengthen its macro-economic management capacity through increased sectoral intervention. To emulate the practice of selective industrial policy in other East Asian economies, China in 1989 formulated its first comprehensive industrial policy. The policy targeted a range of industrial sectors crucial for sustainable and balanced economic development. They include the machinery and electronic industry, especially high added value machine and electronic products; high technology industries; high foreign currency earning export sectors; infrastructure, including transportation and telecommunication; and basic industries, including energy and chemical industries. This selective industrial policy was created by the new SPC soon after its creation in 1988. In August of the year, SPC circulated a draft of the policy at the National Planning Conference. After revision it was further discussed in the State Council and the important Finance and Economic Committee of the CCP at the end of 1988. In March of 1989 the policy was announced in "The Resolution of the State Council on Current Industrial Policy."[15]

However, China's most recent and the most significant effort in rebuilding its state capacity was the 1994 fiscal reform. The goal of the reform was to strengthen the state capacity in resource mobilization and allocation. The reform intended to reverse the trend of declining central control over revenues since the 1980s through a recentralized fiscal regime. This reform was the most significant institution building effort since sufficient revenues are the foundation of effective state. This paper below examines the policies of the 1994 fiscal reform. It also studies the political and economic conditions that facilitated the adoption of this major reform.

Recentralizing China's Fiscal System

This section will first briefly review fiscal decentralization in the 1980s and the necessity of strengthening central control over the fiscal system. It will then examine the policies of 1994 fiscal reform.

Problems of Fiscal Decentralization

The fiscal system before the reform was highly centralized. Local governments were merely agents of revenue collection and remitted almost all they collected to the central government. The central government then allocated a budget for local governments.[16] However, this system left little incentive for local governments for revenue mobilization. The system also left local governments with meager resources to pursue their own economic activities

During the 1980s, as part of the general decentralization package, the fiscal system was decentralized with the purpose of providing incentives for local tax collection and economic development. Provinces were given much greater authority and responsibility in revenue mobilization and were allowed to retain a certain amount of revenue above a preset level negotiated with the center. Several systems were instituted respectively at 1980s, 1985, and 1988.[17] The final system created in 1988 had six subsystems. For sixteen poor provinces, their revenue remittances to the center were fixed in nominal amounts and any additional efforts for revenue mobilization would be kept by these provinces. Three provinces (Shanghai, Shandong, and Heilongjiang) transferred a relatively high portion of their total revenue to the center. These transfers were fixed in nominal terms, so as to give them additional resource mobilization for shared taxes. For Guangdong and Hunan, where the central share was small, a high rate of growth of revenue to the center was provided but was also fixed in nominal terms, thus leaving the provinces all the revenue above the specified growth rate. For six provinces, the earlier system of sharing at certain percentages, either uniform or variable, was retained though for two of them the marginal rate of remittance was higher than the average. For ten provinces, the formula was a mixture of the above two systems with a fixed rate of sharing up to a certain rate of growth of revenue, and 100 percent retention by the provinces of any revenue above the specified growth rate.[18]

Fiscal decentralization of the 1980s provided strong incentives for local governments to mobilize revenues since they could now retain significant revenues above a level contracted between them and the central government. The phenomenal growth of Chinese economy to a large extent benefited from fiscal decentralization since local governments now had much more effective control over resources to promote their own economic development.[19]

However, fiscal decentralization also created long term macroeconomic problems. The greatest problem has been the decline of revenue as a percentage of GDP. As a result of high economic growth generated by fiscal decentralization and a number of other factors, the share of revenue as percentage of GDP declined over the reform years. The table below shows the trend.

Table 1: Development in Government Revenue in China (as a percentage of GDP)

1978	34.4	1986	25.2
1979	31.6	1987	22.7
1980	29.4	1988	19.9
1981	29.0	1989	20.4
1982	27.2	1990	19.1
1983	27.4	1991	16.9
1984	26.4	1992	14.7
1985	26.7	1993	14.1

Source: World Bank, 1995, *China: Macroeconomic Stability   in a Decentralized Economy*, Table 7.3.

This decline of revenue as share of GDP shows the weakening role of the Chinese state in the economy, since government needs sufficient revenues to effectively manage the macroeconomy. International comparison shows that the although China used to have a highly centralized and state controlled economy, the current government's control of resources is even far below the standards of established market economies. Table 2 shows the revenues as percentage of GDP of some advanced market economies.

Table 2: Total Revenue As a Percentage of GDP in 1992

Australia	25.61	Germany	30.53
Japan	21.42	Italy	41.41
United States	19.84	Norway	49.30
Austria	35.70	Spain	32.17
Belgium	43.80	Sweden	43.21
France	40.82	United Kingdom	36.01

Source: IMF, *Government Statistics Yearbook*, 1995

These figures show that the Chinese transitional economy has a relatively weak state if we accept the conventional view that government's ability to collect revenues is an important sign of state capacity.[20] More important however, is the decline of central share of revenue in China as result of fast growth of local revenues. For some of the major contributing provinces to central revenue, tax contribution to the center was fixed in nominal terms for three years. Provinces retained revenues above the nominal terms. For other provinces, if they could increase revenue above certain moderate rates, all revenues were retained by the provinces. Since local economic growth and, as a result, local revenues have been growing very fast, the central share of revenues in China has declined from 59% in 1978 to 38% in 1993.[21] By contrast, central government's share of revenue in leading market economies is much higher. For example, in Japan the central government controls 64% of all revenues. Although Australia is a federal state, its central government's share of revenue is 80%.[22] According to a study by the Finance Ministry of advanced market economies, central government's share of revenues in countries with unitary system is on average 56%, with France and Spain as high as 88% and 84%. In countries with federal system, the average of the central share of revenues is still about 50%.[23]

The decentralized fiscal system first of all caused problems for China's transition to a market economy. The 1988 system was put on a more negotiated basis whereby different provinces were able to establish different marginal retention rates for the tax revenues concerned. Since the fiscal contracts varied across regions and over time, the system lacked standardization and clarity across the board. Thus, the system strongly encouraged particularistic bargaining between a province and the center concerning the rate of retention of revenues.[24] This works against market economy which uses universalistic rules by which everyone must play. As observed by Moise Naim, who once served as minister of industry of Venezuela, one of the most important tasks of market reform is building institutions that effectively enforce universalistic rules. In many countries going through economic transitions, unfortunately, sectoral interests are able to get particularistic favors at the expense of public interest.[25]

Another problem is that the decentralized fiscal system allowed local governments to have de facto control over the fiscal policy of the country. As the World Bank points out, "Unlike most countries, China has not had a national tax administration service. Although the central government determines tax rates and the tax base, all taxes, with the

exception of excise tax, have been collected by local tax authorities."[26]
As a result:

> This has allowed local governments to enjoy de facto control over
> tax policy. Regardless of statutory tax rates, local administrations
> have been able to negotiate contracts with local enterprises to provide
> these enterprises tax relief and grant them tax incentives nor
> authorized by the center. Local governments have also been able to
> urge the local tax bureaus to be less vigorous in their collection of
> taxes to be shared with, or remitted to, the central government.[27]

According to another World Bank study, unlike most other
countries, in China it is the central government that is on the receiving
end of revenue distribution. Elsewhere it is local governments on the
receiving end and the central government has the responsibility of
collecting taxes and then distributing grants to local governments.[28]
The de facto control by Chinese local authority over fiscal policies of
the country deprived the central government of many resources and
caused the declining central share of revenue.

However, there are larger problems caused by the declining share of
revenue in GNP in general and central share of the revenues in specific.
Because of weakened control over resources, the center has been
unable to effectively macro-manage the economy. One unique feature
of the Chinese economy during the reform years is the cycle of boom
and bust. The primary cause was that the central government could not
control the level of investments which were done mostly by local
governments. With their increased resources as a result of fiscal
decentralization, various local governments embarked upon ambitious
local industrialization.[29] This caused a tendency of the Chinese
economy to be periodically overheated with strong inflationary
pressures. The 1992-1993 phenomenal growth of the Chinese economy
and the resulting double digit inflation was the latest example. In
advanced market economies, fiscal and monetary policies are the major
tools of macroeconomic management. In China however, the
financially starved central government lacked resources to
macromanage the economy through either of the tools. It could only
use harsh administrative measures to slow down the economy. This
usually results in a sudden and strong contraction of the economy,
namely a bust.

Another macroeconomic problem caused by fiscal decentralization is
that local governments tend to use their newly acquired resources to
invest in certain industries only. These are primarily light and
processing industries that have low entry barriers in terms of

technology and capital. These industries also generate quick economic returns and thus provide local governments with the much needed revenues. The problem of this pattern of industrialization is that China's industrial structure lacks rationality.[30] High-tech industries that could make China a strong power in the future and infrastructures that are important for sustainable growth are underinvested. From the point of view of local governments, it is economically irrational to invest in these areas due to their risks and slow economic returns.

To rationalize China's industrial structures, the central government in recent years has tried to use selective industrial policy to promote key sectors.[31] This practice of industrial targeting was to some extent copied from Japan and South Korea. However, the implementation of the policy has generally been a failure. The explanation is quite simple. The central government simply does not have the necessary resources to support the key sectors while local governments continue to pour investments into light and processing industries. The success of South Korean industrial policy was due to the fact that the government once owned all the banks and therefore was able to control the bulk of economic resources and support key sectors.

The third macroeconomic problem caused by fiscal decentralization is uneven regional development. Some coastal provinces, such as Guangdong and Fujian, received preferential fiscal contracts with the center and were thus able to retain a larger portion of their revenues. These provinces then used their new resources to promote rapid economic growth.[32] Other provinces, especially those inland, did not benefit as much as coastal provinces. Many of them had to remit a relatively high portion of revenue to the center. Combined with other generous policies from the center to coastal provinces, fiscal decentralization created very disparate regional growth rates, with inland provinces lagging far behind. According to the World Bank, this conflicts with the equity objective of economic development.[33] The results are growing differences in living standard and political resentment by some provinces.

The Fiscal Centralization of 1994

Although fiscal decentralization of the 1980s provided important incentives and opportunities for local government to create the great Chinese economic take-off, its defects also grew increasingly obvious. In fact, the declining central fiscal position has generated a number of serious macroeconomic problems that threaten China's economic future.

Since the early 1990s there have been extensive discussion by fiscal experts and administrators about the problems of contract based and bargaining oriented system.[34] The consensus of these experts was that the system was over decentralized. Many also agree that a new revenue sharing regime with universalistic standards and a stronger role for the central government was the only way out.[35] The Finance Ministry also came to the conclusion that declining central share of revenue, a rising state budget deficit, and the macro-economic problems they caused mandated an overhaul of the decentralized fiscal system.[36] As noted by Finance Minister Liu Zhong-li on the need of reform:

> The weak financial capability of the country seriously compromised the fulfillment of various government responsibilities. Not only could we not adequately invest in infrastructures, defense, agriculture, science, and education, many regions could not even pay salaries on time. Under the situation of central financial hardship, investment in country's key projects faced serious problems. The central government found it very difficult to play macromanagement roles in rationalizing economic structures, coordinating regional development, and overcoming major obstacles of reform.[37]

The World Bank strongly supported strengthening the role of the Chinese central government in macroeconomic management, including fiscal centralization. As one report argues, "First and foremost, the primacy of the central government in the area of macroeconomic management needs to be clearly and permanently established."[38] The Bank specifically supported centralization of the fiscal system. It argued that in a multilevel fiscal system as existed in China, "for the sake of efficiency and equity, most of the major taxes have to be collected centrally.[39] The Bank further suggested three options for reform in China. One is that the center levies and collects all the revenues and gives a portion of the revenues to provincial governments as grants. Option two is that the center levies and collects all taxes but then shares the proceeds of some or all taxes with the provinces on the basis of a formula or a set of formulas. Option three allows the center to levy and collect most of the more important taxes, but the provinces have autonomy to levy and collect other taxes; in addition, the provinces get a share of one or more central taxes and/or receive grants from the center.

With increasing policy consensus on the need of recentralizing the fiscal system and support from the World Bank, a far reaching fiscal reform was adopted by the Third Plenum of the 14th Congress of the CCP in November 1993 with implementation beginning in 1994. The reform was nothing short of, according to the World Bank, "historical proportion," since it sought to fundamentally restructure the fiscal relationship between the center and local governments.[40] The reform abolished fiscal decentralization by a single stroke and could have profound impact on the future of central-local relations.

The fiscal recentralization of 1994 had two components. One was the creation of a new tax sharing regime between the central and local governments. The other was the reform of tax administration with the creation of a National Tax Service. The contents of tax reform and revenue sharing reform is quite complicated and technical.[41] Below is a summary of the major points of the reform.

Basically, the reform followed the third option recommended by the World Bank. Under this option, a tax sharing regime is created in which the central government has sole control of the most important taxes while local governments have control over less important taxes. Moreover, the central and local governments also share certain taxes according to a formula with the central government having the lion's share. So the system mixes tax assignment with tax sharing. The figure below shows the tax assignment to the central and local governments as well as the shared taxes.

Figure 1: The New Tax System

Central Taxes:
Tariffs
Income tax of centrally owned enterprises
Tax on revenues generated by railways, banks, and insurance companies
Consumption tax
Offshore oil resources taxes
Local Taxes:
Business tax (exclude those generated by banks, railways, and insurance companies)
Income tax from locally owned enterprises
Personal income tax
tax on land and property sales
Estate duty
Stamp duty
Shared Taxes:
Value-added tax (VAT)-central government 75% and local government 25%
Security trading tax-central government 50% and local government 50%
Resource tax other than offshore oil tax- mostly to local government

Source: This table is adapted from Tsang and Cheng, 1994

The new system gives the central government control of the most important tax sources, such as income tax from centrally owned enterprises (which tend to be the largest enterprises in China and largest revenue contributors) and a lion's share of the newly created and very important VAT, which, according to the World Bank, is likely to attract 40 percent or more of total tax revenues.[42] The Bank observes that a "good feature of the system is that taxes applying to mobile economic bases, including some that can usually generate very large revenues (for example enterprise profits tax and VAT) have been assigned to the central governments. By contrast, taxes on immobile factors of production (such as land and property taxes, agricultural and husbandry taxes), have been assigned to subnational governments."[43]

The second part of the reform is the creation of a National Tax Service (NST). As already mentioned, China, unlike most other countries, did not have central tax collection capability. Instead, the central government relied on local tax collection administrations which often tried their best to collect less tax for the center. To take the hands of local governments out of the tax sources of central government, the 1994 fiscal reform created two separate tax collection channels to correspond to the new tax assignment system. The National Tax Service has the sole responsibility of collecting all central taxes and all shared taxes, including the very important VAT. Local Tax Service (LTS) only collects local taxes. To ensure the authority of NST in dealing with local governments, especially provincial governments, the agency was given the status of a central ministry, on the same level with the Finance Ministry. To further strengthen the authority of the agency, the first Director of NTS is Finance Minister Liu Zhong-li himself. The Deputy Director and the de facto top administrator of the agency is the former Deputy Finance Minister Xiang Huai-cheng, who played an important role in the fiscal recentralization. To ensure the loyalty of local heads of the NTS, the central government directly appointed all directors of the regional NTS.[44]

This complete restructuring of fiscal system seeks to restore the primacy of the center in central-local fiscal relations. The new system intends to raise the revenue to GDP ratio through more effective revenue mobilization. More importantly, with the center in control of major taxes and with the help of NTS, the new system seeks to increase the central share of revenues and its weight in the economy. The goal is to increase the central share of revenues from the 38% of 1993 to the international standard of 55-60% by the year 2000. Under the new system, parts of the increased revenues for the central government will be returned to local governments in the form of grants. This will strengthen the strategic management role of the center, since it will be able to dictate the use of these grants according to its macroeconomic objectives. This will thus create a financial dependency by the local governments on the center, enabling the latter to set the perimeters of Chinese economy.

The 1994 reform was very bold indeed. The reform measures were, according to a World Bank study, "extremely ambitious in their scope-- more so, it can be argued, than those in any other countries."[45] Even though the reform represents a complete overhaul of China's fiscal system, its implementation was a success judged by strong revenue increases in 1994 and 1995. A report by the Finance Ministry claimed that the success was of historical proportion. In 1994, the first year of implementation, total revenues grew by 86.9 billion *yuan* over 1993, a 20% increase. Moreover, central revenue increased by 25.6%.[46] In the first eight months of 1995, according to Finance Minister Liu Zhong-li, central revenue again grew by 18.7% over the same period of 1994.[47]

The most important indication of the success of 1994 reform was that the central government achieved the goal of raising its share of revenues to the 55-60% level. This goal was in fact accomplished in the very first year of the reform. The 1994 central share of revenues was 55.7%. According to a study by the Finance Ministry, this showed that "the mechanism that attributes most revenues to the central government has already been established."[48] Another research also comments on the success of the 1994 reform:

> The fiscal relationship between the central and local governments went through a fundamental change. The central government has reestablished its preeminent position. Between 1985 and 1993, central and local shares of revenues were on average 38% and 62%. In 1994 the ratio changed to 55.7% and 44.3%.[49]

In 1995 the trend of increasing central share of revenues continued. The total revenue income of the year was 618.773 billion *yuan*. Total central revenue was 384.513 billion while total local revenue was 234.26 billion. As result of this, central share of revenues jumped to 62.14%.[50] This was indeed a fundamental change from the 1993 situation when local share of revenues was 62%.

The success of the 1994 fiscal reform could also be demonstrated by the cooperation from local governments, particularly those larger coastal provinces. The Finance Ministry in early 1994 sent nine separate inspection teams to various provinces to monitor the implementation of the new system. The conclusion was, "Situations indicate that all regions paid great attention to the fiscal reform and the overall implementation is good."[51] Local leaders also openly endorsed the reform measures. For example, the Head of Finance of Liaoning Province observed that "although the old contract based fiscal system once played a positive role, it became increasingly incompatible with the new situation. The contract system limited the growth of revenues. The new tax sharing regime is necessary." The Head of Finance of Shanghai said that "the fiscal reform is long overdue and we sincerely support the measures." The Governor of Fujian added that fiscal reform "is a major measure concerning the reform of the entire economic system. If the fiscal reform could succeed, it will promote the overall progress of reform." The Governor of Shandong even said that "we raise both hands to support the increase of central revenues."[52]

Guangdong Province, which perhaps benefited most from the old contract system, also saw successful implementation of the reform. During the era of fiscal contract, Guangdong remitted only 4-5% of the revenues above the contract to the central government. Because of this, provincial revenue increased from a meager 3.4 billion yuan in 1979 to 34.6 billion yuan in 1993. This greatly aided the economic take-off of the province in the 1980s. However, under the new system Guangdong has to surrender 45-50% of any revenue increase to the center. Nonetheless, Xie Fei, the Party Secretary of Guangdong, openly endorsed the reform. As he said, "We must not allow parochial interests to compromise the reform. We must fully follow the decision of the center and resolutely implement it."[53]

Both the adoption of the 1994 fiscal reform and its success were largely unexpected. Although there had been policy discussions about the need of a new revenue sharing regime, very few, both in and outside China, expected that the reform would be adopted at the end of 1993. In fact, according to Shirk, a rationalization of China's fiscal system was impossible to accomplish. So why and how the recentralization of 1994 took place?

Conditions favoring the Fiscal Reform

Obviously, the 1994 fiscal recentralization was not a minor policy change. It was a bold restructuring of central-local relations in China. Not only is its significance profound, the reform also had a comprehensive and coherent plan. According to the World Bank, this reform was systematic and rather unique since the Chinese economic reform tends to be partial and incremental.[54] This paper argues that it was the favorable political and economic conditions of the 1993-1994 period that made the fiscal reform possible. Specifically, in this period of time a new pattern of political alignment emerged among top leaders that promoted policy consensus, while an economic crisis created opportunities for central leaders to push through the reform.

Political Realignment in the Center

Although problems of fiscal decentralization led many to the belief that a new, more centralized fiscal regime was neede, a policy shift to recentralization was not easy. Indeed, as one article on fiscal reform in China points out, vested local economic and political interests generated by the decentralized system made systematic reform very difficult.[55] Having local governments giving up fiscal decentralization required a favorable political situation.

This favorable political situation was ripe at the end of 1993 when a unified and determined central leadership emerged for the first time in the reform history. In the past, the political center of China was always divided into two camps, those favoring more decentralization and those favoring stronger macroeconomic management by the center. Except for periods of recentralization which occurred after each round of economic overheating, the camp favoring decentralization graudally had the upper hand. Susan Shirk's model of reform policymaking in China could work well in this period. Leaders favoring more decentralization, such as Zhao Zhi-yang and Deng Xiao-ping, struck deals with local leaders. They gave more decentralization in return for support of their power struggle with those central leaders who were economic centrists or conservatives.[56]

This pattern of political alignment, with radical reform leaders and local interests on the one side and economic centrists and conservatives on the other, weakened the central authority. Specifically, it weakened the central efforts to build a new macroeconomic management system which was perceived by many, including the World Bank, as necessary for managing China's transitional economy. Because of the political division at the center, central institutions could only periodically use ad hoc and often purely administrative measures to control the cycle of boom and bust in the Chinese economy. Systematic institutional reform was compromised and delayed. The central response after the 1988 economic overheating and the 1989 political crisis (which was in part the result of high inflation) achieved only temporary results in trying to control the cycle of boom and bust. In 1992 this effort quickly collapsed when Deng Xiao-ping made a last ditch but successful try to mobilize local governments and pressure the economic centrists in Beijing to institutionalize decentralization. The result was another boom and bust cycle with an inflation rate never seen in the history of PRC.

The political center of China was politically divided until the middle of 1993 when a new pattern of political alignment emerged. A unified central leadership that favored more centralization emerged for the first time. The emergence of this new central political alignment was triggered by the quickly deteriorating health of Deng Xiao-ping in 1993. For the first time, the aging leader really lost his physical capacity and no longer exercised political control. Since power is relative, a loss of power by Deng Xiao-ping meant an increase of power for others, especially those who controlled formal powers and but were previously overshadowed by Deng. Jiang Zhe-min and Li Peng no longer faced a competing source of central power that constrained their exercise of authority. This relative ascendance of the power of Jiang Ze-min and Li Peng was aided by the rise of Vice Premier Zhu Rong-ji, who since 1993 exercised enormous power in economic management.

The new leadership team for the first time showed central political unity, since all three favored more centralization. Jiang Ze-min, Li Peng, and Zhu Rong-ji share similar views regarding the problems of the Chinese economy and their solutions. Premier Li Peng is a classic centrist who owes his career to Chen Yun, the patriarch of the centrist economic approach. Li has always supported the policies of recentralization of macroeconomic management. Jiang Ze-min also turned out to be a classic centrist. Although he was the Mayor of Shanghai during the 1980s, he also spent a significant amount of time in Beijing before he was transferred to Shanghai. During the 1970s he worked in the First Ministry of Machinary. From 1982 to 1985 Jiang served as the Minister in the Ministry of Electronics Industry. More importantly, as institutional theories argue, role defines interests and preferences. Precisely because Jiang is the top central leader, he must consolidate central authority to secure his own political future. In recent years we have seen a systematic campaign of "supporting the central authority" (wei hu zhong yang quan wei). Since Jiang perceived potential challenges from local powers, his only choice was to strengthen the authority position of the central government.

The most interesting development was that Zhu Rong-ji turned out to be the most vigorous economic centrist. When he was appointed Vice Premier in charge of the economy, Western media speculated that he was the Gorbachev of China. This was a gross misperception. In fact, although Zhu had a short stint as the Mayor of Shanghai, he spent the rest of his career in central planning institutions (including the State

Planning Commission), ultimately rising to the position of the Vice President of State Planning Commission. After he took charge of daily management of the Chinese economy, especially after becoming the economic czar in the summer of 1993, he was the most visible and energetic proponent of economic recentralization.

Not only did the three top leaders share a similar perception of the problems of Chinese economy, namely excessive economic decentralization and the need of strenghthening central macroeconomic management, but the power relationship among them also favored unity. Although they share similar policy preferences, they could still have been divided if there is a struggle among them over personal powers. This scenario in fact could result in the alignment pattern described by Shirk, when some central leaders formed coalitions with local leaders to combat their central rivals.

However, such an alignment did not occur. The official top leader Jiang Ze-min has already consolidated his power and made his leadership basically indisputable. This is partly because he holds control of all the top formal powers of the party, the state, and the military. As institutional theories of politics imply, as opposed to behavioral theories of politics, formal authority relationship indeed means something. This is especially so when Deng Xiao-ping was near his death and had genuinely lost his political influence. Jiang has also proved to be much more skillful politically than expected. As being observed, he has created a credible power base of his own. One indication of Jiang's power consolidation was the fact that he has changed the entire top echelon of the military several time in recent years.[57]

Jiang's consolidation of power was also due to the fact that his potential competitors are not in positions to realistically challenge his power. Li Peng is basically a technocrat and in fact wanted to resign his position of Premier in the summer of 1993, primarily because of heart problems. Zhu Rong-ji's power is restricted to economic management. He simply does not have the full range of power as enjoyed by Jiang in the party, the state, and most importantly, the military. Some Western reports mentioned Qiao Shi, the President of the People's Congress, as a potential power contender. However, the People's Congress remains a rubber stamp institution. Although Qiao used to be the head of security apparatus, this is not of much help. The Chinese security apparatus, unlike those in Stalin's Soviet Union, is politically insignificant. It has never played a prominent role in the power struggles within the top leadership.

The result of Jiang Ze-min successful consolidation of power is that others, as Goldstein argues, must bandwagon with him and support his policies of strengthening central power.[58] This is not a problem for economic centrists Li Peng and Zhu Rong-ji, who after all shared similar views of the problems of a weakened central government. Thus, since 1993 with the fading of Deng Xiao-ping from Chinese politics, the consolidation of Jiang Ze-min's power, and the rise of classic economic centrist Zhu Rong-ji, a unified central leadership that favored a stronger central authority emerged for the first time in the reform history of China.

This new pattern of central alignment is extremely important to any efforts to reshape the central-local relations in China, including fiscal recentralization. This is because that, as the World Bank emphasizes, a united center in China is more powerful than any resistance.[59] And as Liberthal argues, Chinese political power at the top is still highly concentrated.[60] If this center is unified and has a clear policy agenda, local government will have great difficulty in defeating major policy changes initiated by the center.

The Economic Crisis of 1993

Major policy change could be further facilitated by crisis situations.[61] As Gourevitch argues:

> It is the crisis years that put the system under stress. Hard times expose strengths and weakness to scrutiny, allowing observers to see relationships that are often blurred in prosperous periods, when good times slake the propensity to contest and challenge. The lean years are times when old relationships crumble and new ones have to be constructed.[62]

Although the political center of China was politically unified and enjoyed a policy consensus regarding fiscal recentralization, it still needed a crisis situation to upset the present policy equilibrium and create political opportunities to push through the reform. A crisis situation facilitates major reform both by establishing a sense of urgency for policy change and by discrediting the present policy paradigm.[63] Armijo, Biersteker and Lowenthal particularly emphasize the importance of reformers seizing the moment of crisis to push through their their progrms. They call this strategy "awaiting an economic trough."[64]

Two related crisis occurred around 1993. One was the real or perceived crisis for Chinese central authority and the future of political stability in China. The second was the immediate economic crisis developed in the middle of 1993. Both helped legitimatize a reversal of fiscal decentralization at the end of the year.

The crisis or the perceived crisis by the central leaders concerning the future of political stability of China was associated with the rise of local economies and the decline of central power. One important development in recent years was that Chinese policy experts began to link central economic weakening to potential central political weakening. Or we can say that these were attempts of political analysis of economic problems. One prominent effort was made by Wang Shao-guang, a Chinese political scientist teaching in the United States, and Hu An-gang, a researcher at the Chinese Academy of Social Sciences. They wrote an influential report on the political consequences of fiscal crisis.[65] They argue that historically speaking, declining state extractive capacity leads to weakened ability of governance in general. The result could be fundamental political crisis for the state. The report allegedly reached the Politburo of the CCP and was circulated widely among the political elites.[66]

The perceived political crisis accompanying a fiscal crisis was amplified by the political succession in China. With Deng Xiao-ping near death, the ability of his successors to maintain political stability was a big question. Indeed, in recent years the central ability to implement national policies have been compromised by increasingly powerful local governments.[67] This led to widespread doubts about the future of the Chinese authority. Thus, the idea of a pending political crisis as a result of central fiscal weakening was readily received by the new leaders. Improving central fiscal position became an urgent policy goal. The fiscal recentralizaiton thus became part of the larger movement of "Supporting the Central Authority" that was pushed by the leadership team of Jiang Ze-min, Li Peng, and Zhu Rong-ji.

Beside the real or imagined political crisis as perceived by the Chinese leaders, the 1993 economic crisis also facilitated the fiscal reform. Deng Xiao-ping's 1992 tour of southern China led to new economic decentralization and truly phenomenal economic growth from the second half of 1992 to the first half of 1993. However, this round of economic boom inevitably led to another round of overheating. The result was the highest inflationary pressure in the economic history of PRC. The main cause for this overheating was the dramatic increase in unregulated investment by local economies. The 1993 crisis once again and perhaps ultimately discredited those who supported economic decentralization. The crisis proved that lack of effective macroeconomic management by the center could only create economic chaos and threaten China's transition to market economy.

The economic crisis of 1993 created opportunities for central leaders to push through fiscal reform. First of all, Zhu Rong-ji, the most energetic and dedicated centrist, became the economic czar in the summer of the year and announced an economic austerity plan to cool down the economy. His first effort was to assume the control of the Central Bank and thus cut off capital for local investment. Zhu then personally pushed for the fiscal reform. He not only organized the planning of the reform through the Finance Ministry, but also traveled throughout China to force local governments to support the reform. His personal role in the process was instrumental for the adoption of the reform.[68]

The 1993 economic crisis definitely weakened local resistance to fiscal reform by discrediting excessive economic decentralization. It also upset the policy equilibrium by giving economic centrist Zhu Rong-ji the opportunity to assume enormous economic power as against those supporting decentralization.[69] Zhu and his supporters, both his colleagues in the central leadership team and the central economic bureaucracy, seized the political opportunity offered by the crisis situation and formally adopted the reform at the Third Plenum of the 14th Congress of CCP in November 1993. As Zhu himself observed about the importance of the 1993 situation, "Being able to push through such a comprehensive and fundamental reform fulfilled a goal that we wanted to accomplish for many years but had been unable to do."[70] Xiang Huai-cheng, Deputy Finance Minister and a key promoter of fiscal reform, even more bluntly emphasized the importance of 1993 situation. As he observed in an interview in December 1993, "Proposing the fiscal reform now represents a historical opportunity. The moment is just right. We had considered fiscal reform before the 14th Party Congress. However, the opportunity was not ripe at the time."[71]

Therefore, the crisis situation around 1993 paved the way for the fiscal reform which was adopted at the end of the year. Within the policy community, there was a perceived forthcoming political crisis as a result of central fiscal crisis. This perception of pending political crisis was amplified in the context of political succession. This made fiscal reform an urgent policy goal for the new central leadership team. The 1993 economic crisis ultimately proved that weakened macroeconomic management by the center could only lead to chaos and instability in China's development. The crisis situation upset the equilibrium of policymaking by allowing economic centrist Zhu Rong-ji, with the support from his colleagues, to seize control of economic power and pushed through the reform.

Conclusion

Fiscal reform in China was triggered by the realization that the decentralized system created systematic problems both for China's transition to market economy and for balanced and sustainable development. A very important development that faciliated the reform was the emergence of a unified center which was not seen during most of the reform years, and the fading away of Deng Xiao-ping, the ultimate defender of decentralization. The crisis situation around 1993 also upset the balance of power and allowed centrist leaders to seize control of economic decisionmaking and push through the fiscal reform.

The efforts by China since the late 1980s in strengthening strategic planning, sectoral intervention, and resource control were intended to rebuild its state capacity in economic management.   In certain ways this resembles the East Asian model of development. Fiscal reform, designed to increase central control over resources and their allocation, was the most systematic and could have profound impact on China's state capacity. Strategic planning and industrial policy in the long term could both become more effective if the fiscal reform is successful. Basically, their effectiveness depend on central control over resouces. As the World Bank observes, the effectiveness of Korea's strategic industrial policy was based on government control of resources (for example, the Korean government once owned all the banks before the financial liberalization), and thus its ability to direct them to the targeted sectors.[72] The current limited utility of strategic planning and industrial policy in China is caused by the central government's lack of resources to achieve strategic goals. Therefore, the new fiscal regime could substantially strengthen China's capacity in pursuing strategic economic goals.

Until recently there was a tendency to see every policy change in China as result of struggles between market reformers and economic conservatives. This view was highly simplistic. It saw any renewed centralization as efforts to drag Chinese economy back to central planning. The fact was that recent centralization efforts were intended to rebuild necessary state capacities to manage a developing country with a transitional economic system. Therefore, the 1994 fiscal recentralzation does not mean that economic reform in China has been reversed. At the same Third Plenary of the 14th Congress of the CCP was adopted, establishing a socialist market economy was for the first time proposed as the goal of reform. The fiscal reform only strengthens the capacity of the Chinese government in macroeconomic management. After all, market economy can see varied roles for government in macroeconomic management. This role can range from the relatively hands-off approach of the U. S. government to the statist system of Japan to essentially planned capitalism of South Korea. In fact, China's attempts to rebuild its macro-economic management capacity was supported by the World Bank.

Economic reform is itself a learning process. Maintaining the proper balance between economic decentralization and necessary state macro-economic management is an art and takes time to master. China's fiscal reform since the late 1970s reflected this experience. It moved from high degree of fiscal centralization to exessive decentralization and then back to restoring the fiscal preeminence of the central government. This experience with fiscal reform closely conforms to China's reform ideology of "crossing the river by feeling the stones."

Notes

1.   For studies that emphasizes the role of the state in East Asian industrialization, see Robert Wade, *Governing the Market: Economic Theory and the Role of Government in East Asia* (Princeton: Princeton University Press, 1990); Alice Amsden, *Asia's Next Giant: South Korea and Late Industrialization* (New York: Oxford University Press, 1989); The World Bank, *Korea: Managing the Industrial Transition* (Washington, D. C., 1987).

2.   Pradumna B. Rana and Wilhelmina Paz, "Economic Transitions: The Asian Experience," in Chung H. Lee and Helmut Reisen, eds., *From Reform to Growth: China and Other Countries in Transition in Asia and Central and Eastern Europe* (Paris: Organization for Economic Cooperation and Development, 1994, p. 119.

3.   Juan Linz and Alfred Stepan, *Problems of Democratic Tansition and Consolidation: Southern Europe, South America, and Post Communist Europe* (Baltimore: Johns Hopkins University Press, 1996), p. 436.

4.   Ibid., p. 139. Maravall made similar argument about the positive role of strengthened state in Southern Europe. See Jose Maria Maravall, "The Myth fo the Authoritarian Advantage," in Larry Diamond and Marc Plattner, eds., *Economic Reform and Democracy* (Baltimore: Johns Hopkins University Press, 1995).

5.   Lieslie Elliot Armijo, Thomas J. Biersteker, and Abraham F. Lowenthal, "The Problems of Simultaneous Transitions," in Larry Diamond and Marc Plattner, ibid.

6.   Moises Naim, "Latin America: The Second Stage of Reform," in Larry Diamond and Marc Platter, ibid.

7. For the history of economic bureaucracy in China, see Baohui Zhang, "The State Central Economic Bureaucracy and Systematic Economic Reform: An Institutional Explanation for the Soviet and Chinese Experiences," *Governance*, Vol. 5, No. 3 (July 1992).

8. This resolution of 1989 was selected in State Economic System Reform Commission, *Zhongguo jingji tizhi gaige nianjian* (*The Yearbook of China's Economic System Reform, 1990*)(Beijing: Gaige shuban she, 1990), p. 54.

9. World Bank, *China: Industrial Policy for an Economy in Transition* (Washington, D. C., 1992)p. 15.

10. World Bank, *China: Between Plan and Market* (Washington, D. C., 1990), p. xvii.

11. See Zhou Shulian, "Reform of the Planned Economy and the Planning System," in Geore Totten and Zhou Shulian, eds., *China's Economic Reform: Administering the Introduction of the Market Mechanism* (Boulder: Westview Press, 1992), pp. 26-27.

12. For these measures to institutionally strengthen the new SPC, see *Zhongguo jinji nianjian, 1989* (*The Yearbook of Chinese Economym, 1989*) (Beijing: Jingji guanli chuban she, 1990), p. III-9.

13. Robert Wade, *Governing the Market: Economic Theory and the Role of Government in East Asia* (Princeton: Princeton University Press, 1990), p. 257.

14. See *Zhongguo jinji nianjian, 1989* (*The Yearbook of Chinese Economy, 1989*) (Beijing: Jingji guanli chuban she, 1990), p. III-9.

15. For the 1989 industrial policy, see State Planning Commission, *Wuo guo dangqian ci chan ye zhengce wenti* (*The Current industrial Policy of China*)(Beijing: zhongguo jihua chuban she, 1990).

16. For discussion of China's fiscal system before the reform, see Tian Yi-nong and Xiang Huai-cheng, *Lun zhongguo caizheng tizhi gaige yu hongguan tiaokong* (*The Reform and Macro-Management of China's Fiscal System*)(Beijing: Zhongguo caizheng jingji chubanshe, 1988).

17. For fiscal reforms, see Michael Oksenberg and James Tong, "The Evolution of Central-Provincial fiscal Relations in China, 1971-1984: The Formal System," *The China Quarterly*, No. 125. (March 1991); Christin Wong, "Central-Local Relations in an Era of Fiscal Decline: The Paradox of Fiscal Decentralization in Post-Mao China," *The China Quarterly*, No. 128 (December 1991).

18. For this part on different arrangements between the central government and provinces, see World Bank, *China: Reforming Intergovernmental Fiscal Relations* (Washington, D. C.: World Bank, 1992), pp. 4-5.

19. For the impact of fiscal reform on local industrialization, see Christin Wong, 1991.

20. For this view of state capacity, see John Campell, "The State and Fiscal Sociology," *Annual Review of Sociology*, Vol. 19 (1993).

21. For this discussion of the central fiscal decline, see World Bank, *China: Macroeconomic Stability in a Decentralized Economy* (Washington, D. C.: World Bank, 1995), p. 32.

22. For central governments' control of revenues in Japan and Australia, see World Bank, *China: Reforming Intergovernmental Fiscal Relations*, pp. 21-23.

23. For this study by the Finance Ministry, see Xiang Huai- cheng, *Zhongguo caizheng tizhi gaige* (*The Reform of China's Fiscal System*)(Beijing: Zhongguo caizheng jingji chubanzhe, 1994), p. 24. Xiang Huai-cheng was then the Deputy Minister of the Finance Ministry.

24. For more discussion of this problem, see Alan Roe, "Intergovernmental Fiscal Relations in China: Report of a Senior Policy Seminar," in World Bank, *Macroeconomic Management and Fiscal Decentralization* (Washington, D. C. 1995), p. 7.

25. Moises Naim, "Latin America: The Second Stage of Reform," in Larry Diamond and Marc Platter, eds., *Economic Reform and Democracy* (Baltimore: Johns Hopkins University Press, 1995), p. 33.

26. See World Bank, *China: Macroeconomic Stability in a Decentralized Economy* (Washington, D. C.: World Bank, 1995), p. 29.

27. Ibid..

28. World Bank, *China: Reforming Intergovernmental Fiscal Relations* (Washington, D. C.: World Bank, 1992), p. 28.

29. See Christin Wong, 1991.

30. For the negative impact of local industrialization on China's industrial structures, see World Bank, *China: Industrial Policies for an Economy in Transition* (Washington, D. C.: World Bank, 1992).

31. For the practice of industrial policy by China, see ibid..

32. For the advantages for Guangdong and Fujian, see Jiang Zhuo-zhong, "Guangdong tuijin fen shui zhi chengxiao xianzhu" ("Gongdong Making Remarkable Progress in the Implementation of Revenue Sharing System"), *Liao Wang*, June 7, 1994.

33. See World Bank, *China: Reforming Intergovernmental Fiscal Relations* (Washington, D. C.: World Bank, 1992), p. 13.

34. For research criticizing the fiscal contract system, see Qin Feng-xiang, "Lun caizheng baogan tizhi di deshi jiqi gaige di xianshi xuanze"("The Success and Failure of the Fiscal Contract System and Its Reform"), in Wang Shi-ding, ed., *Quanguo youxiu caizheng keyan chengguo xuan, 1989-1990*(*Selected Works of Outstanding Fiscal Research, 1989-1990*) (Beijing: Zhongguo caizheng jingji chubanshe, 1993); Research Institute of Fiscal Science, Shandong Province, "Caizheng tizhi gaige ruogan wenti di renshi jiqi sikao"("On the Reform of the Fiscal System"), in ibid.; Research Group of Fiscal Science, Zhejiang Province, "Guanyu tigao caizheng shouru zhan guomin shouru bizhong di yanjiu baogao"("A Report on Raising the Revenue to GDP Ratio"), in ibid..

35. For research supporting a new revenue sharing regime, see Jia Kang, "Fen shui zhi xia di zhongyang yu difang zhengfu zhijian di guanxi"("Central and Local Governmental Relations under a Fiscal Sharing Regime"), in ibid.;

Yu Xiao-ping, "Zai wuoguo shixing fen shui zhi di jiben gouxiang"("A Preliminary Plan for the Fiscal Sharing Regime"), in ibid.; Yan Zhen-wui, Shi lun shixing chedi fen shui zhi caizheng tizhi di kexing xing"("The Possibility of Implementing a Fiscal Sharing Regime"), in ibid..

36. See Xiang Huai-cheng, *Zhongguo caizheng tizhi gaige (The Reform of China's Fiscal System)*(Beijing: Zhongguo caizheng jingji chubanzhe, 1994), pp. 19-23.

37. See Liu Zhong-li, "Xu yan" ("Preface"), in ibid., p. 5.

38. World Bank, *China: Macroeconomic Stability in a Decentralized Economy*, p. xi.

39. World Bank, *China: Reforming Intergovernmental Fiscal Relations*, p. xiii.

40. World Bank, *China: Macroeconomic Stability in a Decentralized Economy*, p.60.

41. For reform policies published in Chinese, see "Guowu yuan guanyu shixing fen shui zhi caizheng guanli tizhi di jueding" ("The Decision by the State Council on the Implementation of Fiscal Sharing Management System"), published in *Caizheng*, No. 2, 1994; For discussion of the reform policies in English, see Tsang Shu-ki and Cheng Yuk-shing, "China's Tax Reforms of 1994," *Asian Survey*, No. 9, Vol. XXXIV (September 1994).

42. See Alan Roe, "Intergovernmental Fiscal Relations in China: Report of a Senior Policy Seminar," in World Bank, *Macroeconomic Management and Fiscal Decentralization* (Washington, D. C. 1995), p. 6.

43. Ibid..

44. For central control the appointment of regional bureau heads of NTS, see Xiang Huai-cheng, "Speech at the Meeting of Bureau Adminstrators of National Tax Service, August 2, 1994," in National Tax Service, *Shui shou gongzuo wenjian fagui xuanbian (Selected Documents and Regulations of Revenue Collection)* (Beijing: Zhongguo caizheng jingji chubanshe, 1995).

45. See World Bank (ft. 42), p. 11.

46. See "Xin shui zhi yunxing chengxiao" ("Results from the New Tax System"), *Caizheng*, No. 11, 1995. *Caizheng* is a monthly publication by the Finance Ministry.

47. See Liu Zhong-li, "Cai shui gaige dadao le yuqi mudi"("Fiscal Reform Achieved Expected Results"), *Caizheng*, No. 10, 1995.

48. See "Dui wen shan fen shui zhi wenti di ji dian kan fa"("Comments on Improving the Revenue Sharing System"), *Caizheng*, No. 11, 1996, p. 23.

49. For this research, see Gai Jian-ling, "Zai shui tizhi gaige hou zhongyang yu difang fenpei guanxi di bianhua"("Changes in the Distribution Relationship between the Center and Locals after the Fiscal and Tax Reform"), *Jingji guanli*, No. 7, 1997, p. 15.

50. For the 1995 figures, see Liu Zhong-li, "Guanyu 1995 nian zhongyang he difang yusuan zhixing qingkuang di baogao"("Report on the Implementation of 1995 Central and Local Fiscal Plans), *Caizheng*, No. 5, 1996, pp. 4-5.

51. See "Cai shui gaige jinzhan qingkuang di diaocha"("Report on the Implementation of Fiscal Reform"), *Caizheng*, No. 4, 1994.

52. For the comments by provincial finance administrators, see "Caizheng ting ju zhang tan fen shui zhi gaige"("Finance Bureau Heads of Commenting on the Revenue Sharing Reform"), *Caizheng*, No. 2, 1994. For the comments by provincial leaders, see "Difang dang zheng lingdao tan cai shui gaige"("Local Party and Government Leaders Commenting on the Fiscal Reform"), *Caizheng*, No. 3, 1994.

53. For the implementation of fiscal reform in Guangdong, see Jiang Zhuo-zhong, "Guangdong tuijin fen shui zhi chengxiao xianzhu" ("Gongdong Making Remarkable Progress in Implementing the Revenue Sharing System"), *Liao Wang*, June 7, 1994.

54. See World Bank, *China: Macroeconomic Stability in a Decentralized Economy* (Washington, D. C.: World Bank, 1995), p. 59.

55. See Zhang Liang-qing, "jide liyi: caizheng gaige zhong di nan dian"("Vested Interests: Obstacles for Fiscal Reform"), in National Association of Young and Middle Aged Scholars of Fiscal Theories, *Quan guo zhong qing nian caizheng jingji lilung wenxuan* (*Selected Works of Fiscal Research by Young and Middle Aged Scholars*)(Beijing: Zhongguo caizheng jingji chubanshe, 1992)

56. See Susan Shirk, *The Political Logic of Economic Reform in China* (Berkeley and Los Angelos: University of California Press, 1993).

57. See Sha Ming, "Jiang zemin gonggu quanli"("Jiang Ze-min's Consolidation of Power"), *Jiu shi nian dai*, November, 1995.

58. See Avery Goldstein, *From Bandwagon to Balance-of-Power Politics: Structural Constraints and Politics in China, 1949-1978* (Standford: Standford University Press, 1991).

59. See World Bank, *China: Macroeconomic Stability in a Decentralized Economy* (Washington, D. C.: World Bank, 1995).

60. Kenneth Liberthal, "Introduction: the Fragmented Authoritarianism Model and Its Limitations," in Kenneth Liberthal and David Lampton, eds., *Bureaucracy, Politics, and Decision Making in Post-Mao China* (Berkeley and Los Angelos: University of California Press, 1992).

61. For the role of crisis in major policy change, see Peter Katzenstein, *Small States in World Markets: Industrial Policy in Europe* (Ithaca: Cornell University Press, 1995).

62. Peter Gourevitch, *Politics in Hard Times: Comparative Responses to International Economic Crisis* (Ithaca: Cornell University Press, 1986), p. 9.

63. For more systematic discussion of the role of crisis in the initiation of reforms, see Michel Oksenberg and Bruce Dickson, "The Origins, Processes, and Outcomes of Great Political Reform: A Framework of Analysis," in Dankwart Rustow and Kenneth Erickson, eds., *Comparative Political Dynamics: Global Research and Perspectives* (New York: Harper Collins, 1991).

64. Lieslie Elliot Armijo, Thomas J. Biersteker, and Abraham F. Lowenthal, "The Problems of Simultaneous Transitions," in Larry Diamond and Marc Plattner, eds., *Economic Reform and Democracy* (Baltimore: Johns Hopkins University Press, 1995).

65. See Wang Shao-guang and Hu An-gang, "Zhong guo zhengfu jiqu nengli de xiajiang jiqi houguo"("The Declining Extractive Capacity of Chinese Government and Its Consequences"), *Er shi yi shiji*, No. 21 (February 1994).

66. The impact of this report on Chinese leaders is discussed by Wu Guo-guang and Wang Zhao-jun, *Deng Xiao-ping zhi hou di zhongguo (China after Deng Xiao-ping)* (Taipei: Shi jie shu ju, 1994), pp. 206-207.

67. See Maria Hsia Chang, "China's Future: Regionalism, Federalism, or Disintegration," Studies in Comparative Communism, Vol. XXV, No. 3 (September 1992).

68. Zhu Rong-ji's personal role in the fiscal reform was discussed by Jian Yan, Deputy Director of NTS, in his speech at an important meeting of NTS administrators. See Jin Yan, "Speech at the Meeting of Bureau Adminstrators of National Tax Service, March 3, 1994," in National Tax Service, *Shui shou gongzuo wenjian fagui xuanbian (Selected Documents and Regulations of Revenue Collection)*(Beijing: Zhongguo caizheng jingji chubanshe, 1995); Also see Yan Hua, "Zhu Rong-ji tuixing fen shui zhi zao wuigong"("Zhong Rong-ji under Attack for His Push for Revenue Sharing System"), *Jiushi niandai*, No. 12, 1994.

69. For the rise of Zhu Rong-ji during the 1993 economic crisis, see Susumu Yabuki, *China's New Political Economy* (Boulder: Westview Press, 1995), pp. 214-220.

70. For this comments by Zhu Rong-ji, see "Guowu yuan fu zongli zhu rong-ji zai quanguo caizheng gongzhuo huiyi he shuiwu juzhang huiyi shang di jianghua"("Speech by Vice Premier Zhu Rong-ji at the National Meeting of Fiscal Works and the Meeting of Bureau Administrators of National Tax Service, August 4, 1994"), in National Tax Service (fn. 68), p. 8.

71. See "Xiang Huai-cheng fu bu zhang tan caishui tizhi gaige"("Vice Minister Xiang Huai-cheng Commenting on the Fiscal Reform"), *Caizheng*, No. 1, 1994, p. 8.

72. See World Bank, *Korea: Managing the Industrial Transition* (Washington, D. C., 1987).

PART THREE

REFORMING
OR
REVOLTING SOCIETY

Chapter 7

The Effects of Structural Changes in Community and Work Unit in China

ZHANG Lening and DENG Xiaogang

Since China started its economic reform in 1979, it has experienced enormous changes in every aspect of people's lives, ranging from employment and living conditions to social relations. These changes reflect the fundamental structural transformation that has accompanied China's quest for modernization and industrialization. These changes are well documented by Western scholars.[1] However, one important area, crime and social control, has not generated sufficient academic research. As China moves towards modernization, the crime rate has also increased rapidly.[2] Although crime has become a major national concern, few studies have examined the relationship between structural changes in community and work unit and crime control in China.[3] This examination may help the Chinese to develop effective control for crime and delinquency. It is also valuable for criminological theory because the Chinese experience offers a unique opportunity for comparative study.[4]

The present study is an attempt to explore theoretically the relationship between the structural changes in community and work unit and crime/delinquency in China. As many scholars have observed. [5,6] Chinese community and work unit are two fundamental social units which are responsible for a low rate of crime before the 1970s as well as for an increasing rate of crime after the 1980s in China. In this paper, we describe structural changes in community and work unit and their possible effects on crime control in China, and then we apply the social disorganization model, developed in the United States, to explain these effects. Further, we specify theoretical models to capture unique characteristics of the Chinese community and work unit in social control.

Characteristics and Changes in Community and Work Unit in China

China has been traditionally seen as a relatively crime-free society.[7,1] However, since the late 1970s and early 1980s, China has been undergoing a significant increase in crime and youth crime in particular. For about a decade, the total crime figure has almost tripled from 890,261 in 1981 to 2,365,709 in 1991.[8] China's changing picture of crime and delinquency and unique social context provide a magnificent opportunity for criminologists to investigate crime and social control.[9] Because "the key to understanding Chinese society's low crime is the controls exerted over citizens at the grass-roots level"[10], any change at this grass-roots level would produce significant and profound effects on Chinese social control for crime and delinquency. As many Western scholars have emphasized, the neighborhood and work unit are two basic social establishments that serve as key bases in maintaining strong social control and preventing crime and delinquency.[11, 5, 6] As the economic reform and "Open Door" policy (which promotes foreign investment and trade) have been fully implemented since the late 1970s in China, these two basic social establishments at the grass-roots level have been undergoing significant change. Therefore, it is imperative to assess the effects of structural changes in community and work unit on crime and delinquency in China.

The Changing Characteristics of Neighborhood in China

In any Chinese city, a neighborhood is not only a residential area, but also a social organization managed by the grass-roots branch of Chinese government, the City Street Office, through the Neighborhood Committee. A City Street Office usually has political and administrative control over several neighborhoods, deals with social affairs, and runs some small business and firms. In addition to the City Street Office, the neighborhood police station is another important government agency that exerts social control over neighborhoods. Traditionally, the police station has had the power to control household registration records that give residents legal right to live in an area. In addition to this power, the police station has extensive responsibility for public safety and the well being of neighborhoods. It not only keeps watch on a "beat" in the area, but also mediates neighborhood and family disputes, participates in rehabilitating and educating offenders, directs neighborhood efforts to prevent crime, and provides assistance for residents who are in trouble.[12, 13] These organizational mechanisms allow the Chinese government to monitor residents' behavior and activities directly, and to facilitate a variety of crime control programs to be carried out at the grass-roots level.

In addition to the structure described above, a Chinese neighborhood traditionally has some important characteristics that promote crime control. First, geographic and residential mobility has been highly restricted from one city to another and from countryside to urban areas. Each citizen has a registration record in his or her neighborhood police station. Moving one's residence without special reasons is forbidden by the police. Furthermore, the shortage of housing to rent or purchase makes residential mobility fairly difficult. Finally, since the job market is planned and controlled by the state, restricted job mobility impedes residential mobility. Thus, many people live in the same neighborhood for life. This low residential mobility results in very stable neighborhoods which allow residents to develop a sense of responsibility for the well-being of their area and a sense of participation in local affairs. According to Braithwaite[14] , these social conditions are conducive to effective control of crime and delinquency.

Second, because apartments are very small, the limited living space makes it difficult for residents to escape the company of other residents, and thus individuals' activities are visible to the entire neighborhood. In addition, mutual knowledge among neighbors is intimate and extensive.[5] This lack of privacy means that wrongdoing or indeed any type of deviance, is readily observable.

Third, the Chinese people are much more homogeneous in culture, thought, economic status, and social activities because of the powerful influences of the traditional culture, state ownership of property, and the extensive state control in people's daily lives. "Such homogeneity is conducive to widely shared values and common definitions of social problems and solutions" at the neighborhood level.[3]

In summary, a neighborhood's organizational characteristics -- stability, dwelling structure, and homogeneity -- are responsible for the low crime rate, and provide a solid foundation for social control in China. However, these characteristics and conditions of community have changed somewhat in recent years due to the economic reform and the open door policy. These changes can be summarized in the following ways.

First, the Chinese government has been loosening its control of population mobility in response to the requirements of economic development and the free market economy. In the countryside, the new "responsibility system" (which allows farmers to profit directly from their labor) has significantly stimulated production, and generated a large surplus labor force which migrates to cities to find work. When millions of rural migrants move into cities, especially large cities, the once stable urban community structures are disturbed. In addition, as the centralized economy has given away to the market economy, geographical and occupational mobility between cities has continued to increase. Thus, the old stability of urban communities is being further broken down.

A second source of change is the variety of new housing projects which has been implemented in an attempt to improve poor living conditions in the cities. These projects usually involve the replacement of traditional one-story dwellings with multi-story apartment buildings. This structural change in residential conditions has implications for social control: (1) people in large apartment buildings are less likely to interact with neighbors than people who live in traditional one-story dwellings; (2) social interaction may also be low because some new residential areas are inhabited by residents who are not familiar with each other; and (3) rental and purchase of new apartments make geographic mobility possible. All these changes may undermine the community base for social control.

Third, although many would doubt that the Chinese government's identification of "Western spiritual pollution" as a major cause of crime and delinquency [8], this argument may have some merits. In pre-reform China, the social values, beliefs, and customs of the Chinese society were almost homogeneous. However, once China ended its isolation and started to have more economic, political, and cultural exchanges with the West, a large variety of foreign values, beliefs, and customs also penetrated. These foreign influences have dramatically decreased the homogeneity of the Chinese society, and make it difficult for the Chinese communists to control people's thoughts and behavior as they once did, but it is also harder for people to reach agreement about social problems and their solutions. Concerted efforts become increasingly difficult at the neighborhood level. Therefore, the functions of community in social control may be weakened.

Finally, inequality has gradually developed because the economic reform has created opportunities for some Chinese people to become richer than others. Consequently, inequality in economic status has replaced the communist "egalitarianism," and the once-homogeneous community in the Chinese society has been further diminished.

In summary, the increasing population mobility, changes in residential conditions, development of multiple values and cultures, and growing inequality may have had unanticipated effects on the capacity of the local community to provide a foundation for social control in China.

The Characteristics and Change in Work Units in China

In China, a work unit (*danwai*) is an institution in which people are employed for pay. It is similar in certain respects to a business establishment in the U.S. that every "employee' has an occupational position and is paid by his or her work unit. However, the work unit also differs from a simple business institution in the U.S. in several important ways [11, 6] : First, a work unit is not an independent economic or social body; rather, it is an agency of Chinese government which responds to orders from the government and whose operation is largely controlled and directed by the government. Thus, the relationship of workers with their work units links these workers to the government. Second, the relationship between workers and work unit is also political. The Communist Party sets up its branch in each work unit and implements its political control for workers through the branch. Workers are attached to the Party through their work units.

Third, the relationship between workers and their work unit is also social because the work unit performs some important social functions, such as providing health care, housing, leisure activities, and assistance in family disputes. Finally, the work unit has an educational function. Each work unit conducts political and moral education and provides political guidance for workers' lives. Moreover, many large work units offer occupational training for young workers through evening and weekend classes. Therefore, as most Westerners observe, a work unit has a profound effect on an individual's life in China.[5]

Before the economic reform in the late 1970s, there were two common types of work units: the state and the collective. The government takes full control and direction of state work units. In contrast, a collective work unit is owned by its employees who have some control over the operation of the unit. Even in this case, however, the operation of the unit largely depends on the government's guidance and support.

In pre-reform China, the "work unit" occupational structure was very stable and provided a mechanism through which the government could exercise control in the following four dimensions. First, for most Chinese workers in the past, the initial work-unit assignment was often a lifetime placement. Occupational mobility was rare. Second, because the majority of work units were run by the state, the government was responsible for people's employment. Consequently, unemployment was also rare. Third, the economic, political, and social functions of work units led to people's heavy reliance on their work units. The heavy reliance provides a solid basis for the government to control people's lives. Fourth, the simple and homogeneous structure of work units also facilitated the operation of social control by the state.

However, China's reform and the open door policy may change the situation somewhat. As the centralized economy is gradually changing to a market economy, the state's grip on the job market has been loosened. Work units have been permitted to independently hire workers based on a contract that allows workers the right to leave for other jobs. The unemployment rate is increasing due to the fact that many state-owned firms fail to compete in the market and go bankrupt. At the same time, new forms of ownership such as private enterprises, foreign companies, and joint ventures are developing. Increasing occupational mobility and new forms of ownership seriously challenge the ability of the state-controlled work unit system to perform its traditional social control functions.

Theoretical Perspectives and Explanatory Models

Westerners are witnessing and Chinese people are experiencing these changes in the community and work unit system. Both Western and Chinese commentators have suggested that there may be an association between these changes and the increasing rate of crime and delinquency. In this paper, we will attempt to explore its mechanisms and processes. This theoretical exploration will be valuable for developing criminological theory and for helping China to deal with its crime problem.

When assessing the effects of the structural change in the community and work unit on crime and delinquency, a relevant theoretical perspective is the social disorganization theory developed in the U.S. The social disorganization perspective has been developed in the pioneering work of Shaw and Mckay [15, 16] and then refined by the contemporary scholars [17, 18, 19, 20, 21, 22, 23, 24, 25, 26]. Initially, the social disorganization perspective attempted to capture the association between the changing community structure and the crime/delinquency experienced by the American society. However, insights derived from this perspective also have some universal implications for other societies which have experienced similar changes in community due to urbanization and industrialization. In this paper, we attempt to apply the social disorganization perspective to the Chinese context by examining the association of changes in community and occupational structure with crime/delinquency in China. We employ two kinds of theoretical and analytical strategies. First, we apply a typical social disorganization model developed in the U.S. to the analysis of Chinese society and assess its applicability and generality. Second, we develop two theoretical models that reflect respectively the unique characteristics of community and work unit in the Chinese society.

Applying U.S. Social Disorganization Models to Chinese Society

Generally, social disorganization refers to "the inability of a community structure to realize the common values of its residents and maintain effective social control".[25] The social disorganization model generally includes three sets of variables that are causally correlated. [18, 27, 28, 25, 26] The first set of variables (referred to as exogenous sources of community disorganization) includes low economic status, ethnic heterogeneity, residential mobility, and family disruption. The second set of variables includes the intervening variables that reflect the degree of community organization and cohesiveness indicated by prevalence of local friendship networks, street corner teenage peer groups, and organizational participation. The last set of variables is crime and delinquency rates. The model predicts that the first set of variables (structural factors) directly affects the second set of variables (organizational level of community), and in turn affects crime and delinquency rates. Sampson and Groves [25] used these three sets of variables to develop a model of social disorganization. We adopt their model for analyzing community change and crime in China (see Figure 1).

Figure 1. An Adopted U.S. Model of Structural Change in Community and Crime

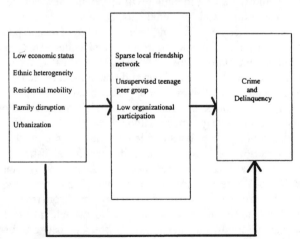

Theoretically, this social organization model can be used to analyze structural changes in the Chinese community. As previously noted, the structure of the urban Chinese neighborhood is undergoing significant changes, as revealed by the indicators such as dwelling structure, residential mobility and heterogeneity, and economic status. These structural changes reduce the organizational cohesiveness in community, resulting in fewer personal associations and networks, less involvement in supervision over adolescent activities, and less participation in community activities. As a result of these changes in participation level, crime and delinquency rates are likely to increase. While it is to some degree useful, this model also has some problems in reflecting the unique characteristics of the Chinese social and cultural context. We argue that it is necessary to make some modifications to capture these features within the basic social disorganization model. For instance, ethnic heterogeneity may not be a significant structural factor in China because 95% of Chinese people belong to the same "Han" race and most minority groups have separate residential areas that are far away from where most "Han" people live. On the other hand, new factors such as changes in the work unit or dwelling structures should be added in the models to make them more applicable to China.[1]

Chinese Models

New theoretical models that can seize the distinctive features of community and work unit in China will contribute new perspectives to theory construction and criminal justice practice. The Chinese traditionally rely less on formal and legal control by laws and punishment and more on informal and inner control by moral codes and extra-judicial groups and organizations. This preference for informal and inner control is based on the idea that formal laws and punishment make people fear, but give them no sense of shame. People may make every effort to avoid punishment but cannot escape from the sense of shame imposed by moral codes and their intimate groups.[29] Although the post-Mao leadership has realized the importance of laws and legal control in the modernization, and has made efforts to establish a more formal criminal justice system (as reflected in many new laws promulgated since the late 1970s), it is not the case, as some Western scholars claim, that China is undergoing "a concerted shift from informal to formal control, and from rule by custom to rule by law".[8] The unique combination of formal and informal control in China may not follow the dichotomized distinction between formal and informal control posited by Western scholars: "as one increases, the other must decrease".[30]

This unique combination is revealed in the "total society strategy" for controlling crime, initially formulated in 1981 and developed and reconfirmed in 1991.[31] The basic objective of this strategy was expressed in the "Decision of the Chinese Communist Party Central Committee and the State Council on Strengthening Systematic Control of Public Security" in 1991: "Under the leadership of the Party committees and governments at various levels and relying on the masses, all social organs and organizations make a concerted effort to control public security, combat against crime, and prevent crime by employing political, economic, administrative, judicial, cultural, and educational measures in order to stabilize social order and create a good social environment for the reform and the construction of socialist modernization".[31, 3] Therefore, the emphasis on a formal social control does not mean the abandonment of an informal model.

Based on this "total society strategy," the Chinese people and government have developed some distinctive measures of informal control in community and work unit, such as *bangjiao* (a community crime control program) and *tiaojie* (a community mediation program). The effectiveness of these measures largely depends on the stable structure of community and work unit. However, as described above, these structures are becoming less stable. Thus, although the Chinese government is struggling to maintain informal controls, structural changes in the community and work unit are undermining the foundation informal controls rely on. It is important to investigate how structural changes in the community and work unit render informal mechanisms inactive and unable to control people's behavior, thus resulting in a rise in rates of crime and delinquency. Two models of community and work unit are developed here in an effort to show how the three sets of variables might work in the Chinese context.

The Chinese Community Model

In the new model we develop (see Figure 2), the exogenous (the first set) and endogenous (the third set) of variables are similar to those defined in the U.S. model, but the intervening variables are different. The Chinese model contains a set of new intervening variables which reflect informal control mechanisms at the community level. This set of variables includes active neighborhood committee, *tiaojie*, *bangjiao*, public legal education, and neighborhood watch.

Figure 2. A Chinese Model of Structural Change in Community and Crime

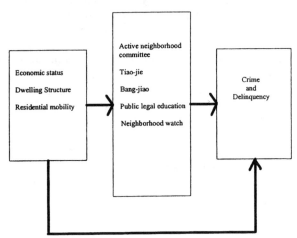

Active Neighborhood Committee

A neighborhood committee is formed in a residential area of 100 to 600 households. Its members, who are usually senior residents, are elected from the residents of the neighborhood. The committee is instructed, supervised, and given a modest allowance by the City Street Office, which is the grassroots branch of the Chinese government. Thus, the neighborhood committee, a social body organized and controlled by the government, differs from the usual conception of a voluntary association in the U.S..[5, 6] However, although the neighborhood committee is sponsored by the government, it is not a formal official agency, and its members are not formal government employees. Its activities largely depend on members' voluntary efforts in carrying out official tasks. In the past, when the neighborhoods were stable and homogeneous in population structure, economics, and culture, it was not too difficult for the neighborhood committee to perform its functions. However, changes in the neighborhood have made their work more difficult. Although neighborhood committees still exist in response to the governmental requirements, they can no longer successfully perform many of their traditional social service functions such as mediating family conflicts and monitoring the neighborhood.

Tiaojie

Tiaojie refers literally to "mediating and solving disputes that arise in daily life among neighbors and family members. It entails a community effort to deal with conflicts that may lead to crime".[3, 12, 9, 32, 29] Although this social control mechanism is sponsored by the Chinese government, it is basically a voluntary activity. A basic form of *tiaojie* is the neighborhood *tiaojie* committee consisting of reputable and senior residents. Its activities are guided by the grassroots branch of the Chinese government, district courts, and neighborhood police stations. Persuasion through discussion is the principal means employed to handle disputes and conflicts. Using data from China, Zhang et al.[3] have found that *tiaojie* has a significant effect on controlling neighborhood crime. However, they have no data to assess the effect of the structural change in neighborhood on the functioning of *tiaojie*. We argue however that the structural change has affected the effectiveness of *tiaojie* committees since this mechanism largely relies on community stability.[3]

Bangjiao

Bangjiao, which means "assisting, helping, guiding, and directing offenders, especially juvenile offenders"[3], represents a social effort to prevent and control crime and delinquency informally rather than through judicial or administrative disposition. There are two basic goals of *bangjiao*: (1) preventing the development of minor offenses to serious offenses and single offense to multiple offenses; and (2) rehabilitating officially released offenders. Although, in principle, the targets of bang-jiao include offenders from all age groups, the common targets are young offenders aged at 13 to 28 years old.

Although forms of *bangjiao* vary nationwide, one of the popular forms is *bangjiao* groups located in the neighborhood. "These groups normally consist of the delinquent's parents, a member of the Neighborhood Committee, an officer from the neighborhood police station, a head of the work unit where the youth formerly was employed (if the youth is an ex-employee), and the head of the school where the youth (if an ex-student) once was a student".[3] The routine activities of these groups include heart-to-heart talks with the delinquent as well as practical assistance in various areas such as employment, schooling, and marriage in which the delinquent may encounter difficulties.

Theoretically, *bangjiao* can be viewed as an organizational and structural mechanism that conducts "reintegrative shaming".[14] It condemns the wrongdoing with a gesture of reacceptance, and thus provides a "channel" for the delinquent to return to normal life smoothly in a way which prevents further involvement in delinquency. A recent study by Zhang et al.[3] indicates that *bangjiao* is a significant barrier against neighborhood crime and recidivism. However, due to data limitations, their study has not addressed the effect of the change of the community structure on *bangjiao*.

Public legal education

In contrast to the Western belief in original sin, the Chinese traditionally believe that human nature is basically good, that all humans have equal potential for moral growth[33], and that proper education and training are key in shaping people's thoughts and behavior. Another traditional belief is that thoughts precede and guide actions. Thus, a person's thoughts must be guided and changed before his/her actions can be affected.[9, 34, 35] Chinese communists have assimilated these traditional beliefs in constructing their mechanisms of social control. During Mao's era, the government relied on political education as a control strategy to prevent social deviance. As Johnson[36] observed, "political education for all Chinese is part of the drive to mobilize collective effort in building a socialist society, but raising political consciousness also is the tool for correcting deviance." Mao's method of political education has been subjected to serious critiques for its authoritarianism and for its techniques which resemble brainwashing.[37]

Since Mao's death, DENG Xiaoping and his colleagues have lessened political education and launched public legal education as they have attempted to develop law and formal social-control mechanisms.[38, 39, 8, 40] Public legal education is "an attempt to teach virtually every citizen about law and the legal system"[40] because "China does not subscribe to the legal fiction that everyone knows the law" as does American society .[41] The Chinese authority believes that once people have learned about the law, they will avoid criminal acts.[42, 29] One can escape the external control of law and relevant punishment, but inner control is hard to escape. Only through education could a person form inner control.[43] Therefore, the Chinese authority believes the effectiveness of this legal education while

Westerners may be skeptical.[40]

In the legal education, because the Chinese law speaks directly to the general public rather than professionals, "many Chinese 'laws' would appear to a Western observer to resemble statements of general principles or policies rather than a set of detailed rules".[41] It represents a striking contrast with the U.S. situation. As Victor Li [41] pointed out, in the U.S., "to a considerable degree, the legal system is something detached from the public, existing in a world of its own."

In China, legal education takes place at various levels --national, provincial, local, community, and family -- through media, posters, pamphlets, education programs, and so on. One of the most important components of public legal education is at the community level. The routine legal education in a neighborhood is charged by the City Street Office, the grassroots branch of the Chinese government, and legal education activities are actually organized and conducted by the neighborhood committee. These activities are supported and directed by the district court and the neighborhood police station. Routine activities include group meetings in which citizens learn basic facts about laws and examine their own thoughts and attitudes toward the laws, distributing written materials and posters in the community, inviting the district court judge and a local policeman to explain the law and legal system, and organizing a contest of legal knowledge.

Neighborhood watch

Neighborhood watch is a voluntary activity organized by the neighborhood committee. Generally, people who engage in a neighborhood watch are senior and retired residents. The neighborhood watch, whose effectiveness depends on neighborhood stability, patrols the neighborhood area every day. People who are responsible for the neighborhood watch generally know well their neighbors' working schedule and life circumstances. Thus, it is fairly easy for them to identify strangers and abnormal situations. However, as the community becomes less stable, it becomes harder to maintain a high level of familiarity with everyone in the area.

In summary, the new intervening variables shown in Figure 2 reflect the unique informal controls at the community level in China. These measures of informal control largely rely on a stable and homogenous community. As the community is undergoing significant changes in economic status, dwelling structure, and residential mobility, these changes may undermine the foundation of informal control. Consequently, the crime rate is likely to increase.

The Chinese Model at Work Unit Level

As previously discussed, a work unit is a distinctive economic and social institution that is largely different from a business organization in the U.S. In the past, the work unit was a major agency of social control and carried many functions of social control. This was possible because all economic activities were strictly controlled by the state, because there was very low occupational mobility, and because work units were responsible for the political, social, and economic aspects of workers' lives. These functions of social control include activities of political organizations and labor unions, *bangjiao*, *tiaojie*, legal, moral, and political education for workers, model worship, and sponsoring leisure activities. However, with changes in ownership of economic enterprises, work units become more like business establishments which, like their counterparts in the West, simply pay employees a wage. Private companies or joint venture enterprises do not perform these social and political functions beyond economic activities. The result is that once the work unit has no or fewer functions of social control, the crime and delinquency rate is likely to increase. Significantly, this disorganization and reorganization process of work units is unique to the Chinese society. Neither the social disorganization perspective nor other perspectives developed in the U.S. can provide an adequate explanation of this unique process and its effect on crime and delinquency. However, following the logic derived from the social disorganization perspective, we argue that the structural change in work unit may prevent or reduce work unit's ability to perform various social control functions they used to do, and thus lead to a higher crime rate. The work unit model is as follows (see Figure 3). Similarly, the model includes three sets of variables. The first set of variables includes change of ownership, occupational mobility, and change of the relationship between workers and work units. This set of variables refers to structural changes in work unit which constitutes exogenous sources of the disorganization of the old work unit system. The second set of variables includes the intervening variables -- activities of political organizations and Labor Union, *bangjiao*, *tiaojie*, legal, moral, and political education, model worship, and sponsoring leisure activities. The last set of variables are crime and delinquency. We discussed the first and the last sets of variables previously. We explain the second set of variables -- intervening variables -- as follows.

Figure 3. A Chinese Model of Structural Change in Work Unit and Crime

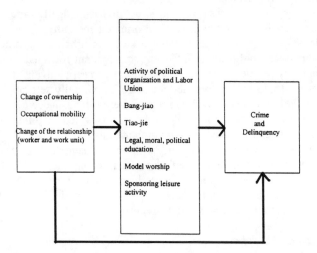

Activities of political organizations and labor unions

Since work units in China were political as well as economic entities, various organizations within the work units had explicit political purposes.[44] First of all, the Communist Party had virtually established branches at all levels of work units. All important decisions were made by the party secretary. Thus, the Party apparatus effectively controlled the whole work unit and every employee. If any deviant behavior was found, the party network could quickly mobilize its resources to nip deviance in the bud. Moreover, since leaders of labor unions, the Youth League, and Women's Federation within the work unit were usually appointed by the Party (or at least had to have party membership), these organizations worked together to help the Party ensure that employees were in line with the Party's policies. Leaders of the Youth League usually tried to find out what practical problems young workers might have and help them solve these problems. They also organized regular youth meetings to praise model young workers and criticized those who might show some signs of deviance.[44] In a like manner, labor unions were actively involved in employees' lives by providing assistance in housing, promotion, mediation in family disputes, and marriage. Combining its grassroots support with the endorsement of various social organizations, the Communist Party could utilize various resources to maintain social control of workers' behaviors.[45]

However, when China's economic structure has gradually shifted from the centralized economy to the market oriented economy, the Party has gradually lost its total control over workers. In urban areas, since the government can not provide sufficient employment for a nation of 1.2 billion, many people have to rely on themselves to earn a living. In 1993, there were 15.43 million people who were individually self-employed, and 139,000 privately owned companies were established. Moreover, Western investors constructed 84,000 foreign owned or joint venture companies where no party or even union activities are allowed.[46] Even in state-owned enterprises, the Party's influences have declined because the economy is not monopolized by the state enterprises anymore. In many foreign-owned or joint ventures which limit their involvement with workers to paying a wage, the Party apparatus and multiple controls for workers' behaviors no longer exist anymore.[46]

Bangjiao and Tiaojie

The general principles and functions of *bangjiao* and *tiaojie* in the work unit are similar to those in the community. A major target of a *bangjiao* group in a work unit is to help offenders, particularly young offenders who were ex-workers and were re-employed by the work unit after released from criminal justice institutions. A *bangjiao* group in the work unit commonly consists of a Labor Union leader in the work unit, a manager, and a family member related to the offender. The purpose of *bangjiao* is to educate and reform the offender's deviant thoughts and behavior, and then help him or her to return to normal work and social life. *Tiaojie* in the work unit is to help and assist the neighborhood committee to solve conflicts in which an employee of the work unit gets involved. It also plays a role in mediating employees' family disputes. A *tiaojie* committee in the work unit is commonly sponsored by the Party branch and has Labor Union and employee's representatives as members.

Bangjiao and *tiaojie* in a work unit are often powerful and effective because such activities are closely associated with employment.

Legal, moral, and political education

In work units, various task oriented departments and organizations frequently provided legal, moral, and ideological educational programs through routine group meetings.[47] The purpose of these programs was to teach appropriate values which would lead individuals to commit themselves to the Party's policies. For instance, the propaganda department in work units publicized Party policies and state rules, guiding employees' ideology, directing them to obey the laws, and praising good persons and good events within the unit. The education department offered educational programs and legal education seminars that trained employees to become obedient workers. Similarly, the Youth League and labor unions often used various propaganda means to influence employees' thoughts. Usually, they set up propaganda posters, wired radio, wall news, newsletters, and blackboard news to distribute officially endorsed policies or the official version of "better" reality.[48] Since these departments and organizations shared the same goals (such as maintaining social order), they could effectively coordinate their efforts to work with potential rule violators. However, the rapidly changing economic structure and declining or non-existent political organizations in work units have significantly reduced this traditional function.[45] Consequently, as workers lose their multiple attachments to, commitment to, and involvement in their work units, deviant behaviors increase.

Model worship

For the Chinese, a (role) model is an exemplary person who has the power to influence people's thoughts and behaviors because he/she is admired and honored by the society. Therefore, since Confucius' time in China, learning from models or heroes has been an important means of guiding and educating people to develop socially desired behavior. During Mao's era, LEI Feng, a PLA soldier of the 1960s, was a national model. People, especially young people, were encouraged to learn Lei's hard work, selflessness, love of socialism, and patriotism.

After Mao's regime, the types of models have been changed somewhat, but learning from models is still an important technique by which the Chinese authority attempts to promote desirable attitudes and behaviors among the youth. There are national and local models. At the national level, the Communist Youth League of China selects "Ten Best Youths" who have achieved great success in political, economic, cultural, and military areas each year. At the local level, cities and regions follow the national practice and select their own youth models. At the work unit, model workers are selected each year according to their achievements in political activity, moral growth, and job performance. The pictures and achievements of these model workers are posted at the work unit and the work unit encourages workers to learn these model through self-criticism and mutual criticism in group meetings, thereby promoting desirable political and social attitudes and behaviors.[49]

Sponsoring leisure activities

In the past, the Youth League and labor unions sponsored various leisure activities that include films, shows, performances, sports events, speech contests, and other entertainment. In large work units, labor unions usually had their own libraries, performance troupes, and sports clubs. Because they were provided with various constructive leisure activities, employees' lives were heavily involved with their work units. This limited their time and opportunities for deviant behavior. However, as previously described, these activities may not be offered by many private and foreign companies, or joint ventures. Consequently, workers' involvement in their work units are reduced.

In summary, these social control measures in the work unit are rooted in a uniform state-run employment system and stable occupational structure. As many scholars have observed [10], work units indeed played a significant role in keeping the crime rate low in the past. However, the fundamental changes in the economic system may make it difficult for a work unit to implement these social control measures. The result is an increase in the crime rate.

Summary and Discussion

The present study is a theoretical attempt to explore the association between structural changes in the community and the work unit and crime in China. This attempt is built upon the common observation that China's social control is rooted at the grassroots level. As many scholars observe, the community and the work unit system are two fundamental establishments which function as major social control agencies at the grassroots level. Therefore, to understand the increasing rate of crime/delinquency in China, an important approach is to examine how the structural changes in community and work unit resulting from economic reform have implications for crime control. To assess this association between the structural changes in community/work unit and crime, we proposed several explanatory models based on theoretical perspectives developed in the U.S. and the unique features of Chinese society.

In our first model, the social disorganization perspective is used to assess the structural changes in community and crime. We argue that the social disorganization perspective is applicable in general, but should be modified according to the Chinese circumstance. Some variables specified and identified by the social disorganization perspective, such as community heterogeneity, may not be generalized to the Chinese situation. Further, we develop other two explanatory models to reflect the unique features of the Chinese community and work unit in social control. These models specify some intervening variables which capture unique informal control measures in Chinese community and work unit, such as public legal education, *bangjiao*, and *tiaojie*. We point out that these distinctive measures are rooted in the stable and homogeneous structure of the community and work unit, and they are responsible for low crime rate in China. However, the structural changes in community and work unit may make these control measures non-existing or less effective, and in turn the disappearance of these control measures may lead to a higher crime rate. These models may have implications for developing a more general theory which would be able to explain social change and crime across different social and cultural contexts.

In practice, these models may offer insights for crime control in China. The Chinese people are expecting inevitable industrialization and modernization. However, the unanticipated consequences of industrialization and modernization may undermine the traditional structure in the community and the work unit, both of which have played important roles in controlling people's behaviors at the grassroots level. In turn, this may lead to significant increase in criminal behavior. The challenge is how to solve this dilemma. As Clark[9] comments, "it remains to be seen how this process will actually develop and what the Chinese response will be."

We close with a final comment. Although these two kinds of models may be useful for understanding the increasing rate of crime/delinquency in China, we definitely need solid data to test these models. It will be an important task to conduct sophisticated survey research for addressing these issues in the years ahead.

Notes

1.   Significantly, the U.S. model of social disorganization is not applicable to the analysis of the association between the structural change in work unit and crime rate in China because the model addresses the change of community

structure and crime rate. As described previously, work unit is a unique employment establishment embedded in the social and economic contexts of Chinese society.

2. Fairbank, J. K. 1987. *The Great Chinese Revolution: 1800-1985.* New York: Harper and Row.

3. Guo, X. 1996. "China: Social Transformation and Crime Control." *Journal of Juvenile*

4. *Delinquency Study* (in Chinese) 171: 2-7. Zhang, L., Zhou, D., Messner, S. F., Liska, A. E., Krohn, M. D., Liu, J. and Zhou, L. 1996.

5. "Crime Prevention in a Communitarian Society: Bang-Jiao and Tiao-Jie in the People's

6. Republic of China." *Justice Quarterly* 13: 199-222.

7. Adler, F. 1996. "1995 presidential address: Our American Society of Criminology, the World, and the State of the Art." *Criminology* 34: 1-10.

8. Troyer, R. J. 1989a. "Chinese social organization." Pp. 26-33 in Social control in the People's *Republic of China,* edited by Ronald J. Troyer, John P. Clark, and Dean G. Rojek. New York: Praeger Publishers.

9. Whyte, M. K. and Parish, W. L. 1984. *Urban Life in Contemporary China.* Chicago: University of Chicago Press.

10. Dutton, M. and Tianfu L. 1993. "Missing the Target? Policing Strategies in the Period of Economic Reform." *Crime and Delinquency* 39: 316-336.

11. Rojek, D. G. 1995. "Changing Directions of Chinese Social Control." Pp. 234-249 in *Comparative Criminal Justice: Traditional and Nontraditional Systems of Law and Control,* edited by Charles B. Fields and Richter H. Moore, Jr. Prospect Heights, Illinois: Waveland Press.

12. Clark, J. P. 1989. "Conflict Management outside the Courtrooms of China." Pp. 57-69 in *Social Control in the People's Republic of China,* edited by Ronald L. Troyer, John P. Clark, and Dean G. Rojek. New York: Praeger.

13. Troyer, R. L. and Rojek, D. G. 1989. "Introduction." Pp. 3-10 in *Social Control in the People's Republic of China,* edited by Ronald L. Troyer, John P. Clark, and Dean G. Rojek. New York: Praeger.

14. Henderson, G. E. and Cohen, M, S. 1984. *The Chinese Hospital: A Socialist Work Unit.* New Haven, CT: Yale University Press.

15. Bracey, D. H. 1984. "Community Prevention in the People's Republic of China." *TheKey: Newsletter of A.S.P.A. Section on Criminal Justice Administration* 10: 3-10.

16. Johson, E. H. 1984. "Neighborhood Police in the People's Republic of China." *Police Studies* 6: 8-12.

17. Braithwaite, J. 1989. *Crime, Shame, and Reintegration.* Cambridge, UK: Cambridge University Press.

18. Shaw, C. R. and Mckay, H. D. 1942. *Juvenile Delinquency and Urban Areas.* Chicago: University of Chicago Press.

19. Shaw, C. R., Zorbaugh, F. M., McKay, H. D., and Cottrell, L. S. 1929. *Delinquency Areas.* Chicago: University of Chicago Press.

20. Bursik, R. J., Jr. 1988. "Social Disorganization and Theories of Crime and Delinquency:

21. Problems and Prospects." *Criminology* 26: 519-551.

22. Bursik, R. J., Jr. and Grasmick, H. G. 1993. *Neighborhoods and Crime: The Dimensions of Effective Community Control.* New York: Lexington Books.

23. Bursik, R. J., Jr. and Webb, J. 1982. "Community Change and Patterns of Delinquency."

23. *American Journal of Sociology* 88: 24-22.

24. Byrne, J. and Sampson, R. J. 1986. "Key Issues in the Social Ecology of Crime." Pp. 1-22 in *The Social Ecology of Crime*, edited by James Byrne and Robert J. Sampson. New York: Springer-Verlag.

25. Gottfredson, S. D. and Taylor, R. 1986. "Person-Environment Interactions in the Prediction of Recidivism." Pp. 133-155 *in The Social Ecology of Crime*, edited by James M. Byrne and Robert J. Sampson. New York: Springer-Verlag.

26. Kapsis, R. E. 1978. "Residential Succession and Delinquency." *Criminology* 15: 459-486.

27. Sampson, R. J. 1987. "Communities and Crime." Pp. 91-114 in *Positive Criminology*, edited by Michael R. Gottfredson and Travis Hirschi. Beverly Hills, CA: Sage.

28. Sampson, R. J. 1988. "Local Friendship Ties and Community Attachment in Mass Society: A Multilevel Systemic Model." *American Sociological Review* 53: 766-779.

29. Sampson, R. J. and Groves, P. 1989. "Community Structure and Crime: Testing Social-Disorganization Theory." *American Journal of Sociology* 94: 774-802.

30. Simcha-Fagan, O. and Schwartz, J. E. 1986. "Neighborhood and Delinquency: An Assessment of Contextual Effects." *Criminology* 24: 667-703.

31. Heitgerd, J. L. and Bursik, R. J., Jr. 1987. "Extracommunity Dynamics and the Ecology of Delinquency." *American Journal of Sociology* 92: 775-787.

32. Kornhauser, R. 1978. *Social Sources of Delinquency.* Chicago: University of Chicago Press.

33. Leng, S. and Chiu, H. 1985. *Criminal Justice in Post-Mao China: Analysis and Documents.* Albany: State University of New York Press.

34. Troyer, R. L. 1989d. "Conclusion." Pp. 188-196 in *Social Control in the People's Republic of China*, edited by Ronald L. Troyer, John P. Clark, and Dean G. Rojek. New York: Praeger.

35. *People's Daily* (Overseas Edition). 1996. March 1. Beijing, China: People's Daily Publication.

36. Johson, E. H. 1983. "Mediation in the People's Republic of China: Participation and Social Control." Pp. 56-57 in *Comparative Criminology*, edited by I. L. Barak-Glantz and Elmer H. Johson. Beverly Hills: Sage.

37. Jan, L. 1983. "Deterrence as Social Control in the United States and China." *International Journal of Comparative and Applied Criminal Justice* 7: 195-200.

38. Munro, D. J. 1977. *The Concept of Man in Contemporary China.* Ann Arbor: University of Michigan Press.

39. Troyer, R. L. 1989b. "Chinese Thinking about Crime and Social

Control." Pp. 45-56 in *Social Control in the People's Republic of China*, edited by Ronald L. Troyer, John P. Clark, and Dean G. Rojek. New York: Praeger.

40. Johson, E. H. 1986. "Politics, Power and Prevention: The People's Republic of China Case." *Journal of Criminal Justice* 14: 449-457.

41. Huang, W. S. W. 1993. "Book Review: Social Control in the People's Republic of China." *International Criminal Justice Review* 3: 161-162.

42. Brady, J. P. 1982. *Justice and Politics in People's China: Legal Order or Continuing Revolution?* New York: Academic Press.

43. Lin, J. 1993. *Education in Post-Mao China*. New York: Praeger.

44. Troyer, R. L. 1989c. "Publicizing the New Laws: The Public Legal Education Campaign." Pp. 70-83 in *Social Control in the People's Republic of China,* edited by Ronald L. Troyer, John P. Clark, and Dean G. Rojek. New York: Praeger.

45. Li, V. H. 1977. *Law without Lawyers: A Comparative View of Law in China and the United States*. Stanford, CA: The Portable Stanford.

46. *Law Yearbook of China* (in Chinese). 1993. The Editorial Committee of Law Yearbook of China. Beijing, China: Law Yearbook of China Publication House.

47. Anderson, A. F. and Gil, V. E. 1994. "Prostitution and Public Policy in the People's Republic of China: An Analysis of the Rehabilitative Ideal." *International Criminal Justice Review* 4: 23-36.

48. 44. Kang, S. (ed.). 1992. *Introduction to Criminology*. Beijing: Beijing University Press (in   Chinese).

49. Zheng, S., (and twelve others) et al. 1996. *1996 Yearbook on Chinese Communism* (in Chinese). Taipei: The Institute for the Study of Chinese Communist Problems.

50. Yu, L. (ed.). 1993. *Research on China's Contemporary Crime Problems* (in Chinese).

51. Beijing: Chinese University of Public Security Press.

52. Reed, G. G. 1995. "Moral/Political Education in the People's Republic of China: Learning through Role Models." *Journal of Moral Education* 24: 99.

53. Shaw, V. 1996. *Social Control in China: A Study of Chinese Work Units*. Westport, Connecticut: Praeger.

54. Zhang, L. and Messner, S. F. 1996. "School Attachment and Official Delinquency Status in the People's Republic of China." *Sociological Forum* 11: 285-304.

Chapter 8

Crime in China's Modernization

CHEN Jiafang

What is "crime"? It is difficult to find a universal definition of the term "crime". Actually, the definition varies in different historical periods, under different social systems, and cultural backgrounds. What could be called "crime" in historical period *A*, place *B*, with a cultural background *C* might be highly appreciated in historical period *X*, place *Y*, with a cultural background *Z*. For example, in ancient Chinese dynasties, joking about the emperor in any verbal, or symbolic action, or both, would be considered the most serious crime termed "insulting the emperor." The punishment would be the death penalty for sure, or, most possibly, the "extermination of the entire family." This is considered cruel and barbaric by the current moral standard in most of the civilized societies. But, it was the law, or the rule at the time in Chinese society. On the other hand, most of the leaders in the Western industrialized societies are elected rather than through inheritance. During their campaign for the position, one candidate can accuse the other candidate, or, sometimes the current leader, with no criminal risk involved. Yet, sometimes, the fact of the accusation is twisted, sometimes, personal attacks are involved. But, unlike in ancient China, these activities are not considered crime since they neither affect the freedom of the public nor interfere with someone else's business. Another example is that joking about the President is common on many U.S. talk-show programs, in essence, this is similar to the "crime" in ancient China, and all these jokes are not considered crimes.

Time and cultural changes are other dimensions to differentiate what is and what was not a crime. More than a thousand years ago, before the Song Dynasty, pre-marital sex was not unusual, and it was not a crime, nor was it an issue against the norm at that time. Therefore, there was no charge nor punishment against this kind of behavior. This situation had not changed until the "Ru" School doctrine dominated China. This fact was not only shown in Chinese ancient literature, but also shown in the Chinese history. Similar change can also be found in Western literature and history.

Even in the modern era, especially in the current societies, the definition of crime also varies by country and cultural background. For example, vandalism is very common in the United States, especially in the large metropolitan areas. A lot of public facilities, such as buses, parks, walls, etc., are vandalized. As part of the American sub-culture, vandals left their marks everywhere. This is definitely not what the American public wants. Since there is almost no punishment for this kind of behavior, there is no way that this kind of behavior can be controlled or stopped, even though the result of this kind of freedom violates the freedom of the public.

A few years ago, an American young man vandalized in Singapore, and he was punished by caning, according to the law of Singapore. The U.S. media had different opinions toward this event, some were for the punishment, some were against it. From another angle, we can see that in different cultures, and different societies, the definition of crime can be completely different. This difference will exist in this world for as long as we have differences in social systems, cultures, legislation, values, and opinions.

All these differences do not mean that there is no universal agreement on the definition of crime. A close look at the categories of the behavior which are classified as crime reveals that, in spite of all these differences, some categories of behavior are considered crime in most of the societies all over the world, such as robbery, homicide, arson, poisoning, theft, and rape. Most of these behaviors are considered against the law, or violate the norm in the society. Therefore, this article will focus on the categories of behavior which are commonly considered as crimes, which are homicide, intentional injury to others, robbery, rape, smuggling (drugs, as well as children and women), theft, etc. Some categories are not included in this study because of differences in political systems, customs and norms, such as political prisoners, since they are classified as criminals merely because of their political opinions.

A Historical Review of Crime in China

Criminal behavior exists everywhere in the world. It is fair to say that with a relatively large enough human population in a given country, criminal behavior is inevitable. Thus far, there is no country in the world without crime. The difference between countries is the number of crimes is large or small; the crime rate is high or low. According to the conflict theory, basic interaction among individuals creates conflict. Therefore, the more interactions in a given society, the more conflicts there will be. Some of these conflicts will turn out to be crimes. Following this logic, the population of China is more than one billion, thus, it is inevitable that China also has crimes.

After more than half a century of civil war and the experience of World War II, the People's Republic of China was founded, yet with a lot of problems, such as poverty, prostitution, drugs, inflation, low level of productivity, starvation, and political instability. In order to maintain the political stability and social order, there were some conflicts between the new government and the remainders of the old government. After that, the Chinese economic development was slowly established. During this period of time, history shows that along with the economic development, the crime rate in China was relatively low also, especially when it is compared with other countries in the world. According to the State Statistics Bureau, there were about 190 thousand criminal cases reported in 1956 nationwide, averaging 3 cases per 100 thousand population. This rate was maintained at the similar level until 1965, the eve before the "Cultural Revolution", in which there were 210 thousand criminal cases reported nationwide. The crime rate was still 3 per 100 thousand population. In other words, the crime rate did not rise nor did it fall [1,2,3,4,5].

During the "Cultural Revolution", China was in complete chaos. There were small-scaled wars among different organizations, fights among individuals, "accidental" deaths due to all sorts of reasons, etc.. There is no way one could tell which was considered crime and which was not. Also, State Statistics Bureau lost the track of almost everything. Since this is a special historical period in modern China, it is understandable that the interruption of the statistics is not due to technical reasons.

After the "Cultural Revolution", the State started to pick up the numbers again. Unlike the situation before the "Cultural Revolution", criminal case numbers were exploded. In 1982, there were 750 thousand criminal cases reported, averaging 7.5 case per 100 thousand population. This rate has already more than doubled the rate at the eve of the "Cultural Revolution". Six years later, the trend of crime keeps on increasing. In 1988, there were 830 thousand cases reported nationwide, averaging more than 7 cases per 100 thousand population. The numbers and the rate were almost doubled those of 1988 in 1994 [6,7,8,9]. The historical trend of crime in China can be seen from Table 1.

Table 1
**NUMBERS OF CRIMES AND CRIMES PER 100,000 POPULATION
IN THE PEOPLE'S REPUBLIC OF CHINA**

Year	Number of Crimes (In 1,000)	Crimes per 100,000 Population
1950		9.0
1951		5.9
1956	190	3.0
1965	210	3.0
1982	750	7.4
1988	830	7.7
1994	1,660	14.3

Sources of data: 1. State Statistics Bureau, 1985, 1986, 1987, 1988, 1989, 1990, 1991, 1992, 1993 edition *"Social Statistics of China"*, Beijing, China: Chinese Statistical Press. 2. China's Law Yearbook Press, 1989, 1990, 1991, 1992, 1993, 1994, 1995 edition "China's Law Yearbook". Beijing, China: China's Law Yearbook press.

Researchers and law enforcement agencies in China were confused by this phenomenon, and several researchers wondered why some of the "model cities", which are traditionally low crime rate areas in Southeast China, also have the problems of increasing crimes. The local government did try to control the increasing trend, but little effect had been seen. In some cities, youth crime rate has been increasing at about 20 percent annually, especially in the newly industrialized cities [10]. The Chinese government admits that if the current trend of juvenile delinquency continues, it will have a great impact on the fast growing economy in China.

Who's Fault?

Usually, when something happens, researchers will try to find out the cause of the event. It does not matter whether in the Western World or the East, scientific studies always do that. But, the recent change in China, economically and socially as well, is not due to a single cause. Crime in China have the following characteristics:

The Increase of the Young Criminals

The numbers of the young criminals are increasing recently, especially along the coastal areas where economic development is faster than the rest of China. Among all arrests due to their criminal behavior, less than 50 percent of the total are under 26 years of age in 1984. After 10 years, the total number of young criminals arrested jumps to more than 820 thousand in 1993, which is 2.28 times of the number 10 years ago. Ever since the 1980s, juvenile crimes along the coastal areas have been consistently maintained at around 60 percent of all the crimes. In the coastal cities, juvenile crimes have been increasing at 5 percent annually [11].

Robbery and Theft are the Main Component of Juvenile Crimes

Statistics indicates that among all the crimes committed by the young people, more than 80 percent of them are robbery and theft. From the goods valued at a few cents to the machinery valued in the millions, there is almost nothing excluded from their robbery list. In 1987, less than 440 thousand robberies and thefts were reported in the whole nation, while in 1994, the reported robberies and thefts increased to more than 1,130 thousand cases [12]. Several researchers suggest that the value system change among the young is suspected to be the cause of this problem. In the People's Republic of China, children used to be taught to "serve the people" when they got their formal education. Since Chinese economy switched to the market economy, money becomes the driving force for almost everything. Driven by pursuing money, the traditional value of "serving the people" has been transformed into "individualism". They conclude that so long as the money pursuing is there, there will be more and more robberies and thefts [13].

The Increasing Trend of Violent Crimes

Another characteristic of the recent trend is that violent crimes such as homicide, is increasing in the whole society. This trend threatens the safety of ordinary people. It is predicted by some researchers that this trend will continue with the industrialization of the nation. There were close to 10 thousand homicides, and around 20 thousands intentional injuries in China in 1987. In a country where population is around 1 billion, the homicide rates is relatively low. Eight years later, according to the Press of Law Yearbook of China, there were almost 30 thousand homicides in 1994, and almost 70 thousand intentional injuries in the entire nation [14]. Compared to some industrialized countries in the world, China's crime rate and homicide rate are not high at all, but, there is definitely an increasing trend in homicide and violent intentional injuries. The increasing proportion of young people in violent crimes calls for more attention. In 1994, almost half of the homicides were committed by people under the age of 25, and more than 60 percent of the intentional injuries involved these young people.

The recent trend of crime in China indicates that, according to most of the researchers, crime in China will continue to increase. If there is no correspondent policy or program to control the situation, the problem of crime will eventually affect the economic growth and social stability. Before any policy can be issued, the question is: what is the cause of this trend? There are many propositions and assumptions, so far, none was tested. A list of some typical propositions will help us to see the current research in China.

Social Change Proposition.

This proposition suggests that during social change the previous dominant element will conflict with the new emerging elements in the society. This conflict will cause a series of change, such as values, behaviors, structures of the society, etc.. The increase of crime during this period of time is only part of the change.

Cultural Conflict Proposition.

This proposition considers that Chinese culture is inward, and conservatively oriented. It is less aggressive, therefore, it will not cause many violent crimes. On the other hand, Western culture is considered outwardly oriented and more aggressive. The consequence of this kind of culture will create more interactions, including violent interactions. After China opened the door to the whole world, it is inevitable that traditional Chinese culture will conflict with Western culture. As a result, more people, especially the young, feel confused. The result of this confusion is, partially, deviated behavior.

Media Misleading Proposition.

This proposition considers that Chinese society had few crimes due to the bond of the traditional Chinese values. Violent movies, programs and criminal stories through the TV and other media gave people a misconception that this society is full of violence. Therefore, people, especially young people, imitate the criminal behaviors on the TV and from the media.

"Money Makes the Mare Go" Proposition.

This proposition suggests that criminal behavior is actually a reflection of the money oriented values in the society. This proposition uses the high percentage of robbery and theft in all crimes to illustrate this point. It also suggests that money oriented value is the product of the market economy and social change, which indirectly causes the rise of the crime in China.

There are some other propositions, such as: the imbalance of the "two civilizations" (the material civilization and the spiritual civilization); the lost of control of the norms in the society; the crises of the traditional families; the corruption of the government; the gap between the rich and the poor is too wide; etc.. From different angles, all these propositions provide different explanations for the current increase in crimes in the society. When comparing the crime in China with crime in some of the industrialized countries when they were experiencing the process of transition (which means the transition from a traditional society to an industrialized society), it is not difficult to find that both China and the Western countries have a lot in common. Almost all countries had the problems of increasing crimes when they experienced social transition from traditional to modern. In many studies, researchers indicated that crime is the problem that comes hand in hand with urbanization, industrialization, and modernization. This problem is universal. If this statement is true, in the case of China, is it worthwhile to try something to control the crime, or just leave the problem of crime as it is? If something needs to be done, what is it?

Any Solution

Whenever there is a problem, researchers or decision-makers will try to find a solution. In the last several decades, some programs were recommended by the government and the educators. The first one is on education. Under this program, reeducation of the youth who committed crimes or with some problems is very important. Forced labor is part of the component of the program, aiming at educating the young and changing their habits to getting used to work. Is it successful? The answer is: yes. According to the Press of Law Yearbook of China, after this kind reeducation, averaging less than 9 percent of them recommitted crimes in the next ten years[15, 16, 17, 18, 19, 20]. Many of them can earn their living and raise their own families later on. This is considered successful comparing to some industrialized countries. For example, in the U.S. where repeated crimes after they served their jail time are more than 50 percent.

The second one is to crack down on all crimes. This program is like a political movement, whenever the government considers that crime is a problem to the whole society, then a crack down will follow. Some of the criminals will receive capital punishments and some of them will serve longer prison time. After the crack down, there is always a period of time where crime rate is lower than it was. This kind of crack down has some impact on the society, seasonally lowering the crime rate. The problem is this kind of crack down cannot be there all the time. Crime rate will rise after a while.

Researchers of social sciences suggest that in order to reduce the crime in the society, early prevention is the first step to reach that goal. In this suggestion, they proposed four incremental and educational layers. The first layer is to educate a child with a given ideal, so the child will pursue this ideal in the rest of his/her life. The second layer is the virtue and the norm, in which traditional Chinese culture is an important part. The third layer is the correspondent administration, which includes the educational institute from preschool to the university, the local community administration, and the society. The fourth, and the last layer is the law enforcement, which will do whatever is necessary to stop crime when the first three layers fail.

Other researchers suggest four barriers each of which will prevent youth from committing any crime. These barriers include the family, the school, the administrative agent, and the society. Actually, these four barriers are not significantly different from the four layers. Both of them emphasize the traditional norm and virtue, and strict control. Under this program, there were several "model" areas and cities in the country, such as the SouthEast model around Su Zhou. Unfortunately, this model was smashed in the 1990s by the increasing crimes in the area, and no reason for the increase was provided by the researchers.

The above two suggestions are not new. During the Cultural Revolution, in which China was in a chaotic situation for about ten years, the government emphasized a similar strategy to prevent crime. Right after the Cultural Revolution, these plans and programs were part of the central tasks of the Communist Party. What happened then? From the statistics, we still see the increase of crimes. The question is how do we perceive the phenomenon? Only when we understand this phenomenon can we consider the way to deal with it.

First of all, let us consider the following facts: 1. The economic development in China. Economic development in the world is an irresistible trend in the future simply because the demand of the people is there. Since this is an irresistible trend, previous models of economy, such as the closed-model and the central-planned model, are no longer adequate for China's situation today. In a closed-model, almost everything is planned and controlled. There are less interactions, few communications, and limited mobility, which in turn produce less effective, slow, and sluggish economic growth. On the other hand, the open and market oriented economy demands more communication, mobility, and adjustment. Therefore, more mobility, adjustment, and communication will bring about more interaction. It is almost impossible to try to control these unplanned interactions. Once one out of one thousand interactions goes wrong, there will be millions wrong, or miscommunication, or deviated interactions out of billions of interactions. In a country like China where the population is over one billion, deviations and crimes which exist in the daily life are expected. Actually, there is almost no country in the world, where the population is large enough that has a crime-free environment. The difference is whether there are a lot of crimes or few of them.

Since China wants its economy to grow, probably, the majority of people will not allow anybody to change the market economy into a closed economy again. When this is inevitable, it is also true with the increasing interactions and communications, therefore, no matter if you want it or not, crime is there. Even when the economy in China was not developing fast, such as during the Cultural Revolution, crime was still there. Thus, economic growth is not to be blamed for increasing crime in China. There maybe some impact from economy, but more studies have to be done to test this proposition.

2. Cultural Impact from Abroad. Western culture is not something that you can stop when you want only the technology and science. Along with economic development, more and more scientists, engineers, technicians, workers, business people, and commercial products flushed into China. All of these brought Western culture with them. They helped the Chinese economic growth. But, it is almost impossible for the Chinese government to import foreign technology without any influence of the foreign culture. Of course, if everybody can follow Confucius' advice to "learn the merit and correct the mistake from any of the three people whom I encountered", this world would be without crime. Unfortunately, this is not an ideal world. Economy must grow, communication must continue, interaction will increase, and foreign culture will arrive with the development. When this is understood, the question is: how can we lower the crime rate to the minimum level.

Possible Explanation and Future Orientation

Criminology as a discipline of learning started centuries ago. The real scientific test study of criminology is only a matter in the last several decades. Researchers all over the world paid attention to the ups and downs of the crime rate, the effect of the economic impact on the criminal behavior, and the pathology of the criminals. Studies started from descriptions to the current quantitative analysis. Yet, findings vary from one to the other. But, most of the researchers agree that the stability of the family, social status, educational attainment, influence of the peer group, childhood experience, and the income of the family have a great impact over human behavior [21, 22, 23,24 25, 26, 27, 28, 29, 30]. Some researchers found, through their macro level studies, the most important factors of crime in the United States are the economic situation and the age-structure of the population [31, 32]. Are these factors universal? If at least one of them is universal, does it apply to the situation in China?

Possible Explanation

One possible factor which has the potential to affect the ups and downs of the crime rates in China is the age-structure of the population. Recent studies indicate that the economic factor and the age-structure in the U.S. determine the ups and downs of the homicide rates in the last 60 odd years [33]. A theoretical rational suggests that there may be a biological factor which affects the violent behavior of human beings. According to recent studies, the biological factor is very important in the study of aggressiveness[34]. Let us have a brief review of this perspective.

In the early stage of our lives, before ten years old, the aggressiveness of human beings, especially as offenders, is not fully developed. Physically, most of children cannot commit violent crimes. Therefore, very few criminal offenders are found in these age groups. This is proved by criminal records everywhere in the world. On the other hand, at the very early stage of our lives, especially as infants, human beings are vulnerable to any criminal offender since they do not have any capability to physically defend themselves. Therefore, it is impossible for them to become offenders at this stage.

The 10 to the 19 year old period is critical and dangerous. Physically, both boys and girls are stronger and bigger. This provides the potential for aggressive behavior. Daily activities are no longer limited to families and schools. There is an increase in the frequencies of interactions among peer groups, between each individual and his/her surrounding environment-- the society. This increased interaction provides another potential for violent behavior towards somebody. They, themselves, are also vulnerable to similar behavior initiated by their peers or criminals in older age-groups. In addition, teens are physically mature, but not mentally mature, or experienced. They tend to respond to temptations easily without considering the consequences. Therefore, they are more likely to be caught by law enforcement agencies for their violent behavior.

From age 20 to 29 is a period in which almost everyone will have a "big" transition from a dependent, affiliated with the family, to an independent. To some extent, one will experience the transition from an unstable, unsure situation to a relatively stable, and settled situation. Once this transition is completed, marriage and child-rearing will follow. During this period of time, physically and mentally, people are more mature than the teenagers. But, this is still a transition period. Since they are mentally more mature and experienced, sometimes law enforcement agencies have more difficulties in catching them even when they committed crimes. A recent study found that in the U.S., this age-group has a great impact on the crime rate in the last 60 odd years.

Life after 30 years old is safer and more stable. Most people settle down and have more interactions within their family circle, and less interactions with their peers than they used to have in their teens and twenties. Since most families are protective of their own members, it is considered that home is "sweet home." It also follows that body-strength related crime rates for people after 30 years old go down because physically older people are not as strong as they were in their twenties. On the other hand, older people are mentally mature and experienced, therefore, they are more likely to avoid being arrested. Since they are mentally matured, they use their brain more than their physical strength. Therefore, also due to their convenience to access something like money and power, there are more "brain" related crimes than "strength" related crimes.

Keeping these characteristics in mind, it is not very difficult to find out that the age-structure has an impact on the human behavior effect. It is true that each case varies, but, at the macro-level, the similarities over a long period of time in our life span give us another picture. A quick glance at the population age-structure in China together with the projected population age-structure in the years to come may help in this extent. Table 2 is the estimated Chinese people ages 20-29 as a proportion of the total population from 1982 to 2010. The proposition is: as this proportion of population goes up, there will be an increase in the crime rate, and vice versa.

One of the previous questions that Chinese researchers raised is that some low-crime-rate "model" cities and townships in the early 1980s in

South-East China experienced an increase in the crime rate in the early 1990s. The problem is: nobody knows why. It follows that more propositions are raised than analyzed or tested. In Table 2, the proportion of people ages 20-29 in the total population started to increase in the late 1980s, and reached the peak in the early 1990s. This ups and downs of the proportion of this age-group is coincidently followed by the ups and downs of the crime rate in China. If there is more detailed information about crime and the crime rate in China, this statement can be tested empirically.

Table 2
PROPORTION OF PEOPLE AGES 20-29 IN THE TOTAL
POPULATION
CHINA, 1982-2010

Year	Proportion	Year	Proportion
1982	16.63	1997	18.75
1983	17.34	1998	17.99
1984	17.71	1999	17.06
1985	17.90	2000	16.20
1986	18.35	2001	15.23
1987	18.43	2002	14.65
1988	18.59	2003	14.12
1989	19.52	2004	13.69
1990	20.24	2005	13.45
1991	21.31	2006	13.36
1992	21.74	2007	13.41
1993	21.16	2008	13.60
1994	20.69	2009	13.81
1995	20.10	2010	14.19
1996	19.34		

Source: Estimation based on the population projection results of Jiafang Chen, 1995. "Relative-Stable Population Theory and Its Empirical Proof." *Shanghai Academy of Social Sciences Quarterly*. Shanghai, P.R. China, and the data from Xinwu Yao and Hua Yin, 1994. *Basic Data of China's Population, Data User Service Series No.1*. Beijing: China Population Publishing House.

The rational of this statement is simple and straight forward: people in their 20s are physically strong, and some of them are not mentally matured, plus this is a period of time in their lives that many thing are being settled, which means this period is a transition period in their lives. The instability will create more interactions, thus, more opportunities for crime. This proposition is proved adequate in the U.S.. When the ups and downs of the crime rate in China are correlated with the proportion of the people in this age-group, this proposition usually holds.

The proportion of the people ages 20-29 in the total population in China will decrease after the mid-1990s. The projection of population and the proportion of this age-group indicate that this proportion is going down right now. This trend will continue after the year 2000. Thus, crime rate in China is expected to go down in the next decade. At least, the age-structure in China suggests so. This trend can also be seen from Figure 1.

Figure 1

PEOPLE AGES 20-29 AS A PERCENT
OF TOTAL POPULATION, CHINA 1982-2010

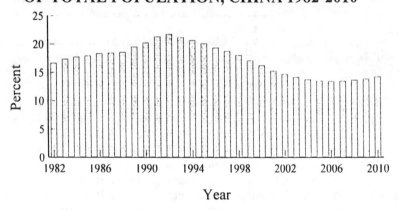

PEOPLE AGES 20-29

Future Orientation

In order to provide a scientific analysis to the legislators and policy makers, to protect the majority of the people, and to continue the economic growth, controlling the crime in a society is necessary. The following suggestions may be useful.

1. Archive the documentation of the criminals and victims, publish the criminal data annually, so the researchers may access the dada and analyze them. The criminals as well as the victims will be categorized by the geographical location, age, sex, race, and the type of crime at the grass roots level, and the information will be sent to the provincial, and the state level each year. With the help of the modern computer, the data entry, and compiling are relatively easier than it used to be. This documentation will provide the foundation for the scientific study of crime.

2. Establish the death registration nationwide. Starting from 1987, China began to provide vital statistics information to the World Health Organization. Yet, only a few cities and rural areas are included in this data. If death registration can be extended to the whole country, the information will greatly benefit the medical and pharmaceutical industries. The effect of modern industry on human health, on the environment, on the migration of the population, on the modernization process of people's fertility behavior, etc. can be analyzed and estimated. This longitudinal data will provide scientific evidence for the legislators and policy makers.

3. The above two suggestions demand money. This may become a problem under the current situation because the legislation cannot catch up with the economic growth in China. The first step seems to be emphasized on the economic legislation and taxation. When the tax collection system is established, the application of the above two suggestions will not be that difficult. This series of applications will create a new market for the labor force, new professions, new laws, new orders, and new development. All these will help China to better accomplish the transition from a planed economy, to the market economy, from a closed society to a modernized society.

Notes

1.   State Statistical Bureau, 1985. *Social Statistical Data of China 1985.* Beijing: Statistical Press of China.
2.   State Statistical Bureau, 1986. *Statistical Data of China 1986.* Beijing:

Statistical Press of China.

3. State Statistical Bureau, 1987. *Statistical Data of China 1987*. Beijing: Statistical Press of China.

4. State Statistical Bureau, 1988. *Statistical Data of China 1988*. Beijing: Statistical Press of China.

5. State Statistical Bureau, 1989. *Statistical Data of China 1989*. Beijing: Statistical Press of China.

6. State Statistical Bureau, 1990. *Statistical Data of China 1990*. Beijing: Statistical Press of China.

7. State Statistical Bureau, 1991. *Statistical Data of China 1991*. Beijing: Statistical Press of China.

8. State Statistical Bureau, 1992. *Statistical Data of China 1992*. Beijing: Statistical Press of China.

9. State Statistical Bureau, 1993. *Statistical Data of China 1993*. Beijing: Statistical Press of China.

10. Guo, Xiang. 1995. "Juvenile Delinquency and Law for the Juveniles." pp 989-990. *Law Yearbook of China 1995*. Beijing, China: Press of Law Yearbook of China.

11. *Ibid.*

12. *Ibid.*

13. *Ibid.*

14. Press of Law Yearbook of China. 1995. "Law Enforcement Statistical Data". *Law Yearbook of China 1995*. Beijing, China: Press of Law Yearbook of China.

15. *Ibid.* 1989.

16. *Ibid.* 1990.

17. *Ibid.* 1991.

18. *Ibid.* 1992.

19. *Ibid.* 1993.

20. *Ibid.* 1994.

21. Adelman, Irma and Cynthia Taft Morris. 1973. *Economic Growth and Social Equity in Developing Countries*. Stanford: Stanford University Press.

22. Ahluwalia, Montek S. 1976. "Income Distribution and Development: Some Stylized facts." *American Economic Review*, 66: 128-135.

23. Archer, Dane, and Rosemary Gartner. 1976. "Violent Acts and Violent Times: A Comparative Approach to Postwar Homicide Rates." *American Sociological Review*, 41: 937-963.

24. *Ibid.* 1984. *Violence and Crime in Cross-National Perspective*. New Haven, CT: Yale University Press.

25. Blau, Peter M. and Reid M. Golden. 1986. "Metropolitan Structure and Criminal Violence." *Sociological Quarterly*, 27: 15-26.

26. Block, Richard. 1979. "Community, Environment, and Violent Crime." *Criminology*, 17: 46-57.

27. Daly, Martin and Margo Wilson. 1988. *Homicide*. New York: Aldine de Gruyter.

28. Henry, Andrew F. and James F. Short, Jr. 1954. *Suicide and Homicide: Some Economic, Sociological, and Psychological Aspects of Aggression*.

London: Free press of Glencoe.

29. Merton, Robert K. 1961. "Social Problems and Sociological Theory." in *Contemporary Social Problems*, ed. Robert K. Merton and Robert A. Nisbet, 697-737. New York: Harbourt Brace and World.

30. Quinney, Richard C. 1965. "Suicide, Homicide, and Economic Development." *Social Forces*, 43: 401-406.

31. Chen, Jiafang. 1996. "Economic Conditions, Age, and Homicide in the U.S.: a Historical and Empirical Analysis." *Lethal Violence,* Washington, D.C.: National Institute of Justice.

32. Chen, Jiafang. 1997. "Determinants of Homicide: Age Factor and Economic Factor."   *Research, Law, and Policy, , 1996,* Washington, D.C.: National Institute of Justice.

33. *Ibid.* 1996 and 1997.

34. *Ibid.*

Chapter 9

The Development of Communication Information Infrastructure: A Revolution in Networking

YU Yanmin

INTRODUCTION

An ancient Chinese saying, "A scholar can learn everything without leaving the house," surprisingly predicted what would happen in modern China thousands of years later. In today's China, in fact, it is not just scholars, but also businesspeople, professionals, and students, and in the future it would be anyone with a computer, a modem, and a telephone line to learn everything without ever leaving the house. Surfing the net, discussing Tang poems and Ming drama, exchanging information on Chinese medicine, sending e-mail messages to friends or strangers, and chit-chatting about Buddhism, Confucianism, or Sunzi strategies with people across the country and around the world on the Internet are some of the leisure activities Chinese people are engaged in these days. As recent as five years ago, World Wide Web was a total novelty to most people in China; today having an e-mail address on one's business card has become a popular status symbol.

With rapid economic growth and increasing personal use of the Internet, the communication information infrastructure in China is changing literally daily. This paper will review the history of the development of the Internet in China, analyze the uses of the Internet and the impact the Internet exerts on people's way of communication, examine the rules and regulations the Chinese government has issued to control the Internet, and evaluate the effectiveness of government control and approaches the Internet users employ to get around the rules and regulations.

GETTING ONTO THE INFORMATION SUPERHIGHWAY

It has been only a few years since China first decided to construct its information infrastructure to join the globalization of information technology. The first reported China network cooperating with the outside world was the China Academic Network (CANET) which was implemented in 1988 and provided minimum e-mail services.[1]

In 1989, the China State Planning Commission and the World Bank started to support a project called National Computing Facilities of China (NCFC). This project included a supercomputer center and three campus networks: China Academic of Science Network (CASnet), Tsinghua University (TUnet) and Peking University (PUnet). The construction of these three individual campus networks was completed in 1992. Two years later, a 64K bit-per-second satellite link was established and full Internet access became available to the users of CASnet, TUnet and PUnet.[2]

With regard to connectivity, the Internet links in China can be divided into two phases. The CANET-e-mail phase from 1988 to 1994 and the IHEP, ChinaNet, China Internet and CERNET (ICCC) full connectivity phase which started in 1994[3] and is still developing today. Direct Internet overseas links from China were established in May 1994 when Chinese Ministry of Posts and Telecommunications gave the Chinese Academy permission to lease a line provided by Sprint, the U.S.-based telecommunications company. The line supports 2,000 terminals at three Beijing institutions—Chinese Academy of Sciences and Qinghua and Beijing universities—and the connection time is cheap, thanks to $130,000 a year in joint funding from the World Bank and China's State Planning Commission.[4] After that, several major Internet links were installed and publicized. These included the links from the Institute of High Energy Physics (IHEP), National Computing and Networking Facilities of China (NCFC), Beijing University of Chemical Technology (BUCT), Chinese Education and Research Network (CERNET) and Ministry of Posts and Telecommunications' China Internet.[5]

In less than four years, the construction of the information superhighway in China has made tremendous progress. According to recent statistics provided by the ChinaNet Information Center at the end of 1997, there are now more than 49,000 host computers and

250,000 personal computers in China, with about 620,000 browsers connected to the Internet. In addition, China has more than 1,000 information service providers (ISP), 1,519 home pages and more than 100 commercial information service suppliers,[6] although most of the users are still intellectuals and businesspeople. ChinaNet, which belongs to the Ministry of Posts and Telecommunications (MPT), now covers 30 provinces and aims to hook up 10 million users by year 2,000.[7] According to another report, the number of Internet users in China has already reached almost 100 million (99.96 million) at the end of 1997 and the number is still growing.[8] The computer market in China has never been better in recent years. Chinese purchased more than one million personal computers in 1995, an increase of 55% from the previous year. After Japan, China is the fastest-growing computer market in Asia with more potential customers than any other country in the world. Equipped with computers, many Chinese seek access to the Internet, send and receive e-mail messages, join newsgroups on Usernet, or visit sites on the World Wide Web to gather information on culture, literature, medicine, politics, philosophy, and history.[9]

It is not just businesspeople or professionals who rely on the Internet, computer networks are now indispensable as tools for the government to manage state affairs, economic construction, defense, and science and technology. They are a pillar of social development because they are able to promote the nation's economic development, cultural exchanges and education due to their international connections.[10]

Computer ownership leads to computer literacy among many Chinese people. According to market watcher China Research Corp., China currently has around 250,000 to 275,000 Internet subscribers and the number of Internet service providers has doubled since the beginning of 1997 from 50 to now 100.[11] A recent survey conducted by the Social Investigation Center of the *China Youth Journal* shows that 81% of Beijing high school students have used computers and that nearly half own a computer. One in every 20 claims to have an Internet connection. This survey also shows that 23% of Beijing secondary school students have read Bill Gates' book, *The Road Ahead*,[12] a book considered by many a source of inspiration to succeed in the cyberworld.

While students in Beijing, Shanghai, and other big cities may have access to computers and the Internet, the majority of the Chinese people are still ill equipped and illiterate when it comes to surfing cyberspace. Based on a survey done by the Yanshi Survey and Consulting Service Center, 86% of Chinese families have never used a computer before and nationally only 1.6% of Chinese families own

computers and just 4.1% plan to buy one.[13] Undoubtedly, the Internet is
still an elite's communication medium.

SIPPING COFFEE IN CYBERSPACE

Cybercafe, a new phenomenon in China, as well as in Singapore,
Malaysia, and other Asian countries, has become trendy recently. With
15 to 20 yuan (about 2-3 U.S. dollars), people can have a cup of coffee
or tea and go on the Internet to set up their own mailbox and send and
receive e-mails. Some cybercafes allow customers to cruise the Net;
some offer 30 minutes of free Internet time to customers who buy ice-
cream, cake or coffee.[14] Zhang Shuxin, a 33-year-old entrepreneur, is
considered a pioneer in the cybercafe industry in China. She caught the
on-line bug while touring America in 1994, and has picked up a few
high-caffeine marketing techniques. In January 1996 she opened the
Cybercafe, a nightspot in the lobby of the Beijing Concert Hall where
both the wired and the wannabes gather to exchange e-mail and breathe
the Internet's libertarian air. David Kao and Eddy Campos, after
operating Casablanca as a restaurant for three years, entered in May
1996 into a joint venture in Shenzhen with Wisdom Computer
Company, who supplied all of the hardware and software for the
cybercafe to promote the Internet.[15]

One cybercafe in Shanghai named itself "3C+T," an unusual name
for a café. The 3C stands for Computer, Communication, and Coffee
and T stands for Training. The purpose of the café, according to its
manager, Lin Zairong, is to provide a relaxing and entertaining
environment for its customers to exchange information, learn new
things, and acquire cyber skills via computers. Although this 3C+T café
has opened for less than a year, it has become a popular place for both
local Chinese, mostly young under 30, and non-Chinese who are either
working in or touring China. What makes this café special is its training
program. The café offers seminars and workshops to people whose
knowledge on the Internet is limited. On lecture days, the room is
packed with eager learners and many have to stand in the hallway to get
bits of cyber information. Recently the 3C+T café has extended its
seminars to primary and secondary school teachers,[16] the implication of
which could be phenomenal.

Still a communication novelty, cybercafes attract mainly
businesspeople and university students and professors.[17] Unlike
traditional cafes, cybercafes combine a relaxed setting with the modern
distractions of the information highway. In these high-tech
establishments, food is a sideline: the real business lies in providing

technical assistance to customers who cruise the Net, download information from Web sites, and send and receive e-mail on the café's computer workstations. Cybercafes are not limited to the regular Internet services, however. They can also offer Net-related services for companies and individuals, such as creating on-line ads, product catalogues, Web pages, data banks that function as virtual shopping centers, and classified ads for job or talent hunters.[18]

The cybercafe industry does have its share of problems. The two immediate roadblocks to the success of the cybercafes in China and other Asian countries are first of all waiting for data to download at a snail's pace and second an aggressive government effort to block material that is pornographic, political, or otherwise controversial.

In addition to cybercafe-goers, the information superhighway has been traveled by many other people. Recently, American pop music superstar Mariah Carey discussed her life and work in an interview with a Beijing newspaper. There was nothing unconventional about the interview except it was conducted on the Internet.[19]

CHANGING THE WAY OF NETWORKING

For thousands of years, Chinese have communicated between each other and among themselves mainly through scribal/print medium and by word of mouth. Dropping by at a friend's home without advance announcement was common. Keeping in touch with people who do not live in the same town is primarily through letters. Telephone started to appear in Chinese homes only about ten years ago. Cyberspace technology took China by surprise, fast and without a warning. Although not a major concern yet, communication scholars wonder what this new technology will do to the way Chinese people communicate: Will they be closer to each other or more isolated from one another?

Walter Ong, an expert in communication medium, points out, that oral cultures tend to be strongly united in a communal, tribal sense; writing and reading are isolating forces, leading to solipsism and privacy.[20] Cyberspace communication, a revolution in communication medium, may have far reaching impact on cultures. Rheingold believes cyberspace technology may erase temporal, spatial and geographical differences since Internet communication can be generated from and lend at any place, location, and time zone in the world. This technological development has raised concerns about how it will affect cultural permanence and stability.[21]

According to medium theory, communication technologies have inherent biases, temporal and spatial, that affect social organization and culture, as well as biases that alter humankind's sensory organization and consciousness by determining how human senses are activated and how human experiences are organized.[22] Cyber technology, in particular, will influence the way how information is originated, transmitted, displayed, shared, stored, and reactivated.

What is fascinating is that the Internet allows communication to cross not only time and space boundaries but also age, gender, ethnicity, power status, sexual orientation, and physical ability boundaries. Cyberspace does not discriminate against people who are confined to wheelchairs, nor does it discriminate against people who are gay or straight, old or young, male or female, white or black, powerful or powerless. "Faceless" net-surfers are less likely to be influenced by cues to status and power or by group pressure to conformity.[23] The Internet also allows people with personal problems to seek help without embarrassment. Cyberspace does have its limitation, but a limitation of a different nature. It confines social networks to communities of common interest, which may lead to retribalization, not in the sense of consolidation into a global tribe, but rather fragmentation into many disparate tribes based on users' interest. Valente and Bardini believe, for example, that virtual reality networks "are likely to split into homogeneous subgroups with little cross-group communication."[24]

Cyberspace fosters learning, encourages research, stimulates thinking, and provides a channel for self-expression. It is an excellent venue where almost any type of information can be located. However, the unlimited amount of information does not guarantee its quality because Internet users are not motivated to circulate their best writing due to problems such as theft and copyright protection. Moreover, material is unchecked and unfiltered as anyone can create a home page and send out information in cyberspace.

Cyberspace anonymity, another aspect of this medium, may change the way people perceive themselves. For instance, the Internet allows people, especially shy ones, who might fear exposing a visceral response in face-to-face interaction, to become emboldened and outspoken, because the Internet lowers inhibitions as Rheingold (1993) and others (Becker, 1994; Goodman, 1994) have pointed out.[25] People with disabilities may also feel more at ease when communicating on the Internet because they are less self-conscious.

Oral cultures allow frequent fact-to-face interaction and this physical encounter encourages friendship and corporation. It also requires commitment be fulfilled once it is made because members of the community tend to live together and therefore have to face the consequences. However, in virtual communities, promises can be made and left unfulfilled with little or no consequence as Internet users subscribe and unsubscribe to newsgroups or listservs as they please.

Some scholars believe Internet communication, which is lateral, citizen-to-citizen, and many-to-many in nature, can revitalize a citizen-based democracy through grassroots activism.[26] China is a country of 1.2 billion people and communicating with, not simply to, the majority of these people via the traditional media is almost impossible. With cyberspace technology, however, this may be accomplished, although a daunting task nonetheless. At the same time, grassroots democracy via cyberspace is exactly the problem the Chinese government is concerned about.

REGULATING CYBERSPACE

With more and more people getting on-line, China embraces the concept of information superhighway with both blessings and agony. Under China's ninth five-year plan, China aims to invest US$ 60 billion in telecommunications by the end of the decade, and US$11 billion alone last year. [27] At the same time, the Chinese government believes that free surfing on the Internet can be spiritually unhealthy to users and ideologically threatening to the country and it is therefore necessary for the government to provide protections for the citizens to use the Internet. On February 1, 1996, China passed a law—The Provisional Regulations for the Management of International Networking with Computer Information Networks—which requires that all Internet users register with the government and all computer networks with international links for both inward and outward traffic run through the channels provided by the Ministry of Posts and Telecommunications.[28] The law allows the use of the Internet, but it prohibits dissemination of any information that the government deems "harmful," which includes sexual material, political material, religious material and other types of news information that might somehow be morally and politically offensive, inappropriate, sensitive and therefore unsuitable to Chinese people.

To better control information flowing into China, China decides to funnel all Internet traffic through the Ministry of Posts and Telecommunications. Together with MPT, the Ministry of Electronics Industry, the State Education Commission and the Chinese Academy of Sciences are now responsible for network management. The Ministry of Posts and Telecommunications is installing software to filter out information from some overseas Internet sites known to disseminate politically sensitive information and pornographic material. According to media reports, as of September 10, 1996, Chinese officials had blocked access of China's thousands of Internet users to more than 100 different sites on the World Wide Web.[29] The banned sites largely fall under the following five categories: (1) English-language sites sponsored by the U.S. news media such as the *Wall Street Journal*, *Washington Post* and CNN; (2) Chinese-language sites featuring news and commentaries from Taiwan; (3) Sites sponsored by Hong Kong newspapers and anti-Beijing China-watching publications; (4) Overseas dissident sites, including those providing data on the restive Himalayan region of Tibet and Xinjiang's independence movement; and (5) Adult-oriented and sexually provocative sites, such as those sponsored by the *Playboy* and *Penthouse* magazines.[30]

China also requires Internet providers to use government phone lines which allow information to be routed to government choke points where access can be blocked. The government also restricts international Internet gateways to those run by the Ministry of Posts and Telecommunications, which clearly is a move intended to make it easier to regulate Internet content.

The registered Internet user has to pledge upon registration that "The user will strictly follow the government's regulations, will not produce, retrieve, duplicate, or spread any information that may endanger national sovereignty or security, or information that is obscene and pornographic. If any such information is found on the net, the user should immediately report to the net supervisor, the Public Security Bureau, or the National Security Ministry."[31] With more and more people connecting to the Web, it is inevitable for the government to regulate the use and control the traffic. As Jeff Smith, president of Bridge to Asia, a non-profit organization aimed at connecting Internet users in China and Southeast Asia, points out, "The new regulations for users to register represent formal acceptance of the Internet by China. ... It's like regulating air traffic."[32]

The Internet user registration form explicitly stipulates that "The user should always be ready to accept supervision and surveillance from the Public Security Bureau, the National Security Ministry, or other relevant authorities. And the user should also actively assist the above-mentioned agencies to carry out the job."[33] Internet users in China also have to prove that they have employed "perfect mechanisms of security and control" when they use the Internet. The government clearly wants to guarantee a "sound development" of the Internet in China without "spiritual pollution," that is, Western ideology, subversive literature, or pornographic material.

In January 1996, China announced that economic news services sold by foreign companies, such as Dow Jones & Co. and CNN, must be distributed by Xinhua News Agency.[34] Specific rules regarding foreign economic news services were released early April 1996. The rules specified that any foreign provider of economic news should provide its service under the supervision of the official Xinhua News Agency and it should pay Xinhua a monitoring fee for supervision.[35]

More recently, the Chinese government has enacted even tougher rules on the Internet access, according to the official Xinhua News Agency. Under the new rule, all units doing business related to the global computer network are required to apply for licenses. As part of the application process, such organizations must provide data on the nature and scope of their networks and all addresses of their computer hosts. Violators of the rules will be ordered to cease networking services and will be fined up to 15,000 yuan (US$1,800). The Leading Group on Information Advancement under the State Council is empowered to oversee the work.[36]

As the Internet becomes more and more popular, the rush to register domain names and the scalping of those names have become a serious problem. As a result, the government issued new regulations intended to put an end to the speculative registration of Internet domain names in June 1997. The new regulations specify the structure of the Internet domain-name system and the procedures by which the domain names will be applied for and approved. Applicants will have to be legally registered organizations with the ability to independently shoulder civil liability. In addition, the government set up the China Internet Information Center, which will be responsible for the management, operation, and service of the Internet in China in order to ensure its stable development.[37]

By the end of 1997, China unveiled yet another set of Internet regulations, aiming at strengthening safety protection of China's computer information system and safeguarding state security and social stability. As Zhu Entao, Assistant Minister for Public Security, explains at a news conference on the regulations that Internet links since 1994 had boosted China's cultural and scientific exchanges with the world. "But the connection has also brought about some security problems, including manufacturing and publicizing harmful information, as well as leaking state secrets through the Internet." According to Zhu, the regulations cover a wide range of crimes, including leaking state secrets, political subversion and spreading pornography and violence.

The rules are also designed to protect against computer hacking, viruses and other computer-related crime. This five-chapter, 25-article regulation was approved by the State Council on December 11, 1997 and became effective December 30, 1997. The law outlines computer management and supervision departments' duties, responsibilities, and obligations of enterprises involved with international connections of computer networks. Under the new regulations, Internet providers would be subject to supervision by Public Security officials and would be required to help track down violators. Internet providers and users who violate the rules—both individuals and business organizations--will be punished as criminals and fined up to 15,000 yuan (US$1,800).[38]

It is not only Chinese individuals and organizations that have to follow the regulations the Chinese government has issued, foreign companies that do business with China also have to comply with Chinese regulations and assist China in its effort to control the Internet. Most recently, Prodigy Inc., an American on-line service, has decided to launch an Internet service in China in a joint venture with China North Industries Co., a state-owned conglomerate. Prodigy enters China's Internet market with the understanding that the Prodigy is going to provide Internet filtering technology to allow the Chinese government to block information deemed inappropriate.

While new rules are being enacted, some of the old ones are becoming annulled. In September 1996, China removed limits on the number of Internet accounts in the country. According to Zhang Weihua, vice president of the Shanghai Posts and Telecommunications Administration, the initial limits imposed by the government was due to the security arrangements that were incomplete and there was a problem with pornographic and politically unacceptable material. Now that the arrangements have been improved, new accounts can be added without restriction.[39]

BYPASSING RULES AND REGULATIONS

The Internet is undoubtedly providing users with unprecedented connectivity to the world; it also is fast becoming the tool of choice for overseas advocacy groups. This new way of networking is probably the reason why some Asian governments, including the Chinese government, are so concerned with the Internet. Amnesty International, for example, posted on its Web site an interactive presentation, designed to be downloaded onto a floppy disk, to commemorate the crackdown in Tiananmen Square.[40] Human rights activists in

Washington are using the Internet to collect submissions about the use of forced labor in Burma. They will then forward these to the European Union, which is weighing whether to restore Burma's trade privileges.[41]

Since there are attempts to disseminate information that is unfriendly to the Chinese government on the Web, it is not surprising that the Chinese government is trying every means possible to curb the free flow of information. Most of the blocking methods so far have fallen into three categories: (1) software that consults a list of known sites and blocks them according to criteria chosen by the PC owners; (2) software that looks for suspect words to decide when to block sites; and (3) the fencing off the portions of the Internet by firms that provide Internet access. None of the three methods can work effectively or can be effective for long. Sites can change their names as fast as list-makers detect them. Word-screening is notoriously ineffective because words like "breast" and "intercourse" can be used in both pornographic descriptions and serious discussions. Blocking a portion of the Internet can lead to unwanted censorship of "newsgroups," a case in point was CompuServe's ban on more than 200 newsgroups in response to a threat from Bavarian prosecutors.[42]

Although technically it is complicated to control the Internet, it is feasible if all international telephone traffic reaches a country through one network, such as in China and Singapore. When that is the case, the authorities are able to monitor anything being sent to Internet servers. Chinese and Singaporeans could still dial abroad and get access to the uncensored Net, but that would be expensive—prohibitively so for most people in China.[43]

While the government is searching for ways to police the Internet, users are trying to get around the rules without being caught. In fact, circumventing the gatekeepers is relatively simple according to Wayne Arnold. All it takes is a little knowledge of how the Internet works or, even simpler, money,[44] although money is not easy to come by for the majority of people in China. Internet censorship poses little challenge to hard-core pornographic enthusiasts or underground dissidents. The real danger is the intimidation censorship creates and intimidation can be quite effective in China. As one Internet service provider says, "The fact that where you go on the Internet can be recorded, can be saved, can be tracked and that factor makes people more hesitant."[45] For those who do manage to dodge the barricades to ogle hard-core porn or incite revolution, the chief constraint is the fear of being caught.[46] And being caught is not just a fear, it does happen from time to time.

While the Internet may prove to be hard to control, Intranet—the internal Internet—Chinese officials believe, may be the answer to ultimate control. The Ministry of Posts and Telecommunications has worked out plans to build up the Intranet starting from Guangdong Province. According to James Chiu, Chairman of China Internet Corp, CIC, a small firm based in Hong Kong which has contracted to develop the Intranet service for China, full Internet access will probably be restricted to foreigners and selected Chinese nationals, while most people in China will be allowed to use the closed network. The network, called GNET, will be more usable, without worrying about breaking the law.[47] Although GNET subscribers will not be able to access international information at will, the GNET, when completed, will provide businesses and individual users in Guangdong area with education, entertainment, shopping, real estate, health, and financial information, as well as news. Some selected information from international businesses will be provided through CIC, which has already established a skeletal closed network using Xinhua's existing infrastructure.[48]

As Jeff Smith, president of Bridge to Asia, predicts that there will be attempts to censor the Internet from the Chinese government but he also believes that censorship will be futile because it is like trying to stop the wind: it will chill Internet use, but those who are clever will be able to get the information they want.[49]

CONCLUSION

Zhu Ling, a chemistry student at Qinghua University, has a personal life-and-death experience about the wonders of the Internet. About two years ago, she was suffering from a mysterious illness and her life was in jeopardy. Her face was paralyzed, she had difficulty breathing, and her whole nervous system was under attack. What was more frightening was that no specialist in Beijing was able to identify the cause of her illness. Desperate, Zhu Ling's friends sent out the symptoms on the Internet and appealed for help. Before long, responses came from all directions and Zhu's life was save.[50]

The Internet is clearly a communication wonder. It does not only save lives, but also allows China to participate in the information globalization process which is indispensable for China's economic, scientific, technological, and academic advancement. The Chinese government is committed to the construction and development of information infrastructure. One of the goals of ChinaNet, according to Tian Shuning, president of U.S.-based AsiaInfo Services who developed ChinaNet, is to become part of the global information infrastructure and to give total coverage of China down to the county level.[51] Although getting one billion people, or even one tenth of them, hooked onto the Internet is no easy task and it will not happen any time soon, the future of the Internet in China is nonetheless bright and encouraging.

The Chinese government has recently planned to use the Internet to promote China's cultural image abroad. As Xinhua News Agency reports, "A program introducing China's 5,000-year-old culture on the Internet is planned, and channels for promoting commercial performances and exhibitions abroad will be created."[52] According to the Ministry of Posts and Telecommunications, the number of Internet users in China is expected to increase further with improved communication networks and lowered access fees. The Ministry hopes to increase on-line users by 150,000 with a 30 percent increase in revenues, equaling $20.5 billions (The number of on-line users has already passed the projected number by the end of 1997). The ambitious projection is backed by a promise of wider telephone coverage and more aggressive recruiting measures. Last year, China spent $11.8 billion on telecom projects, constructed or improved thirty-one ground satellite stations, enabling its mobile telephone service to cover more than 261 cities.[53] CERNET, managed by the National Network Center at Qinghua University, has set an ambitious goal for the year 2000 of linking China's 1,090 universities, as well as 200,000 primary and secondary schools.[54]

As for now, the Internet is still largely the domain for intellectuals and corporations in China. China's scientists, academics, and businesspeople use the Internet to communicate with people across the country and around the world.[55] Although English is still the dominant lingua franca on the Web, advances in Chinese computer software allow more and more Chinese to communication by typing in Chinese characters or pinyin and this will definitely attract more Chinese people whose command of English is limited or none to get on-line.

Notes

1. Tse & Tsang, "Internet and WWW in China: All the right connections," http://www/csu.edu.au/special/conference/apwww95 (April 29, 1997).
2. *Ibid.*
3. *Ibid.*
4. T. Plafker, "China to triple Internet links with commercial hookups," *Science* 267(5195), (January 13, 1995): 168.

5. Tse & Tsang, *ibid.*

6. Yanni Chen, "Regulations safeguards computer information," *China Daily* (December 20, 1997).

7. "China accepts the Internet," (May 6, 1996). http://www/bridge.org/censorship.html.

8. "Internet users near 100 million," *China News Digest* (February 4, 1998).

9. R. Aronson, "Leisure & arts: Net breaches Chinese wall," The *Wall Street Journal* (August 19, 1996), p. A10.

10. Andrew Browne, "China clamps new controls on Internet," *Reuters* (December 30, 1997) and Yanni Chen, *China Daily* (December 20, 1997).

11. Jianguo Wang, "China tightens up domain name procedures," IDG. http://darkwing.uoregon.edu/~felsing/cstuff/shu/html (June 6, 1997).

12. I. Johnson, "International: Thoughts of Chairman Gates attract the interest of China's computer buffs," The *Wall Street Journal* (January 21, 1997), p. A15.

13. I. Johnson, *ibid.*

14. Michael Vatikiotis, "Net police: Asean seeks to control cyberspace," *Far Eastern Economic Review* (March 28, 1996).

15. M. Krantz, "China, wired: A new online service tiptoes past the Party," *Time* (April 22, 1996). p. 3.

16. "Full house at the cyber café," The *World Journal* (January 28, 1998), p. A12.

17. Jianzhong Wang, Personal communication. (April & May, 1997).

18. E. Yun, "Net working," *Free China Review* (July, 1996). p. 56-59.

19. "Internet introduces more choices of life," *China Daily* (October 3, 1997).

20. Walter. J. Ong, *The Presence of the World: Some Prolegomena for Cultural and Religious History* (Minneapolis, MN: University of Minnesota, 1967) and *Orality and Literacy* (London, England: Methuen, 1982).

21. H. Rheingold, *The Virtual Community* (New York, NY: Harper Collins, 1993).

22. G. Gladney, "Some enduring issues of cyberspace technology: A medium theory perspective," *The New Jersey Journal of Communication*, 4 (2) (1996): 110-126.

23. Laurie T. Lee, "On-line anonymity: A new privacy battle in cyberspace," *The New Jersey Journal of Communication*, 4 (2) (1996): 127-146.

24. T. Valente and T. Bardini, "Virtual diffusion or an uncertain reality: Networks, policy, and models for the diffusion of VR technology," In *Communication in the Age of Virtual Reality*, eds. F. Biocca & M.R. Levy (Hilldale, NJ: Lawrence Erlbaum, 1995). p. 308.

25. See H. Rheingold, *ibid.*, S. Becker, *Potholes in the information superhighway* (Salt Lake City, UT: University of Utah, October 20, 1994). [Reprint of B. Auberey Fisher memorial lecture], and D. Goodman, *Living at Light Speed* (New York, NY: Random, 1994).

26. Gladney, *ibid.*

27. S. Kalin, "China telecom: Internet freedom key to China advances, US official says," IDG News Service, Boston Bureau (August 15, 1996).

28. "The Provisional Regulations for the Management of International Networking with Computer Information Networks of the People's Republic of China," Xinhua News Agency, (May 30, 1997). A copy of the exact document of the regulation can be obtained from the author upon request.

29. Congressional Record, (1996).

30. K. Chen, "Marketing & media: China bars access to as many as 100 Internet web sites," The *Wall Street Journal* (September 5, 1996), p.B5.

31. From the Internet Registration Form.

32. "China accepts the Internet," *Reuters* (March 14, 1996).

33. The Internet Registration Form.

34. K. Chen, *ibid.*

35. "Marketing & media: China releases new rules for foreign news agencies," The *Wall Street Journal* (April 17, 1996), p. B8.

36. China News Digest, (May 30, 1997).

37. Jianguo Wang, ibid.

38. Browne, ibid. and Y. Chen, ibid.

39. "Technology & health: China removes curbs on Internet access to many Western sites," The *Wall Street Journal* (January 16, 1997), p. B4.

40. "China: Amnesty International Uses the Internet in the Fight for Human Rights," http://www.pathfinder.com/@@wgDm@gUAq9Kr2vGj/asianweek/95/0908/fe at2.html, (May 24, 1996.

41. "NetNanny states," *The Economist* (September 14, 1996), p. 34.

42. "The Top shelf," *The Economist* (May 18, 1996), p. 84.

43. Asia and the Internet, (1996).

44. Wayne Arnold, "Asia's Internet censorship will be easy to circumvent," The *Wall Street Journal* (September 11, 1996), Sect. B, p. 7A.

45. Wayne Arnold, "Internet censorship in China, Singapore may affect law-abiding citizens most," The *Wall Street Journal* (September 13, 1996), Sect. B, p. 7A.

46. "NetNanny states," *ibid.*

47. C. Smith, "China, unhappy with Internet data, creates own network with limited ties," The *Wall Street Journal* (May 17, 1996).

48. Smith, *ibid.*

49. "China accepts the Internet," *Reuters* (March 14, 1996).

50. "Watch this Cyberspace: China weighs the pros and cons of the Internet," http://www.nando.net/newsroom/ntn/world/090996/world-607.html (September 8, 1995).

51. "China accepts the Internet," *ibid.*

52. "China gets wired as cultural blitz planned," *China News Digest* (February 2, 1998).

53. *China News Digest*, (January 6, 1997).

54. J. Kinoshita, "Scientists hope competition will improve Internet access," *Science* 270 (5239), (1995): 1141-1142.
Arnold, *ibid.*[1]

PART FOUR

CHANGED IMAGE

Chapter 10

Student Attitudes towards Free Markets: China and the United States Compared

Jessie X. FAN, XIAO Jing Jian, and XU Yinzhou

In their 1992 study "Hunting for homo sovieticus: situational versus attitudinal factors in economic behavior," Robert Shiller, Maxim Boycko and Vladmimir Korobov investigated this important question: "Have years of communist rule in former communists countries produced a human character type that is virtually a different species in terms of its motivational stance toward economic activity?" If yes, then this familiar claim would have dire implications for the prospects for transforming the economic system in ex-communist countries to western-style free-market economy. It will take much more than just a system imitation to make the transition work. If not, then one would know that people in former communist countries, as rational economic agents, would respond to incentives in a market economy in similar ways as people in western countries.   Therefore, the successful transition to a western-style free-market economy should just be a matter of time.

Comparing survey data from Russia, Ukraine, former East Germany, the United States, Japan, and former Western Germany, Shiller et al rejected the common belief of the existence of "homo sovieticus," claiming that the differences in attitudes between former communist countries and western industrial countries were mainly situational rather than attitudinal. While attitudinal factors relate to psychological treats, personality, and culture, situational factors relate to people's situations that affect them.[1]   In other words, while attitudinal differences, if exist, are much more difficult to change, situational differences would disappear as soon as the situation around the people, such as the economic system, has changed.

China, yet another communist country on its way of economic system transition, with its unique cultural and historical background, adapted a gradual economic reform rather than a system overhaul. Although the economic reform in China has been quite successful, China still has a long way to go in the transition process.   The smoothness of the transition will depend on many factors, including Chinese people's attitudes towards free-market economy. Do Chinese, under the influence of Confucius doctrine for two thousand years, and communist ideology for more than forty years, have different ideas about entrepreneurial spirits, initiatives, leadership, motivation, and the willingness to take risks and assume responsibilities as their western counterparts, such as the Americans?

The purpose of this study was to collect up-to-date survey data on students' attitudes towards free market at five universities in Guangzhou, China, and compare the survey with the data collected by Hemesath and Pomponio in Shanghai, China, and Minnesota, the United States in 1992-93.[2]   The researchers would like to see whether the two sets of Chinese data led to consistent findings, when compared with the U.S. data.   If yes, then the results of Hemesath and Pomponio's study would be supported and the conclusions would be more generalized; if not, then either there were regional differences in students' attitudes towards free markets in China, or the attitudes have changed in the past few years, or both.   The results of this study, along with other similar studies, can be used as a foundation to develop more generalized and in-depth research projects, such as popular attitudes towards free markets among the general public, and the relationship between attitudinal factors and economic outcomes, which will have direct implications for the design and forecast of further economic reform in China.

Literature Review

Shiller, Boycko and Korobov developed a questionnaire of 36 questions, addressing various aspects of human behavior related to free markets, including opinions concerning whether price changes are fair, attitudes towards income equality, popular theories concerning the importance of incentives, inhibitions against exchange of money, envy or hostility towards business people and the rich, popular understandings of the welfare effects of compensated price changes, and expectations of future government interference. While some questions probed public opinion on certain issues related to free markets, most questions asked the respondents to consider some imaginary situation that they might experience and to describe their behavior in, or judgment of, that situation.[3]

Shiller et al compared data collected from a random sample of 391 residents of Moscow and 361 residents of New York through telephone interview in May 1990. They found some evidence that the Russians were more resistant toward exchange of money and had less warm attitudes toward business than their American counterparts. They also found evidence that the Russians were a little more concerned that the government may later nationalize private business. Other than that, there were very little difference between the Russians and the Americans in their opinions on price changes, income inequality, and other aspects of free markets.

Because the differences they found between these two countries concerning attitudes towards free market were often small or nonexistent, Shiller et al suggested that the pressing and immediate problems facing former Soviet Union countries may be political and institutional in nature, instead of problems with people's attitudes towards free markets.

In 1992, Shiller and his colleagues extended their study by including more questionnaires and administrating the questionnaires to more countries. The major findings of their study were briefly reviewed at the beginning of this paper.[4]

Interested in whether people's attitudes towards free markets might have played an important role in China's successful economic development and Russia's relatively unsuccessful economic reform, Hemesath and Pomponio extended Shiller and his colleagues' 1991 study to include survey data collected from 231 Chinese students in Shanghai in 1992/93, 251 American students in Minnesota in 1992, and 361 Russian students in Krasnodar in 1991, using the same questionnaire developed by Shiller et al.[5]

While similarities were found between Chinese and American students' attitudes, particularly a shared interest in material gain and belief in the importance of material incentives, there were also significant differences. Chinese students were less comfortable with market outcomes and more willing to support government intervention in markets than Americans were. Also, Chinese students expressed more doubts about the characteristics of business people than did their

American counterparts.

When compared to Russian undergraduates, Chinese students were found to be less concerned about the fairness of market outcomes, but they were also more supportive of government interventions. Russian students were found to be more interested in material gain and more supportive of business than their Chinese counterparts.

Russian students, while generally expressed support for markets, tended to be less supportive of market outcomes than American undergraduates. In particular, Russian students had different ideas about fairness, and less trust of government and business, compared to their American peers. On the other hand, despite some misgivings, the Russians seemed to be willing to actively participate in the market. Most of them were willing to accept market outcomes, even if they believed them to be unfair. They were willing to accept even more income equality than American students. Hemesath and Pomponio's study suggested that the differences in the attitudes towards free markets among these three countries did not seem to be big enough to be the main cause of different economic outcomes.

All these studies have rejected the notion that differences in people's attitudes towards free markets were the main cause of differences in economic success in different nations. However, the results of these studies are more suggestive rather than definitive, due to the limitations in sampling and methods. Although it is possible to conduct a survey on national representative samples, it will be very costly. Not all is lost, though. The rule of inter-subjectivity states that if different researchers, using different samples and/or methods, could come to the same conclusion, then the conclusion is closer to the truth. It is the purpose of this research to study another sample of Chinese students, at a different location and a different time, to add some more information to the research in this area.

Data and Methods

Data

Data used in this study were from two sources. The Shanghai, China and Minnesota, U.S. data were collected by Hemesath and Pomponio in 1992-93, and their study was reviewed in the previous section. Details for their data collection procedures can be found in their paper.[6]

The second source was data collected in the summer of 1996 from five universities in Guangzhou, China. The questionnaires originally developed by Shiller, Boycko, and Korobov in 1991 were translated into Chinese and used in the survey. Under the supervision of an international economics professor, college students went to five universities to distribute and collect questionnaires. The five universities were Zhongshan University, Jinan University, Huanan University of Science and Technology, Huanan Normal University, and Guangdong Commercial College. The student investigators were trained by the professor, and had experiences in doing similar field surveys for academic or commercial institutions. Among 407 usable questionnaires collected from the Guangzhou survey, 39% were females, 81% from urban hometown, and 42% economics and business related majors and 6.5% foreign language majors.

Analytical methods

The Guangzhou data were combined with Hemesath and Pomponio's Shanghai and US data for the analysis. Two pairwise comparisons were made, one was the Chinese versus U.S. sample, and the other was the Guangzhou versus Shanghai sample. The Chinese sample was composed of the Guangzhou and Shanghai sample. Probit (for categorical dependent variables) and OLS regressions (for continuous dependent variables) were used to control for the differences in factors other than countries or regions, such as age, gender, academic major (economics and business related, language, and others), and hometown (rural vs. urban). All "don't know" answers were treated as missing values. The findings are presented in a way similar to Shiller, Roycko, and Korobov's 1991 study, in which only the significant levels of the selected variables in the multivariate analyses are presented along with the corresponding descriptive statistics. The complete findings are available from the authors upon requests.

Issues of interpretation

Situational vs. cultural factors

Shiller and his colleagues proposed the framework of situational vs. attitudinal factors to interpret the results in their 1992 paper. Since differences in attitudinal factors were mainly caused by cultural differences, it refers to cultural factors. In this study, the questions designed by them in 1991 were used before they proposed the framework. Thus, the emphases of situational and attitudinal factors were not straightforward in the questions asked in our study. The researchers interpreted the results of the analysis with regard to situational vs. cultural factors based on their judgment of the questions.

China sample vs. U.S. sample

China and the U.S. have very different political, cultural, social, and economic systems. Currently, the major difference is that China is in an economic transition process, from a central-planning economy to a market economy. The U.S., on the other hand, has been in a relatively stable market economy for many years. In addition, Chinese traditional values, mainly a combination of a two-thousand-year old Confucius doctrine and forty-plus-year communism ideology, are quite different from American's values, which are fostered by the doctrine of Christianity and reality of capitalist mechanism.[7] Given the existence of both situational differences and culture differences between these two nations, the differences in people's attitudes could be caused by both.

Guangzhou sample vs. Shanghai sample

Guangzhou is a major Chinese city in southern China, nearby Hong Kong, and Shanghai is the largest industrial city in China, located in the east coastal area of China. One important difference between the two cities is the intensity of the economic reform. Guangzhou is in one of the earliest "economic reform experimental zones," to which Chinese government granted many special reform-policy privileges that were not allowed in other areas in the early years of the economic reform. Because the market economy is developed earlier in Guangzhou than in Shanghai, and the Guangzhou data were collected three years later than the Shanghai data, the Guangzhou sample is expected to be more similar to the U.S. sample, compared to the Shanghai sample. In addition, people from Guangzhou and Shanghai have many different characteristics that constitute regional differences. These differences were taken into consideration during our analysis.

Student sample vs. general public sample

Compared with their counterparts in 50s, 60s, and 70s, today's Chinese college students have changed their value system from communism-loyal to independent thinking.[8] Chinese with college degrees have the most favorable attitudes towards the economic reform, and are more willing to take risks in order to get the benefits that are brought by the reform.[9] Because of the economic reform, social values of the general public in China also have shifted towards values in western countries, although not as much as the young educated generation. The differences between the attitudes of college students and that of the general public should be kept in mind when reading the results.[10]

Results and Discussion

The results are presented in nine sections reflecting nine aspects of students' attitudes towards free markets. These nine aspects are: (1) fairness of price changes, (2) government intervention, (3) understanding of compensated price changes, (4) income inequality, (5) exchange of money and money tradeoffs, (6) attitudes towards business people and speculation, (7) work incentives and initiatives, (8) risk taking, and (9) consumption and saving. In all the tables presenting the results of our analysis, *** are used to denote the two parties of interest were significantly different in their answers to the questions at $\alpha = 0.01$ level, ** is significantly at =0.05 level, and * is significant at =0.10 level.

(1) Fairness of price changes

Questions B2, B11, and A9 were related to whether it's fair to raise the price of a commodity when the demand of the commodity has increased. Question B12 asked whether the factory had the right to raise the price regardless of fairness, and Question 10 was related to whether it's fair for companies to make large profits. Table 1 presents the results of our analysis.

Most students, both in China and in the United States, thought it was fair for sellers to increase the price of a commodity when the demand of the commodity has increased. Furthermore, in both countries, even more respondents seemed to think that the sellers had the right to increase the price of a commodity when the demand has increased, regardless of their perception of fairness. Most students also thought that it was fair for businesses to make profits.

Although significant differences between the respondents in the U.S. and in China existed in their answers to three of the five questions, the magnitudes of the differences were rather small. Overall, the notion of fairness of price changes seem to be neither country-specific nor situation-specific. This finding is somewhat contradictory to the findings of the 1991 study by Shiller et al with the Russia and U.S. sample, where they found that the perception of fairness of price changes were situation-specific, but not country-specific. They also found that most respondents in their sample perceived the price increase in flowers was unfair. Since the sample consisted of only

Table 1. Results of questions related to fairness of price changes

	China vs. U.S.			Guangzhou vs. Shanghai		
	China	U.S.	Sig.	Guangzhou	Shanghai	Sig.
B2. Fair to increase flower price	80.3%	87.9%	•••	78.5%	83.3%	
B11. Fair to increase table price	78.5%	81.6%		81.9%	72.7%	
B12. Factory has right to raise price	81.5%	94.5%	•••	81.1%	82.1%	
C10. Fair to make large profit	79.4%	77.9%		81.8%	75.5%	
A9. Fair to raise rent	80.8%	84.4%	••	78.6%	84.4%	

B2. On a holiday, when there is a great demand for flowers, their prices usually go up. Is it fair for flower seller to raise their prices like this?

B11. A small factory produces kitchen tables and sells them at $200 each. There is so much demand for the tables that it cannot meet it fully. The factory decides to raise the price of its tables by $20, when there is no change in the cost of producing tables. Is that fair?

B12. Apart from fairness, should the factory have the right to raise the price in this situation?

C10. A small merchant company buys vegetables from some rural people, brings the vegetables to the city, and sells them, making from this a large profit. The company honestly and openly tells the rural people what it is doing, and these people freely sell the company the vegetables at the agreed price. Is this behavior of the company, making large profits using the rural people, acceptable from a moral point of view?

A9. A new railway line makes travel between city and summer homes positioned along this rail line substantially easier. Accordingly, summer homes along this railway become more desirable. Is it fair if rents raised on summer homes there?

students, that there might be a generation difference in people's attitude. Overall, the reported evidence suggests that there is actually little ground to believe that Chinese students were characteristically hostile toward free-market price changes.

(2) Government intervention

Questions B3 and C4 asked about attitudes towards government intervention. Questions C7 and B8 were related to the possibility of reversing the reform process. Table 2 reports the results. The difference in attitudes towards government intervention was quite apparent. Chinese students, grown up in a society where government intervention in different aspects of live has been quite common, were much more likely to feel comfortable with that. More than half of the

Table 2. Results of questions related to government intervention

	China vs. U.S.			Guangzhou vs. Shanghai		
	China	U.S.	Sig.	Guangzhou	Shanghai	Sig.
B3. Favor gov. limit on flower price	56.7%	9.9%	***	63.7%	44.4%	***
C4. Favor gas rationing over taxing	17.1%	21.5%		16.8%	17.4%	
C7. Gov. likely nationalize business	17.5%	7.4%	***	17.6%	17.4%	*
B8. Gov. likely prevent use of saving	52.4%	38.5%	***	44.5%	63.8%	***

B3. In the flower price case (see B2), should the government introduce limits on the increase in prices of flowers, even if it might produce a shortage of flowers?

C4. Suppose the government wishes to reduce the consumption of gasoline. They propose two methods of attaining this goal. First, the government could prohibit gas stations from selling, for example, more than five gallons to one person. Second, the government could put a tax on gasoline, and prices of gasoline would go up. From your point of view, which of these methods is better?

C7. How likely do you think it is that in the next few years the government will, in some way, nationalize (that is, take over) most private businesses with little or no compensation to the owners? Is such nationalization (1) quite likely or possible; (2) unlikely or impossible?

B8. How likely is it, from your point of view, that the government in the next few years will take measures, in one way or another, to prevent those who have saved a great deal from making use of their savings? Is it (1) quite likely or possible; (2) unlikely or impossible?

Chinese respondents thought that government should set a limit on the price of flowers, whereas only less than 10% of the American students agreed with that. This difference could be both situational and cultural. Even though China is moving towards a market economy, the government has dominated the production and sales process of almost all consumer goods and services for over forty years, and the proportion of current government intervention in the economy is still substantial. The idea that people should obey the government has a deep root in traditional Chinese values. For example, Chinese philosophy refers a country as a family. In a country, people should obey the ruling officials, just like in a family, children should obey parents. However, when it comes to the way government should use to intervene the market, there were no significant difference between these two countries. Most respondents favored a taxing approach over a rationing approach.

There was also a difference between the Guangzhou sample and Shanghai sample in their answers to Questions B8. This difference reflects the different intensity of the reform process, both geographically and chronically. Guangzhou students were more likely than their Shanghai counterparts to welcome government intervention. This reflects people's wish that government can deal with the problems emerged in the development of the market economy. The problems coming with the early stages of market economy, such as unfair competition due to the lack of an established and enforceable legal system, may be more serious in Guangzhou, which started the reform process earlier than other parts of China. Also, the Guangzhou data were collected three years later than the Shanghai data. As the reform goes further, the problem with the lack of an effective legal system becomes more and more serious, and people may turn to the government for solving these intensified social problems.

(3) Understanding of compensated price changes

Questions C6 and B10 asked about the respondents' understanding of compensated price changes. Table 3 presents the results. Answers to the two questions were similar between the Chinese and American students. With about one third of the respondents saying that they would be worse off in that situation in both countries, economists might wonder how good the assumption of our utility maximization model is. Respondents in both countries seemed to be more comfortable with the price increase of a single commodity than an overall high inflation.

Differences were found between the Guangzhou and Shanghai sample, in which the respondents in Guangzhou seemed to be much more reluctant to a compensated inflation, but less concerned about the price raise of electricity. Note that the answers of Guangzhou students were similar to their American counterparts, which implies that Guangzhou students might have a better understanding about the compensated price changes than students in Shanghai. This finding is consistent with our expectation.

Table 3. Results of questions related to the understanding of compensated price changes

	China vs. U.S.			Guangzhou vs. Shanghai		
	China	U.S.	Sig.	Guangzhou	Shanghai	Sig.
C6.Better off or the same with increase in electricity price &income	63.3%	68.0%		66.4%	57.3%	***
B10.Support high inflation & high income growth	46.7%	46.6%	**	40.3%	57.3%	*

C6. Suppose the price of electricity rises fourfold, from 10 cents per kilowatt-hour to 40 cents per kilowatt-hour. No other prices change. Suppose also that at the same time your monthly income increase by exactly enough to pay for the extra cost of electricity without cutting back on any of your other expenditures. Please evaluate how your overall material well being has changed. Would you consider your situation (1) somewhat better off; (2) exactly the same; and (3) somewhat worse off.

B10. Suppose that economists have come to the conclusion that we could substantially improve our standard of living in the next year if we would be willing to accept a 30 percent inflation rate (increase in the prices of goods by thirty percent). This would mean that our incomes would rise by more than 30 percent. Then we could buy more goods at the new higher prices. Would you support such a proposal?

(4) Income inequality

Questions A4 and A10 were related to people's attitudes towards income or wealth inequality. Table 4 reports the results of our analysis. Chinese students were more likely to support a plan that would cause great inequality than their American counterparts. The difference mainly comes from situational factors. In China, the society is moving from a fairly equal one to a less equal one, which is encouraged by the government. One of the reform slogans is "To let some people get rich first." This slogan is certainly welcomed by college students, who likely will be in the rich group given their skills. In the U.S., the more relevant issue is to decrease the gap between the poor and the rich, given income inequality is getting wider in recent years. American students' answers reflected this situation.

Table 4. Results of questions related to income inequality

	China vs. U.S.			Guangzhou vs. Shanghai		
	China	U.S.	Sig.	Guangzhou	Shanghai	Sig.
A4.Support reform with more inequality but nobody is worse off	73.3%	58.1%	•••	75.6%	68.9%	
A10.mean inheritance tax rate	45.2%	29.4%	•••	45.6%	44.4%	

A4.   Suppose the government wants to undertake a reform to improve the productivity of the economy. As a result, everyone will be better off, but the improvement in life will not affect people equally. A million people (people who respond energetically to the incentives in the plan and people with certain skills) will see their income triple, while everyone else will see only a tiny income increase, about one percent. Would you support the plan?

A10.   In your opinion, what inheritance tax rate for really wealthy people do you think we should have? A tax rate of zero percent means that they can pass all of their wealth to their children, making them as rich as their parents. A rate of 50 percent means that they can pass half to their children. A rate of 100 percent means that they can pass none at all to their children.

Chinese students assigned higher inheritance tax rates than their American counterparts (A10). Since inheritance taxes (or any kind of personal income tax) are more common in the U.S. than in China, Chinese students' answers were more hypothetical. However, this difference is a function of current situation in China and traditional Chinese values. Although the gap between the rich and the poor in China is much smaller than that in the U.S., the majority of Chinese are struggling to fight high inflation with limited resources. Most Chinese are not comfortable to see a minority of people who made a fortune by ethnical or unethical business dealings. A psychology of envy does exist.

The psychology of envy also has its roots in Chinese culture, and the forty-plus years of central-planning economy have intensified that. During the cultural revolution (1966-76), a popular slogan was: "We prefer the poverty of socialism to the wealth of capitalism."

(5) Exchange of money and money tradeoffs

Questions A7, A8, and B7 asked about people's the attitudes towards exchange of money. Question A6 was related to the tradeoffs between money and time. Question B4 asked about the tradeoffs between money and fame. Table 5 presents the results of our analysis. American students were more likely to charge interests when loan money to their friends (A7), and less likely to get annoyed by the exchange of money for a place in a long line (B7). The differences reflect both situational and cultural differences. Compared to U.S., the incidence and intensity of exchange of money in China are still relatively low. It may be commonly acceptable for American students to charge interest on a loan to a friend, but for most Chinese, this would be considered "too greedy." The traditional Chinese values teach people that friendship is priceless. Therefore, charging interest on a loan to a friend would be placing money over friendship, and is therefore not acceptable to many Chinese. In the case of Question B7, the person who offered his place in the long line for money would be considered as "taking advantage of the situation" and therefore considered "unethical" by many Chinese. The differences in attitudes towards exchange of money are more cultural than situational.

There was also a significant difference between the Guangzhou sample and the Shanghai sample in their answers to Question A7. In China, people from Shanghai have the reputation of being more calculating in money matters than people from other parts of China. The result from A8 is not expected, since people from Shanghai were expected to be more likely to clarify financial matters with friends. One possible explanation is that people from Guangzhou are more and more influenced by the western style of money management due to the economic reform, and due to its closeness to Hong Kong.

The results of Question A6 indicate that Chinese students were more likely to trade money for leisure. The difference may be cultural since the old Chinese tradition promotes that money is not the most important thing in the world. The popular doctrine of "golden mean" can be applied to the allocation of time between work and leisure. The difference between these two countries can also be situational given that Chinese people have longer average working hours than Americans.

Table 5. Results of questions related to exchange of money and money tradeoffs

	China vs. The U.S.			Guangzhou vs. Shanghai		
	China	U.S.	Sig.	Guangzhou	Shanghai	Sig.
A7. Charge friend interest on loan	31.1%	36.5%	**	25.4%	41.1%	***
A8. Count shared expenses with friends	52.4%	56.3%		53.4%	50.8%	**
B7.Annoyed at exchange of money for place in line	50.2%	36.5%	***	50.1%	50.2%	
A6. Would trade money for leisure	28.5%	13.0%	***	25.3%	34.1%	
B4. Favor fortune over fame	76.0%	65.0%	**	75.9%	76.0%	

A7. Suppose you have agreed to lend a friend some money for six months, so that he will not miss a good opportunity to buy a summer home. Suppose banks are offering interest rates of three percent per year. Would you charge him interest on the loan?

A8. If you went on a vacation with friends and there were a lot of shared expenses, would there be a careful accounting of who spent what and a settling of accounts afterwards?

B7. You are standing in a long line to buy something. You see that someone comes to the line and is very distressed that the line is so long, saying he is in a great hurry ans absolutely must make this purchase. A person at the front of the line offers to let him take her place in line for $10.00. Would you be annoyed at this deal even though it won't cause you to wait any longer?

A6. Suppose that for certain reasons you are offered a 10 percent reduction of the duties you perform at your work place with the following terms: Your work week will be cut by 1/10 (say you will have an additional half a day free) but your take-home pay will also decline by 10%. If you take this offer, this has no other effects on your prospects for promotion or relations with co-workers. Do you consider it attractive to have more free time, but less money, so that you would take this offer, or would you decide to reject it?

B4. Which of the following achievements would please you more: (1) You win fortune without fame; you make enough money through successful business dealings so that you can live very comfortably for the rest of your life; (2) you win fame without fortune; for example, you win a medal at the Olympics or you become a respected journalist or scholar.

Chinese students were more likely to prefer fortune to fame than their American counterparts. The difference reflects the current popular "money making" mentality in China. Some students put remarks on the margin of the questionnaire, which read "I want both fortune and fame," reflecting the conflicting interaction of traditional value and current popular mentality, since traditional Chinese values emphasize fame over money.

(6) Attitudes towards business people and speculation

Questions C1, C9, C11, and C5 were related to people's attitudes towards business people, and Questions C8 and B6 asked about people's perception of speculation. Table 6 reports the results of our

Table 6. Results of questions related to attitude towards business people and speculation

	China vs. U.S.			Guangzhou vs. Shanghai		
	China	U.S.	Sig.	Guangzhou	Shanghai	Sig.
C1. Friends nice to you if you become rich by business dealings	92.3%	94.7%		92.5%	92.0%	
C9. Friends respect you less if you are in own business	16.8%	8.6%	**	14.1%	21.4%	***
C11. Difficult to make friends with business people	49.0%	14.2%	***	51.6%	44.7%	
C5. Business people often dishonest	58.6%	45.8%	*	59.0%	58.0%	
C8. Speculation causes more frequent shortage	47.4%	30.9%	*	40.4%	59.6%	**
B6. Increase in coffee price caused by speculators	49.7%	11.3%	***	60.8%	31.9%	***

C1.	Suppose that as a result of successful business dealings you unexpectedly become rich. How do you imagine it would be received by your relatives at a holiday family gathering? Would they congratulate you and show great interest, or would they be judgmental and contemptuous? (1) They would show interest, would congratulate. (2) They would be quiet indifferent. (3) They would be judgmental and contemptuous.
C9.	Do you think that if you worked independently today as a businessperson and received profit, that your friends and acquaintance would respect you less and not treat you as you deserve?
C11.	Do you think that it is likely to be difficult to make friends with people who have their own business (individual or small corporations) and are trying to make a profit?
C5.	Do you think that those people why try to make a lot of money will often turn out to be not very honest people?
C8.	Grain traders in capitalist countries sometimes hold grain without selling it, putting it in temporary storage in anticipation of higher prices later. Do you think this "speculation" will cause (1) more frequent shortages of flour, bread and other grain products; (2) no effect on shortage; and (3) shortage less common?
B6.	If the price of coffee on the world market suddenly increased by 30 percent, what do you think is likely to be to blame? (1) Interventions of some government; (2) Such things as bad harvest in Brazil or unexpected changes in demand; (3) Speculators' efforts to raise prices.

analysis. Both Chinese and American students reported that people would be interested in them if they have a successful business. However, the answers for the other three questions related to attitudes towards business people indicate that Chinese students were more likely to have a negative attitudes towards business people, compared to their American counterparts. The traditional Chinese values emphasize agriculture over commerce. A popular Chinese old saying "no merchant is not cunning" reflects the common attitude towards business. At the beginning of the Chinese economic reform, most people who started their own business had low social status and were at the margin of the social mainstream. Naturally, this phenomenon was caused by their low opportunity cost. In addition, since the legal system in China is not very effective, unethical business dealings have been quite common. Now that these people are rich, others who perceive themselves as in the mainstream are having a "sour grape" mentality. The current popular saying of "only bad people has made a fortune" reflects partly the reality and partly the jealousy mentality.

The results of Question C9 indicate that Shanghai students had more negative attitudes towards business than their Guangzhou counterparts. The difference can be regional given the special policy status of Guangzhou. Also, people in Guangzhou have a long tradition of owning small businesses. In addition, Guangzhou is also geographically close to Hong Kong and Macao, and people in Guangzhou have more relatives and friends who are business owners overseas.

In China, speculation is related with unethical business people and has a negative connotation. The negative attitudes towards speculation among Chinese students were reflected in the answers in C8 and B6. However, speculation has a neutral meaning in English, and sometimes speculation is referred to as a technique or skill of doing business. Thus, the attitudinal difference towards speculation is mainly caused by cultural differences.

(7) Work incentives and initiatives

Questions A1, C3, A3, and A5 asked about work incentives. Question B1 was related to personal work initiatives. Table 7 presents the results of our analysis. The overwhelming majority of the respondents in both countries thought material incentives were very important for hard working, with Americans more likely to agree with that compared to their Chinese counterparts (A1 and C3). On the other hand, a significantly higher proportion of Chinese students in the sample seemed to agree that income equality and economic development cannot coexist, given material incentives for hard-working would promote development but create income inequality (A3). This difference may be contributed to Chinese respondents' witnessing of the failure of the old economic system where material incentives were lacking.

Differences were found in the answers to A3 between the Guangzhou sample and the Shanghai sample. Shanghai students were more likely to support to think that there was a tradeoff relationship between economic development and income equality. This finding may be explained by regional and time differences between these two samples. The difference in their attitudes may be a reflection of dissatisfaction to the country's moving to greater income inequality, as the reform furthers.

Table 7. Results of questions related to work incentives and initiatives

	China vs. U.S.			Guangzhou vs. Shanghai		
	China	U.S.	Sig.	Guangzhou	Shanghai	Sig.
A1. Work harder if pay is related	92.1%	95.4%	**	91.2%	93.7%	
C3. Good manager should be strict in enforcing discipline and give incentives to good work	58.2%	32.3%	***	59.1%	56.5%	
A3. Agree with the tradeoff between equality and economic development	75.9%	52.3%	***	71.7%	83.4%	***
A5. Important work benefits the country	81.6%	95.4%	***	78.1%	74.6%	
B1. Well-motivated employee is better than do-as-told employee	76.4%	92.1%	***	77.5%	87.6%	

A1. Do you think that people work better if their pay is directly tied to the quantity and quality of their work?
C3. Which of the following qualities is more important for the manager of a company? (1) The manager much show good will in his relation to workers and win their friendship. (2) The manager must be a strict enforcer of work discipline, giving incentives to hard workers and punishing laggards.
A3. Some have expressed the following: "It's too bad that some people are poor while others are rich. But we can't fix that: if the government were to make sure that everyone had the same income, we would all be poor, since no one would have any material incentive to work hard." Do you yourself personally agree with this theory?
A5. Is it important to you that your work benefits the country, and is not just to make money? (1) Very important or somewhat important; (2) Not important.
B1. In your opinion, which of the following statements is closer to the truth? (1) An employee who works hard and has the best interests of the business at heart can be worth twice as much to his/her company as a less well-motivated employee; (2) As a rule, an employee should generally do just what she/he is told-trying to do much more is likely to do more harm than help.

Question A5 asked if benefiting the country was one of the working incentives. While the American students were more likely than their Chinese counterparts to say yes, the magnitude of the difference was quite small. The answers to this question indicate an important value change for Chinese students, since Chinese were taught at young ages that work was for the country but not for oneself. The findings in this question indicate that Chinese students have adopted western values regarding working incentives.

American students were more likely than their Chinese counterparts to value individual initiatives at work. The difference is both situational and cultural. Under the central-planning economic system, work initiatives were not considered desirable in China. Even in the early years of the economic reform, college graduates had to wait for the government to assign a job instead of looking for jobs by themselves. For the same reason, it was hard for a person to change jobs. In addition, Chinese tradition values call for the obedience to the leader and teach the idea of "static is better than dynamic. " These would discourage individual initiatives at work. However, even with the above factors, over three-quarters of Chinese students supported the statement that encouraged individual initiatives, indicating that people's attitudes have been changing.

(8) Risk taking

Question C12 and B5 asked about people's willingness to take risks. Table 8 reports the results of our analysis. American students were more likely to take risks in the job market, but less likely to take risks in investment. This may be caused by different opportunity costs associated with these two types of risks in these two countries. In China, job securities used to be guaranteed under the central-planning economy system, and in many cases, it still is. Therefore, the opportunity cost of given up a guaranteed job is quite high. Furthermore, even though current college graduates are not very likely to get permanent jobs, the psychological costs of changing jobs are probably higher for Chinese given what they were used to in the past. On the other hand, in the U.S., most jobs don't come with a guaranteed job security, therefore, the opportunity cost of trying another job is much less. However, when it comes to money investment, the opportunity cost in the U.S. may be higher than that in China. In the U.S., the financial market is well established, and people could easily invest in stocks, bonds, mutual funds, and other investment alternatives. In contrast, in China, stock-trading just got started couple years ago and the risks involved in investing in stocks are much higher than that in the U.S. given that the financial market has not yet well-established and inside trading is rather common. Therefore, the opportunity cost of investing in a friend's risky business is much higher in the U.S. than in China.

When comparing to Guangzhou students, students from Shanghai were more likely to take risks both in the job market case and the investment case. As argued earlier, there is a regional difference between people from Shanghai and from other parts of China when it comes to money management matters. Also, the Shanghai universities where the students were interviewed were considered to be better quality universities than some of the Guangzhou universities, therefore, the Shanghai sample might be more confident in their ability to success under an uncertain situation.

Table 8. Results of questions related to risk taking

	China vs. U.S.			Guangzhou vs. Shanghai		
	China	U.S.	Sig.	Guangzhou	Shanghai	Sig.
C12. Take a new job with uncertainty	86.6%	91.6%	**	82.3%	93.5%	***
B5. Invest in a risky business	46.8%	32.6%	**	43.6%	52.1%	**

C12.	Imagine you are offered a new job that increased your salary by 50 percent. The new job is no more difficult than your present job, but not everyone is good at this line of work. It would turn out that after a year or two in this new job, you will be told that you are not doing well in the job and will be let go. Your chances of keeping the job and your changes of losing the job are about equal. Given this situation, would you take the risky, high-paying new job? In answering, assume that if they let you go, you could, after some time, find something more or less similar to your old job.
B5.	Suppose that a group of your friends are starting a business that you think is very risky and could fail but might also make investors in that business rich. Would you be tempted to invest a substantial portion of your savings in it?

(9) Consumption and saving

Question C2 was related to conspicuous consumption behavior. Questions A11 and A12 asked about saving behavior. Table 9 reports the results of our analysis. Surprisingly, American students were more likely to report conspicuous consumption behavior than their Chinese counterparts since conspicuous consumption is an important social problem in today's China. Most of the newly riches would use any available means to show off their wealth. Ordinary people celebrate the major events in their lives, such as wedding, new birth or death, by inviting many guests and holding fancy ceremonies. It is not uncommon for people to spend more money than what they can afford

Table 9. Results of questions related to consumption and saving

	China vs. U.S.			Guangzhou vs. Shanghai		
	China	U.S.	Sig.	Guangzhou	Shanghai	Sig.
C2. Would by extravagant items	46.6%	61.4%	***	35.6%	64.1%	***
A11.Saved money last year	48.8%	70.9%	***	43.8%	58.1%	***
A12. Saved because buying the thing wanted takes too much effort	7.5%	2.5%	**	6.0%	10.5%	**
A12. Saved for retirement or emergency	8.5%	6.5%		9.5%	6.6%	
A12. Saved to buy durable goods	18.5%	31.5%	***	15.5%	24.3%	
A12. Saved for better things in the future	43.0%	16.5%	***	46.7%	35.9%	**

C2.   If you ever became rich, would you really like to spend some of the money by purchasing really fashionable
        clothes, expensive cars, or other extravagant items that make an impression on people?
A11.   Did you save any money from the income you earned last year?
A12.   Which of the following is the best explanation why you saved? (1) Because to acquire the things I want takes
        too much effort. I just couldn't spend the money; (2) I put money away for old age, in case of illness or other
        unforeseeable circumstances; (3) I saved money so that I will have the means to by a vacation home, an
        apartment, automobile, or other such things of long-term use; (4) I hoped that better things will be available
        for my money in future years; (5) Other;

for these events. Even among college students, conspicuous consumption behaviors, such as purchasing brand name clothing, eating in luxury restaurants, and entertaining in expensive kola-okay clubs, have been observed. The motivation of such behavior is related to Chinese ideas of "peer comparison" and "not losing faces." Comparatively, American people are perceived as more practical and have no fear of losing faces.

The unexpected result might be caused by several reasons. First, since the China sample only consisted of college students who were not rich at the time of the interview and were much better educated than most of the newly riches in China, they might be aware that show-off one's wealth is putting oneself in a lower-status and less-educated group. Furthermore, even if they would engage in this kind of conspicuous consumption behavior, Chinese were more reluctant than Americans to give socially undesirable answers. Second, the question asked used as examples expensive cars and houses, which are items that are quite rarely purchased by private individuals in China. The students in the sample might have other more pressing needs in their mind if they do get rich in the future.

The observed difference in conspicuous consumption behavior between the Guangzhou sample and the Shanghai sample might be regional. People from Shanghai are perceived to pay more attention to their appearances than people from other parts of China. One popular perception is that people from Shanghai prefer clothing to food, but vise versa is said people from Guangzhou.

When it comes to saving behavior, American students were more likely than Chinese students to report saving, which is counterintuitive since the saving rate in China is much higher than that of the U.S. However, the difference lies in the limited resources of Chinese students. Unlike American students, Chinese students usually do not work part-time when attending school. Some Chinese students wrote on the questionnaire: "How can I save if I do not earn money?" In China, it is common that the college expenses are paid by the government and/or parents, although the situation is changing now. More and more colleges require families to pay a larger portion of the expenses, and students are starting to have part-time jobs. Some of them even made fortunes when doing business as college students.

The percentage of respondents who saved last year was significantly different between the Guangzhou sample and the Shanghai sample, with a higher percentage of students in Shanghai reported saving behavior. Again, this may be explained by the regional differences in China, where people from Shanghai are well known for their better skills of financial management.

In term of the incentives of saving (A12) , the major differences were shown in options 3 and 4. While American students were more likely to report saving for specific future expenses, Chinese students were more likely to report saving for "better things in the future." These differences are mainly situational, reflecting a lack of availability of high-quality, yet fairly affordable durable goods in the Chinese market. In addition, the example used in this question was again vacation homes and cars, which were not commonly consumed by private individuals in the current China.

Conclusions and Implications

This study reported the results of a new survey in Guangzhou, China, on student attitudes toward free markets. Combined with data collected by Hemesath and Pomponio in 1992-93, this study compared

Chinese students' attitudes with that of American students, while looking at regional and chronological differences in China at the same time. The following significant and substantial differences are found in the attitudes towards market between Chinese and American students:

(1) Compared to American students, Chinese students were much more comfortable with government intervention. However, when it comes to the method of intervention, students in both countries favored a taxing approach than a rationing approach. This difference is attributed to both situational and cultural factors.

(2) Compared to American students, Chinese students were more likely to support a reform plan which will bring greater income inequality. This difference is attributed to situational factors.

(3) Chinese students were less likely to feel comfortable with exchanges of money, compared to their American peers. However, Chinese students were more likely to favor fortune over fame, which is anti-tradition. Chinese students were also more likely be willing to trade money for leisure. These differences are attributed to both situational and cultural factors.

(4) Compared to American students, Chinese students were more likely to have a negative attitude towards business people, and a suspicious attitude towards business speculations. This difference is attributed more to cultural factors than situational factors.

(5) Compared to their American counterparts, Chinese students were more likely to think that there is a tradeoff relationship between economic development and economic equality. They were also less likely to value work initiatives, and the idea of contributing to the society is less likely to be important for them. This is mainly attributed to situational factors.

(6) Chinese students were more likely to take risks in financial investments, but less likely to take risks in the job market, compared to their American peers. These differences are attributed to situational factors.

(7) Compared to American students, Chinese students were less likely to save. The main reason for saving for Chinese students were for "better things available in the future," whereas for American students, the main purpose of saving was to buy a car, a house, or other durable goods. These differences are mainly attributed to situational factors.

When comparing the Guangzhou sample and the Shanghai sample, the following significant and substantial differences are found:

(1) Students in Guangzhou were more likely to welcome government intervention in controlling prices, compared to students in Shanghai.

This is mainly attributed to chronological differences of these two samples.

(2) Students in Shanghai were more likely to think that there is a tradeoff relationship between economic development and income equality, compared to students from Guangzhou. This is mainly attributed to regional differences.

(3) Compared to students from Shanghai, students in Guangzhou were less likely to be willing to take risks, both financial risks and job risks that is also attributed to regional differences.

(4) Compared to students from Shanghai, students in Guangzhou were much less likely to say they would engage in conspicuous consumption if they became rich. They were also less likely to save money. That is mainly attributed to regional differences.

Among other findings, this study confirmed Hemesath and Pomponio (1995)'s conclusions that Chinese students were more willing to support government intervention in the markets than Americans were, and had a more negative attitude towards business people. All the findings in this study suggest that the differences between students in the U.S. and in China are both situational and cultural, yet situational differences are more prevalent. The differences between the Guangzhou sample and the Shanghai sample are mainly regional.

The findings of this study may be used to understand Chinese people's perceptions of current situation in order to predict their reactions to further economic policy changes. Apparently, since cultural differences do exist, it is important for Chinese policy makers to incorporate traditional Chinese values into the economic reform process, not to exactly copy the western-style market economy system. On the other hand, Chinese students in the sample had very similar attitudes towards many aspects of free markets, such as the perception of the fairness of price changes, therefore, borrowing part of the western-style market economy system should have a positive effect. While effective legal system is eminently needed in China to maintain order and ensure fair competition in business, education is also necessary to change people's negative perception towards business people. The differences between students' attitudes towards government control of prices in the Guangzhou sample and the Shanghai sample should be alarming. If the inflation rate keeps on reaching double digits, people's attitudes towards the economic reform and the role of government might change in an unfavorable direction. The findings of this research, along with results from previous studies, can be a starting point for research Chinese people attitudes and behavior in a radically changing social system. Based on the findings, future research should develop questionnaires that apply to the general Chinese population. Future research is also needed to develop variables related to economic outcomes or performances, along with variables measuring attitudes. Future research should also fully utilize the framework of situational versus cultural factors for their research design.

Acknowledgment

We would like to thank Robert Shiller, Michael Hemesath, and Xun Pomponio for generously providing us their raw data and survey materials, and their prompt responses to our questions regarding their surveys. Helpful comments from Robert Shiller and three anonymous reviewers on the earlier version of the paper are highly appreciated.

Notes

1.   Robert J. Shiller, Maxim Boycko, and Vladimir Korobov, "Hunting for Homo Sovieticus: Situational versus Attitudinal Factors in Economic Behavior," *The Brookings Papers on Economic Activity,* vol. 1 (1992): 127-194.

2.   Michael Hemesath and Xun Pomponio "Student Attitudes toward Markets: Comparative Survey Data from China, the United Sates and Russia," *China Economic Review,* vol. 6 (1995): 225-238.

3.   Robert J. Shiller, Maxim Boycko, and Vladimir Korobov, "Popular Attitudes toward free Markets: The Soviet Union and the United States Compared," *The American Economic Review,* vol. 81(1991): 385-400.

4.   Shiller, Boycko and Korobov, *ibid.*

5.   Hemesath and Pomponio, *ibid.*

6.   Hemesath and Pomponio, *ibid.*

7.   Fritz Gaenslen, Fritz, "Culture and Decision Making in China, Japan, Russia, and the United States," *World Politics,* vol. 39 (1986): 78-103.

8.   S. Rosen, "Value Change among Post-Mao Youth: The Evidence from Survey Data," In P. Link, R. Madsen, and P. G. Pickowicz (eds.). *Unofficial China: Popular culture and thought in the People's Republic.* (Boulder: Westview Press, 1989), 193-216.

9.   Bai Nanshen, "Young People's Attitude and Aspirations: Will They Welcome Reform?" In B. L. Reynolds (ed.). *Reform in China: Challenge and choices* (Armonk: M.E. Sharpe, Inc., 1987), 161-187

10.   Jing Huaibin and Xu Suqin, "Wenhua yanjiu zhong ruogan lilun wenti de shizheng quanshi" (Empirical explanations of several theoretical issues in cultural research), *Zhexue dongtai,* 3.

Chapter 11

The Effect of Social Changes on Address Norms in China

LI Jian

Introduction

> "Who is at the door?" Mom asked her two-year-old daughter. The little girl peeped out the widow and said: "It's a *heiyi* (black aunt).[1]

"*Heiyi*", black aunt in Chinese, a powerful term that reveals not only gender, but also race, generation and seniority. This two-year-old Chinese American girl has just created a new term for address that she has never heard before by using her cultural and linguistic repertoire. According to the Chinese custom of addressing, children should always call relatives, neighbors, friends of parents, and even strangers by kinship terms, and children are called by their nicknames or given names in return. The example illustrates the important linkage between language and culture that reflects social norms of a particular community.

This article explores how the changes in address norms involving kinship terms, titles and names reflect the tremendous social transformations in China since the founding of the People's Republic of China in 1949, especially the effects of the recent economic reforms on the use of social, official, and occupational titles.[2] Focusing on the social conditions under which kinship terms, titles, and proper names are used, this study demonstrates how norms of address maintain and re-create social solidarity and hierarchy in China. Furthermore, theoretical implications regarding the relationship between social structure and the use of different forms of address are also discussed in a historical context.

Literature on terms of address as a part of politeness strategy reveals both parallels and differences in the ways scholars conceptualize social meanings of address norms. As a general rule, appropriate forms of address all involve showing respect and deference on the one hand and the demarcation of social status in varying degrees on the other. The Chinese scholars who examine the address rules in China regard the complexities of the rules governing appropriate address terms as a part of the cultural etiquette in the web of social relationships.[3] In modern sociolinguistic investigation of forms of address, Brown and his colleagues pioneered in the field by proposing a "solidarity and power model" to explain the social significance of norms of address in different societies .[4] The central thesis of this model is that reciprocal use of terms of address is an indicator of social solidarity between persons of equivalent power, while non reciprocal use of address terms reflects unequal power between two parties. The classic example comes from the use of *tu* (*T*)and *vous* (*V*) in French: *T* or *V* is used reciprocally between persons of equivalent power and non-reciprocally between persons of unequal power.[5] Associated with the "solidarity and power model" is the hypotheses that the higher the level of social stratification in a society, the more differentiated politeness strategies will be used.[6]

This study suggests that the changes in address norms in China lend some support but also raise some questions about Brown and his colleagues' hypotheses: with the rapid industrialization and high social mobility in urban China today, the younger generation has developed a system of address that reflects both a more egalitarian attitude among peers and close friends and unequal relationships among those who have differential access to economic resources and political power. Thus, the direction of changes in address norms is not always unidirectional: the reciprocal use of terms of address can co-exist with an elaborated form of non reciprocal use of address during a transitional period of a society, with the former signaling equality and solidarity among peers and close friends and the latter marking status and power between the superior and the inferior.

Historical Background

Since address norms in China were developed, codified, and transformed even before Confucius edited classical canons more than two thousand years ago, it is important to take a historical and holistic view to analyze the forces that shape the use of address terms over a long period of the Chinese history.

The first codification of address norms is found in the *Erh Ya*, the earliest Chinese dictionary, variously attributed to *Chou Kong* (BC?-1105) and to the disciples of Confucius, one section of which is devoted to relationship terms.[7] By means of the school system and their connection with the civil service, whereby graduates were qualified for official appointments, this regional system was gradually imposed upon the rest of the country by the Chou period (ended 221 BC). Although the colloquial use of relationship terms has varied throughout China at all times, the standardization of formal address terms based on Confucian principles was adopted as the state policy about 136 B.C. under the Han emperor Wu. This system of terminology represents the ancient usage in Northern China, where the characteristics of Chinese civilization arose. The first set of codified terms of address in Confucian cannons were kinship terms based on a strict differentiation of age, gender, generation and seniority since ancestors and kin were the key relationships in traditional China. Two principles underlying address norms are the principle of propriety and deference. The principle of propriety dictates a strict observation of social hierarchical order and the reinforcement of social status by *zheng ming*,[8], rectifying names, the use of prescribed names relative to one's social roles and status. The second principle, the principle of deference, requires one to humble oneself and elevate the other for social cohesion and harmony. Although much has changed since the relationship terms were first codified by the Confucian canons more than two thousand years ago, the basic structure of kinship terms and the use of principles of deference and propriety are still very much a part of modern Chinese daily lives.

For example, unlike English, in which siblings are addressed by their first names, in Chinese, the eldest brother is always addressed by the younger brother as *"da ge"*, big brother; the second brother as *"er ge"*, and so on. This is also true of the address pattern among older and younger sisters where the eldest sister is called *"da jie"*, big sister, *"er jie"*; for the second sister, and so on. In return, the younger siblings are always addressed by their nicknames or full names. Not only are such kinship terms used daily within the family, they can also be used outside of one's family. To show their deference and propriety, friends, acquaintances, or even strangers of the same generation, will sometimes use the term *"da ge"* (big brother) or *"da jie"* (big sister) as a sign of respect and friendliness.

The following is a typical polite way of introducing one another when two parties meet for the first time:

[1] A: Nin guixing?
　　　A: Your honorable surname?
[2] B: Mian gui. Xing Li.
　　　B: Don't be so formal, (My) surname is Li.
[3] A: Nin zunxing?
　　　A: Your respectable surname?
[4] B: Mian zun, xing Zhang.
　　　B: I am honored, (My) surname is Zhang.

Although the above dialogue may sound strange when it is read in English, it is perfectly proper when it is said in Chinese because the two speakers are observing the principles of propriety and deference with a shared cultural heritage. It is considered a good manner to pay respect to the other by asking "your esteemed (or respectable) surname?", and respond with modesty "I am honored".

Kinship terms remain relatively stable in the course of Chinese history despite minor changes introduced to the system because of the changes in marriage systems, mourning rituals, and more recently, social mobility and changes in women's status.[9] With the development of modern education and growing specialization of social and economic functions, there is an increasing trend toward using personal names for addressing one another among urban Chinese. The most dramatic changes in address terms are in the use of titles – social, occupational, and official. The popular use and later the gradual disappearance of the social title "*tongzhi*", comrade, is a vivid reminder of how terms of address can be shaped by ideological concerns in a relative short time period and serve as a barometer for detecting directed social change in human relations.

What follows is an analysis of those kinship terms, titles and names used in China that reflect people's changing attitude towards gender, age, seniority, generation and social status.

Kinship Terms

Since excellent descriptive and historical studies of Chinese kinship terms have been already made by numerous writers,[10] the present study is mainly concerned with how the kinship terms are applied and negotiated to non-kin by using the appropriate social rules regarding gender, age, seniority, generation and social status.

Chinese children, whether in mainland China, Taiwan or Hong Kong, are socialized from early age to use kinship terms in addressing neighbors, friends and colleagues of their parents, even strangers.[11] Learning to extend kinship terms to non-kin persons helps children to respect the elder and to find their place in a well established social hierarchy at a very early age. The general rule for extending the kinship terms to non-kin is similar to the way address terms are used within the family. For example, children are taught to call those who are older than they are but of the same generation as "*gege*" (older brother) or "*jiejie*" (elder sister), and they are free to use names to call those who are younger than themselves. For those who are of their parents' generation, children are required to use "*shushu* " (younger paternal uncle) for a male who is about the age of one's father, or "*bobo*" for a male who is older than, and/or having a higher social position than one's father. The single term "*ah yi*" (mother's sister) is used to address women of one's parents' generation. Some of these kinship terms with slight variations, such as "*da ge*" (big brother), "*da jie*" (big sister), are also used among adults to fortify a sense of solidarity.

Negotiation of "*SHUSHU*" and "*BOBO*" to non-kin

The difference between "*shushu*" and "*bobo*" is subtle since both terms apply to a male of one's father's age. "*Bobo*" literally means "elder paternal uncle" as opposed to "*shushu*", "younger paternal uncle. "*Bobo*" is conceptualized in the following by Hong[12]:

    male [+]
    patrilineal [+]
    generation [+]
    relative seniority within the generation[+]

In modern China, there is an increasing trend for using "*shushu*" to replace the term "*bobo*" as in the following example when the father (or mother) introduces a school-age son (or daughter) to a male friend of the parent:

    A: ... Jiao Wang bobo
    (Come and call *Wang bobo* –elder paternal uncle)
    Wang interrupts:
    B: ... Zenme keyi? Bu gandang, bu gandang. ...
    (Oh, no, you do me too much honor.
    ... Jiao shushu jie xingle

(Just call me *shushu* –younger paternal uncle).[13]

This example shows how people negotiate their social relationships by adjusting their proper address terms. It is likely that this friend of father's is not only a little older than the father but also of similar or higher social status than the father since "*bobo*" is a respectful term that denotes both age and seniority. The term "*bobo*" is becoming a less frequently used term among young urban Chinese. As Hong pointed out that "negotiation over the use of this term (leveling down from "*bobo*" to "*shushu*") is a success story for camaraderie in the Chinese social context".[14] This is significant because by merging the term "*shushu*" and "*bobo*", it obscures the line of age and seniority and violates the traditional principles of deference and propriety: neither the child nor the parent needs to humble himself by elevating the other who is, after all, of the similar age of the parent.

Women's Independence and the extension of "*AH YI*" to non-kin

Before the turn of the century, women's place in China was at home and they did not have their separate social identities apart from their father, husband and son. This is clearly indicated by the folk saying: "A woman depends on her father before she is of age. She depends on her husband at marriage, and she depends on her son after her husband's death".[15] Because of their dependence on men, married women had no address terms apart from their role as wives and mothers. In a patrilineal and patrilocal system, a woman would join the husband's family after marriage and she would most likely to be addressed as "*saozi* ", wife of a paternal elder sibling, or "*shenzi*", wife of paternal younger uncle, by both kin and non kin. The term "*yi*" or "*ah yi*" (a regional variation of *yi*) is reserved for mother's sisters. These kinship terms are often extended to non-kin according to a woman's affiliation with the husband's family or her natal family. Thus, a woman is addressed with "*saozi*", by both kin and non-kin when she is in her husband's village, and addressed with "*ah yi*" when she is in her natal family. This system of address is still in use to address women in many parts of rural China.

In urban centers of mainland China, Taiwan and Hong Kong, however, the common term for a child to address a woman of his/her parents' age is "*ah yi*" instead of "*shenzi*" . The following is a pragmatic profile for "*ah yi*":[16]

female [+]
matrilineal [+]
generation [+]
relative age within the generation [-]

The above diagram of *ah yi* is exactly the mirror reflection of *shushu:*

male [+]
patrilineal [+]
generation [+]
relative seniority within the generation [-]

Since the term *"shushu"*, paternal younger brother, is commonly used to refer to a man of one's parents' generation, it would be logical to expect the term *"shenzi"*, wife of paternal younger uncle, to be used for women of one's parental generation. But this is not the case. The only term for children to address women of their parents' generation in urban China, be they close friends of the family or strangers, is "*ah yi*"(maternal aunt). Bonlivian interprets the use of *ah yi* for addressing non-kin as a sign of showing lower status for Chinese women since *ah yi* labels a relative on the mother's side, which automatically carries less prestige than the father's kin".[17] I disagree with her interpretation. Extending kinship terms from mother's side often means a closer bond between the addresser and addressee. For example, a male friend of mother's can be called either as *shushu* , father's brother, or *jiujiu* , mother's brother. It is considered much more intimate and respectful if the child calls the male friend of mother's as "*jiujiu*" instead of " *shushu* ". By calling the man "*jiujiu*", the family treats the man as someone special and dear to the family.

The extended use of *ah yi* to non kin females of parental generation signaled women's independence and breaking away from the traditional patrilineal and patriarchal system, where women's status was defined as a wife and mother. Conducting her fieldwork in China between 1935 to 1937, Lang had already detected the changes in the Chinese women's social status:

The modern women– factory workers, career women, and educated housewives– have won a position in family and society far superior to that of their grandmothers or of those of their own contemporaries who have continued to live under the old conditions. The modern wife is often her husband's equal and not infrequently has acquired a dominant position in the family[18].

The fact that the term *ah yi* is used not only in mainland China, but also in Taiwan and Hong Kong suggests that *ah yi* is not a recent cultural invention under the influence of the Communist ideology. Its roots can probably be traced back to the Republican Revolution of 1911 and the May 4th Movement of 1919.[19] The term "*ah yi*" was probably first used to address the women who gained their independence through modern education and employment outside the family and later gradually spread to the middle class and the working class people in urban centers of China.

Titles

A title is a polite way of addressing a person by showing his/her rank, occupation, status, etc.. According to the functions served, titles can be divided into three categories: social, official, and occupational. The most commonly used titles are social titles, for example, Mr. and Mrs., to be used to address any adult as a sign of respect. Official titles are reserved for persons who hold governmental/ bureaucratic offices, and occupational titles are for persons who are trained in some specialized professions. Titles used as address terms can be viewed as sensitive indicators of levels of social stratification since titles reflect one's relative position in a given social structure. The major social transformations in China in the past century, ideological or economic, all left their marks in the ways titles are used.

Before delving into the discussion of titles, it is useful to distinguish three levels of meanings of titles as analytical units: literal meaning, referential meaning and social meaning.[20] Literal meaning of a title involves its lexicon definition. For example, the English title "Mr." originally means "master", Chinese title *xiansheng*, (Mr.) literally means "first born". The literal or lexical meanings of a title become indeterminable or lost over time, and a title simply becomes a referent – a term used to designate a person. Lastly, social meaning is the most prominent component in the semantics of titles because the social component consists of speaker-addressee relationship, speaker's evaluation of addressee (and situation), and of speaker's social background, as expressed in the use of a given form of address. The changes in social titles from *xiansheng* and *xiaojie* to *tongzhi* and back to *xiansheng, xiaojie* illustrate this interplay between the literal meaning and social meaning.

Social Titles: *XIANSHENG, XIAOJIE* AND *TONGZHI*

Before the Communist revolution of 1949, the most general title used to refer to a gentleman was *xiansheng*, literally, 'first born', since seniority is a compliment in China. There are two referential meanings attached to *xiansheng*: one can address a stranger on the street as *xiansheng*, 'Sir', or address one's teacher as *xiansheng*, (or *laoshi*), 'Master'. [21] Like 'Mr.' in English, one can use *xiansheng*, together with a name, such as *Wang Hua xiansheng*, or *Wang xiansheng*. The social title *xiansheng*, was originally reserved for someone who is senior or having higher status than the addresser, and it was later generalized to general public as in the case with "Mr."

The terms for women corresponding to *xiansheng*, are *xiaojie* , literally 'little miss', for unmarried women, and *taitai* , literally 'grand grand' for married women. A professional woman, such as a school teacher, is often addressed as *xiansheng*, followed by her surname, as the word is not gender specific.[22] In pre-1949 China, *xiaojie* and *taitai* were restricted titles reserved for gentry families which could afford servants. This explains why the use of *xiaojie* and *taitai* was gradually abolished after the Communist Revolution of 1949 in mainland China since it is incompatible with the Communist ideology based on explicit egalitarian principles.

After 1949, the social title *xiansheng, xiaojie* and *taitai* were gradually replaced by *tongzhi*, 'comrade'. Fang and Heng pointed out that the word *tongzhi* as a term of address is by no means the invention of the Chinese Communist Party; it was used by Sun Yat-sen to address his colleagues.[23] In the beginning, *tongzhi* was generally accepted as honorific terms of address characteristic of revolutionary solidarity, equality, and respect as well as intimacy among the high ranking officials. Since the literal meaning of *tongzhi* implies equality and solidarity and can be used regardless of one's gender, wealth, rank, and social status, the government encouraged the use of *tongzhi* among officials and soon it was spread to the urban population at large. The following are some examples of how *tongzhi* has been used on various occasions:

1. LN (Last Name) +tongzhi
2. *Lao* (old) or *Xiao* (young) + tongzhi,
3. *Nan* (male) or *Nu* (female) + *tongzhi*
4. *Tongzhimen* (plural of tongzhi)

Tongzhi loses its literal meaning when it is used indiscriminately to strangers, male or female, superior or inferior as a social title. In many cases, *tongzhi* is reduced to being a referent for "person", as in the case "this book belongs to that *nu tongzhi* . Literally, *nu tongzhi* means "female comrade", which eventually becomes a simple referent for "woman".

The popular use of *tongzhi* diminished its ideologically motivated social meaning until some new social meanings crept into it by a political movement. During the height of the Cultural Revolution (1966 to 1972), many government officials, professors, teachers and other outspoken citizens were labeled as "counter-revolutionaries" and were persecuted. Consequently, they were disqualified to be addressed as *tongzhi* . Some older officials and professors were barred from being called *tongzhi* when they were sent to labor camps. Some of them were moved to tears when they heard themselves being addressed as *tongzhi* again by a friend or a colleague. Under these trying circumstances, the title *tongzhi* became an honor again.

Toward the end of the Cultural Revolution, many people became ambivalent about using the term *tongzhi* indiscriminately. The term *shifu* , master, became fashionable in Shanghai and many other parts of the country from the mid 1970s to the mid 1980s. Unlike *tongzhi* which has a certain political connotation, the title *shifu* is a respectful term originating from the apprentice-master relationship prior to 1949. *Shifu* was/is a popular term to be used to address older store clerks or strangers on the street for asking directions in many parts of the country. Although it can be used as a neutral term free from gender, age and rank, *shifu* is most likely to be used to address a male and an elder person than a female or young person. Occasionally, an older person may address a young store clerk, male or female, as "*xiao shifu* ", "little master". But unlike *tongzhi,* one seldom hears *nu shifu* (female master) or *shifumen* (plural of *shifu*). *Shifu* is never used among colleagues and neighbors either. In a word, *shifu* never attains the full status of *tongzhi* as a referent for "person".

With the introduction of the economic reform and increasing contacts with overseas Chinese since 1976, some traditional social titles, *xiansheng, xiaojie, taitai*, experienced a come back in major cities, such as Guangzhou, Shanghai, Beijing and Tienjin. To many people in urban centers, *xiansheng, xiaojie , taitai* sound "modern" and carry a more deferential flavor than either *tongzhi* or *shifu*. In order to get courteous services in prestigious department stores, many customers feel compelled to use *xiansheng* and *xiaojie* to address clerks. A woman in her fifties recounted her recent experience in a department store in Beijing:

I went to a department store to do some shopping. To get the attention from a busy clerk, I called out *"xiaojie"*. Upon hearing *xiaojie,* the young woman clerk looked at me with surprise and served me promptly. She must think this old woman is quite modern and she deserves good service.

While many young people in urban centers do not hesitate to use *xiansheng* and *xiaojie* for public services, some government officials and older people who are used to *tongzhi* and proud of its egalitarian connotations are critical of the revival of *xiansheng* and *xiaojie*. They regard such social titles as residuals of the "semi-feudal and semi-colonial" China prior to the 1949 revolution, in which *xiansheng* and *xiaojie* were reserved mostly for those in the privileged class. This controversy over the use of *Tongzhi* versus *xiansheng* and *xiaojie* arises from the confusion between the literal meaning and social meaning. Braun pointed out that sometimes certain forms of address are discarded because the 'meaning' expressed is not liked, and others are introduced or supported because they seem to express something desirable, e.g., comradeship, civil rights, solidarity, brotherhood, equality, or friendship.

Despite the good intentions, the question arises as to whether status differences are abolished by abolishing certain linguistic expressions for them, or whether people regarded each other as equals, friends, brothers and sisters, etc., because they address each other with the respective terms".[24]

During a transitional period, people may feel uneasy about using one social title over another. In a long run, the etymological ingredient of any superiority will eventually be neutralized and the formal literal meaning will become irrelevant. The key issue to be examined in the future is not the use of *"tongzhi"* and *"xiansheng"* by themselves, but how these social titles are used, that is, if they are used reciprocally to create social solidarity or used in non reciprocal fashion as indicators of asymmetrical human relationships based on differential social status.

Official Titles and Occupational Titles

The importance of official titles and occupational titles in China is reflected in the range of the terms available to address persons who hold offices or who have skills in some professions. The official titles range from president, chairman to bureau chief and section chief. Here are some examples of official titles that are used as terms of address: *bu zhang*, minister, *sheng zhang*, provincial governor, *ju zhang*, bureau chief *ke zhang*, section chief, *chu zhang*, division chief, *shu ji*, secretary, etc. The occupational titles that can be used for address are as varied as official titles: *dai fu* or *yi sheng* , doctor, *lao shi,* (old master) teacher, *gong cheng shi*, engineer, *ji shu yuan*, researcher, *da sh fu*, a cook in a restaurant, *cai feng* , tailor, *jin li*, manager, *laoban/laoban niang*, an owner of a small business/wife of an owner of a small business, etc.. All the titles mentioned above can be used by themselves or prefixed with a surname, for example:

1. One greets a neighbor who happens to be a division chief by saying: "*Wang chu zhang, zhao!* (Good morning, division chief Zhang!).
2. A student greets his/her teacher: "*laoshi, nin hao!*" (Teacher, how do you do!).
3. One goes to a tailor for making a dress and greets him by saying: "*Wang Cai Feng, ni mang ah?*" ("Tailor Wang, you are busy?").

Although official policy makers often frown at the use of official and professional titles, their effort in encouraging the use of *tongzhi* as a sign of social solidarity and equality met with little success: the Chinese have never ceased to use these honorific titles which are useful tools in showing deference to one's rank and position.[25] Shortly after the economic reform, there is an increasing tendency for people not only to use official and professional titles but also to elevate the titles in order to flatter the addressee: an engineer is sometimes called "*zhong gong*", chief engineer with or without a surname, an administer at a college or a company is also sometime called "*zhong* ", chief, a shop keeper "*laoban*", boss, even an assistant to a shop keeper is called "*er laoban*", second boss, or more respectfully, "*jing li*", manager, a vice bureau chief "*ju zhang*", chief, etc.. Commenting on the declining use of *tongzhi* and recent trend of exaggerating the use of official and professional titles, Fang and Heng lamented:

> This suggests that the gap between those of higher social status and lower social status has become wider, and the kind of comradely relationship which was established during the Armed Revolution Period of the 1930s has been weakened.[26]

Proper Names

Unlike the use of kinship terms and titles, personal names by themselves are free of implications of social status and hierarchy. In a society where proper human relations are ranked by age, generation, gender, seniority and social status, names are the least functional categories to be used for terms of address. As a general rule, names are to be avoided in addressing elder relatives, neighbors, and even friends who were older than the addressee. This "no naming" situation is gradually changed with young people going to school where they are called by their names by teachers and classmates. Thus, it becomes more and more common for school children and college students to use names to address one another.

In introducing oneself, a Chinese person is more likely to say his/her surname than given name since many feel their first names are too personal and intimate to be revealed to a stranger. It is regarded more polite to ask "*nin gui xin?*" (what is your honorable surname?) than to ask plainly "*ni jiao she mo minzhi?*" (What is your name?). However, a monosyllabic surname is not a free form and must be bounded to something else to form a complete term of address. Therefore, one never hears a surname being used alone except when it is disyllabic, such as *Ouyang* or Murong. Disyllabic names are very rare in Chinese, less than about dozen are still in use in China today.[27] Knowing only the surname, the addresser has to make a decision as to how to combine a title with a surname to address a person. Here are some choices:

1. LN +xiansheng (Mr.) or LN+xiaojie (miss)
2. LN+tongzhi (comrade)
3. LN+lao (old)
4. Lao+LN/Xiao (little)+LN
5. LN+Official/Occupational Title
6. LN+KT (kinship term)

Currently, choice 1 is most commonly used to address an overseas Chinese or a senior member of a democratic party or a religious organization. It is also becoming accepted in addressing people who provide services, such as those working in hotels and stores. Choice 2 is not common except on some formal official occasions with a law enforcement personnel or in the army. Choice 3 is usually reserved for the aged with status (usually to men). Choice 4 is common in urban centers on informal occasions with people of similar social status.

Depending on their age, an older person may address a younger person as "Xiao+LN", while a younger person may address an older person (only a few years older and with similar status) with Lao+LN. Although it is gender free, people are more likely to use Lao+LN to address a man than a woman. Choice 5 is common on both formal and informal occasions when people feel a need to show deference either because of social distance or the difference in social status. Choice 6 is common on informal occasions when people feel a need to strengthen solidarity. In summary, choices 4 to 6 are more commonly used address terms than choices 1 to 3. It is always safe to use choice 5, that is, LN+Official/ Occupational Title, when one is introduced to a person for the first time. With all these choices available, a person has to choose a form of address that is most appropriate for that particular occasion based on his evaluation of the addressee's age, gender, seniority, and social status.

The most common form of address in schools and colleges is to call and refer to each other by one's full name. First names are not commonly used because they confer a special sense of intimacy, which is reserved for family members and special friends only. It becomes more and more common to use full names to address one another among young people in urban China, Taiwan, and Hong Kong since the young have been socialized in schools where full names are used by teachers as wells as classmates.

Summary and Theoretical Implications

In the past century, many drastic social changes occurred in China: the republic revolution of 1911, the May 4th Movement of 1919, the Communist revolution of 1949, the Cultural Revolution between 1966 to 1976, and the recent economic reforms and open-door policy since 1978, which all left their marks on the way people address one another. Although all three forms of address, kinship terms, titles, and names, have co-existed in China for thousands of years, the centrality and the conditions under which each category is used vary with time, place and social status.

The numbers of kinship terms used to address kin and non-kin have been reduced greatly due to high social mobility and changes in family structure.[28] With the simplification of kinship systems, the use of social, official, and occupational titles is on a rise since 1949. In pre-1949 China, titles were used much less frequently than kinship terms. The social titles "*xianshen, xiaojie, taitai*" were usually reserved for the gentry class. The use of official and occupational titles were also limited since most people turned to their kin or fictive kin for networking and support. The increasing specialization of social and economic functions promoted the use of social, official and occupational titles in cities.

The economic reform since 1978 has provided opportunities for social mobility as well as creating a new form of social hierarchy. Official titles and occupational titles enjoy new popularity especially among young people who are eager to court favors from those who have access to economic resources and political power. The reciprocal use of *tongzhi* motivated by egalitarian ideology lost its favor when the economic reform swept through the whole country. Many traditional social titles, such as *xiansheng, xiaojie, taitai,* became fashionable in major cities in China, which caused alarm among some officials in the government. However, the use of these social titles is not likely to threaten social cohesion and solidarity if they are used reciprocally. Asymmetrical human relationships is created only when the titles are used non reciprocally.[29]

The reciprocal use of personal names is the most democratic form of address, which has been the least favored form of address in China since it is void of the principles of deference and propriety based on the prescribed social order. Compulsory education has promoted the use of names among classmates and close friends of the same generation. To what extent the reciprocal use of names will prevail is hard to ascertain since social mobility and egalitarian ideology do not always go hand in hand and do not necessarily promote the reciprocal solidarity as proposed by Brown and Gilman.

The changes in address norms in China lend both support and raise questions about Brown and his colleagues' hypotheses on two accounts. Social mobility and changes in family structure have helped to simplify kinship terms. However, the recent economic reform which brought the development of an unequal distribution of economic wealth and political power facilitated the proliferation and exaggerated use of official titles and occupational titles. Thus, contemporary China shows signs of social development that is both more hierarchical and democratic at the same time on different accounts as reflected in the way address terms are used. Furthermore, although social mobility and egalitarian ideology have a leveling effect on the use of social titles, they have little effect on the non reciprocal nature of kinship terms, official and occupational titles, whose main function is to acknowledge the status of a person based on his/her age, gender, generation, seniority and social status. The experiences of other East Asian countries that share a Confucian heritage also indicate that the non reciprocal use of kinship terms, official and occupational titles is not likely to change despite the industrialization and democratization processes.[30] With an emerging social order based on both the cultural tradition and a new market economy, the Chinese are facing a transitional period in which many forms of address co-exist; thus, a rich tapestry of address terms, encompassing kinship terms, social, official and occupational titles and personal names, are available for people to experiment, choose, and manipulate for paying deference, marking social status and affirming social solidarity for a long time to come.

Notes

1.   This anecdote is from my personal experience. My daughter was born in the United States, but she was taught to address people by kinship terms according to the Chinese custom before she went to day-care after she was two years old.

2.   The Chinese characters in this articles are transcribed according to *hanyu pinyin*, the romanization of the Chinese phonetic alphabet, which was officially endorsed in the People's Republic of China in 1958.

3.   The three categories of titles: social, occupational, and official, are useful analytical units introduced by Y. R Chao, "Chinese Terms of Address", *Language* 32 (1) (1956), 217-41.

4.   This is especially evident by the earlier Chinese scholars, for example, Chen and Shryock, Feng, Chao, all analyzed the significance of Chinese terms of address from historical and anthropological perspectives. T.S. Chen and J. K. Shryock, "Chinese Relationship Terms", *American Anthropologist*, 34 (1932), 623-69, H. Y. Feng, "Teknonymy as a Formative Factor in the Chinese Kinship Terms", *American Anthropologist*, 38 (1936): 59-66, Y. R Chao, "Chinese Terms of Address", *Language* 32 (1) (1956), 217-41.

5.   Brown and his colleagues laid a theoretical foundation for studying forms of address by publishing a number of influential articles on the theory of address. In "The Pronouns of Power and Solidarity". Brown and Gilman developed a theory of "power semantic versus solidarity semantic" which was applied to the use of pronouns, and was later extended to terms of address in general. Roger Brown and Albert Gilman, "The Pronouns of Power and Solidarity", in T.A. Sebeok ed. *Style in Language*. (MA: MIT Press, 1960), 253-276.

6.   Brown and Gilman ibid., 255-265. For a more detailed analysis, see also Roger Brown and Marguerite Ford, "Address in American English", in Dell Hymes ed. *Language in Culture and Society*. (New York: Harper and Row Publishers, 1964), 239-243. The use of *tu* and *vous* in French parallels the use of *ni* and *nin* in Chinese. *Ni* is used among the equals and toward the inferiors whereas *Nin* is used to strangers and superiors.

7.   Penelope Brown and Steven Levinson, *Politeness: Some Universals in Language Use*. (Cambridge University Press, 1987), 24.

8. Chen and Shryock pointed out that the Confucian canon contains "practically all the relationship terms, recognized today, except for colloquial use". Chen and Shryock, ibid., 623.

9. *Ming* in the Confucian sense encompasses, in contemporary terminology, sociological definitions and values of an individual's social roles and status. To *zheng ming* is to put each individual in his/her place according to his/her social positions. Yueguo Gu, "Politeness Phenomena in Modern Chinese", *Journal of Pragmatics* 14 (1990), 238.

10. Both Chen, Shryock and Chao provide a detailed description of how certain kinship terms become simpler and more inclusive due to the disappearance of some ancient institutions of the sororate, junior levorate and cross-cousin marriage; the elaboration of mourning rituals. Chen and Shryock ibid., 628, Chao ibid.,160-163.

11. Chen and Shryock ibid., Feng ibid., Chao ibid.,1956.

12. This practice probably stems from the traditional close-knit clan structure and name avoidance ritual in rural China. Paul Chao, *Chinese Kinship*. (London: Kegan Paul International, 1983), 6-27.

13. Beverly Hong, "Politeness in Chinese: Impersonal Pronouns and Personal Greeting", *Anthropological Linguistics,* 27 (1985), 207.

14. The example is provided by Gu, the translation from Chinese to English is mine. Yueguo Gu, "Politeness Phenomena in Modern Chinese", *Journal of Pragmatics* 14 (1990): 237-257.

15. Hong, Ibid., 107.

16. Paul Chao, ibid., 61.

17. Hong ibid., 209.

18. Nancy Bonvillain, *Language, Culture, and Communication.* (New Jersey: Prentice Hall, 1993), 65-96.

19. Olga Lang, *Chinese Family and Society,* (New Haven: Yale University Press, 1946), 338.

20. The term "family revolution" was introduced into the public consciousness during the New Culture Movement of Renaissance, which started in 1917, broke out in full force in the May 4th Movement of 1919. Inspired by the western democratic ideals, the youth in the May 4th Movement demanded a new role for women in the family as well as in society in general terms of gender equality; it also demanded marriage by free choice and love, not by parental arrangement. Lang ibid.,12-13, 16.

21. For a detailed analysis of the three levels of meanings involved in forms of address, see Braun, ibid., 253-264.

22. Y.R.Chao, ibid., 223.

23. Y.R.Chao, ibid., 224. This use of *xiansheng* to refer to teacher is no longer practiced today, instead, the common term for teacher is "*lao shi*" in China, Taiwan and Hong Kong.

24. Fang and Heng 1983:496.

25. Frederick Braun, *Terms of Address: Problems of Patterns and Usage in Various Languages and Cultures.* (Berlin:Mouton de Gruyer, 1988): 262.

26. The Chinese in the mainland, Taiwan, Hong Kong , and the peoples in Singapore, Japan and Korea, all have extended forms of address based on official and occupational titles.

27. Fang and Heng, ibid., 498.

28. For more details about names, see Y.R. Chao 1956, 221-223.

29. Based on the hierarchical social order, Chao divided the kinship terms/names into seven categories: 1. Superior: of a higher generation than ego, even though sometimes younger in age; 2. Equal Older: of the same generation and older; 3. Equal younger: of the same generation and younger; 4. Inferior: of a lower generation than ego; 5. Stranger: stranger or slight acquaintance; 6. Friend: friend, schoolmate, or close acquaintance; 7. Lower: child, servant, beggar, or the like. One hundred and fourteen kinship terms were listed under this system of the one hundred and fourteen kinship terms listed, probably less than half of them are still in active use in China today. . Y.R. Chao ibid., 232-233.

30. Cf. Brown and Ford, ibid.. for a detailed discussion of the relationship between the reciprocal and non reciprocal use of titles and how it affects human relationships.

31. Matsumoto, and Hijirida, Kyoko and Ho-min Sohn demonstrated that both Japan and Korea still use highly elaborated systems of address that acknowledge status differences between the addresser and the addressee despite the industrialization and democratization processes. In fact, Japan and Korea use more linguistic devices to mark honorifics to mark status differentiation than either the mainland China or Taiwan or Hong Kong. Yoshiko Matsumoto, "Reexamination of the Universality of Face: Politeness Phenomena in Japanese", *Journal of Pragmatics*. 12 (1988), 403-426. Kyoko Hijirida and Ho-Min Sohn, "Cross Cultural Patterns of Honorifics and Sociolinguistic Sensitivity to Hornorific Variables: Evidence from English, Japanese, and Korean", *Papers in Linguistics.* Vl 19 (3) (1986), 365-401.

Chapter 12

The Resurgence of Chinese Anti-Americanism in the Post-Cold War Era

XU Guangqiu

Anti-Americanism, hostile activities or sentiments against the United States, can be seen in many parts of the world as well as in China.[1] Anti-Americanism in China is understood to refer to those feelings of disapproval, hostility, or condemnation that are found among the Chinese people against American foreign policy, society, cultures, and values. The Chinese have always had mixed sentiments about America. While many Chinese are still friendly to Americans in person, they do not hesitate to criticize the United States from a distance. Why was the anti-U.S. public sentiment rising again in the 1990 while China was not threatened by the United States? This article first reviews the anti-Americanism in China after the Chinese Communists came to power in 1949, then examines the shaping of pro-Americanism from 1979 to 1989, and finally study the sources of the anti-Americanism in the 1990s.

Anti-Americanism in China, 1949-1979

After the Chinese Communists took over China in 1949, Marxist-Leninism dominated the Chinese society. According to Marxist-Leninism, the whole world was divided into two camps, socialist and capitalist. The United States was the leading imperialist power. Working men of all countries would unite and overthrow the U.S.-led capitalism. In his book, *Imperialism, the Highest Stage of Capitalism,* Lennin argued that when capitalism reached the final stage of its development, the monopoly stage, a dominant financial oligarchy would be created. In this stage, a great economic crisis would arise and socialist revolution would be unavoidable. Most Chinese intellectuals accepted this interpretation of the world including the United States after 1949. The negative image of the United States articulated in the official media was seen in scholarly publications. America was considered as a greedy and violent nation struggling to remain the wealthiest and strongest in this world. But it was racked by internal class struggles between the proleteriats and capitalists. A revolution in United States would be inevitable and U.S. imperialism would collapse in the end. These negative images reinforced in the Chinese society.

In addition, the Chinese government carried out a number of campaigns against the United States after 1949. Beijing first waged nationally the "Resist America, Aid Korea" campaign during the Korean War from 1951-1953, attacking the U.S. imperialism at the city, town, village, factory, and neighborhood level. Many Americans who did not want to leave China after the Communists took over power in 1949 were sent to prisons as spies.[2] Calling to "Liberate Taiwan," Beijing condemned Washington of supporting the Nationalist government in Taiwan during the 1954 and 1958 Taiwan Straits crisis.

When the "Anti-Rightist" Campaign started in 1957, many American-trained intellectuals got into trouble because of their "bourgeois American outlook" and pro-American attitude. Some of them were sent to prisons, or labor camps, or countryside. After the United States was involved in the Vietnam War in 1964, the Chinese government escalated attack on U.S. imperialism, claiming America's bombings of North Vietnam was a prelude to invade China. In 1965, Marshal Lin Biao delivered his famous speech, "Long Live the Triumph of People's War," calling the people all over the world to fight American imperialism. The United States became not only the number one enemy of the Chinese but the people of the world, according to the Chinese government. As the Cultural Revolution started in 1966, the anti-Americanism campaign reached to a very high point. Thousands of the Red Guards besieged Beijing as well as other cities with mass demonstrations, shouting, "Down with U.S. Imperialism." Uncle Sam was burned in effigy on the streets in many big cities and Americans were vilified in the official media and scholar works. The Chinese who had relations to the United States were regarded as American agents, "running dogs," or spies. They were then criticized and insulted before mass criticism gatherings. Many of them were forced to committed suicide, sent to prisons, or tortured. The horrible persecution was not over until President Nixon's visit to Beijing in 1972. Since then severe criticism of the United States in the official press were toned down and anti-Americanism began to decline toward the late 1970s when the relations between China and United States were improved. In sum, motivated by Marxist-Leninism ideology, the Chinese government played an important role in promoting the anti-Americanism campaigns from 1949 to 1979 in order to continue the Communist revolution against Western capitalism and imperialism.

Wary Pro-Americanism in China, 1979-1989

Since the normalization of diplomatic relations between China and the United States in 1979, anti-Americanism had gradually given way to cautious pro-Americanism in the Chinese media and professional publications. Following Mao's death in 1976, the official critical image of Americanism continued, but a more admiring image emerged among the intellectuals and average Chinese people, especially after 1979 when both China and the United States established formal diplomatic relations. From 1979 to 1989 there were two kinds of images of the United States in China, positive and negative. The conservative leaders still insisted that although the Communist established official relations with capitalist United States, but the ideological and political struggle between socialist and capitalist system in the world was not over. The ultimate objective of American foreign policy was to destroy Communism in the world. The United States, a rotten capitalist country still posed a security threat to China and American policy toward China was hostile. The Chinese had to resist American cultural and ideological influences when opening its door to the West. Many Chinese scholars and professors expressed this official orthodox opinion in their professional publications.

But this critical picture coexisted alongside a more positive and, to some extent, a favorable view of the United States in the 1980s. The United States was regarded as a strategic ally offsetting the military threat from Soviet "social imperialism" after 1972 and was seen as a precious resource of money, technology, and managerial expertise for China's industrialization after 1979. Pro-American images in the official media and professional publications grew in number before the Tiananmen Square crisis in 1989. During this period, non-Marxist scholars began to appear as a new school of interpretation of U.S. foreign policy, economy, ideology, and society, admiring American advanced science and technology, political system, values, and society. At the level of the mass populace, there was a more deep reservoir of pro-Americanism. Many Chinese, especially the youth, considered America as a land of wealth, freedom, equality, mobility, and opportunity. They praised Americans for their industriousness, creativity, and friendliness.

Wary pro-Americanism was surging because the Chinese understood more the United States than ever before. Since the first official contact between Beijing and Washington in 1972, especially the establishment of formal diplomatic relations between these two countries, official, academic, and public exchanges between the Chinese and Americans had been increased. It was in early 1979 that Americans as well as other foreigners began to enter China in substantial numbers for the first time since 1949. From 1979 to 1989, hundreds of official Chinese delegations were visiting Washington, New York, Los Angeles, and other American cities each year while about 25,000 American tourists were in China annually. Many books on American society and hundreds of translations of American literature were published. Millions of Chinese youth listened to the 'Voice of America" every day for news and features about American people as well as for English lessons. Thousands of hundreds of Chinese youth enjoyed watching American films in Chinese theaters. Sponsored by the U.S. government, academic institutions, public organizations, and private foundations, hundreds of American professors, scholars, and students were teaching, doing research, and studying at the Chinese universities while more than 30,000 Chinese students and a large number of Chinese visiting scholars were in the United States each year from 1979 to 1989. Multiple channels of learning about Americans resulted in a better understanding of the United States. More importantly, the pro-American scholars and professors who interpreted the America for the Chinese leaders also contributed to a better official image of Americans during the 1980s.

The Resurgence of Anti-American sentiments after 1989

After the Tiananmen Incident of 1989, pro-Americanism began to decline and anti-Americanism started to rise among the ordinary people, especially the youth. The anti-American sentiments were in the most popular books and T.V. series. One of the indications of this resentment of Americans was the popular autobiography, *Manhadun de Zhongguo Nuren* [Chinese women in Manhattan] by Zhou Li, which intrigued many Chinese people. Describing a Chinese woman migrating to New York City and making a quick fortune, this book concluded that American society was a dishonest society. Dishonest was the only way to succeed where you made money. If you did not make money, you were a loser. Scoring and rejecting American values and cultures, the book tried to convince readers that American spiritual life was relatively empty and poor. This book became one of the most popular boos and was sold about 200,000 copies in 1993.

In the same year, a television series, *Beijing Ren Zai Niuyue* [A Beijing man in New York], attracted a record viewing audience in China. This series became the most popular tele-series in China in 1993. *Beijing Ren Zai Niuyue* involved a trip by a Chinese hero to the United States where he overcame adversity and obtained fortune. Wang Qiming, the major actor of the series, was forced to surrender all his Chinese values to succeed in the United States. Some Chinese viewers emphasized the aspects of conflicts between the Chinese and American cultures.[3] Some said that this series tried to show the audience that there were no ground rules and no morality in the United States where the strong ate the weak and the fittest survived.[4] Some critics further pointed out that the major theme of this series was anti-Americanism.[5]

In 1995, the China Youth Research Center, the China Youth Development Foundation, and the Historical Materialism Society conducted jointly a public opinion poll. The survey indicated that over 50% of respondents believed that the United States was a country hostile to China, and among the countries most disliked by the Chinese people, the United States was ranked first, followed by Japan and Vietnam. This survey showed the rising feeling against the United States among the Chinese citizens.[6]

The popularity of a new book simply testified to the strong anti-U.S. sentiment among Chinese people. In May 1996, five young Chinese authors, who were in their 30s and worked as reporters, lecturers, and/or poets, finished a book, *Zhongguo Keyi Shoubu* [China can say no], which quite unexpectedly attracted much attention both in China and abroad. The 50,000 copies of the first edition sold out immediately, becoming an instant best seller in the Beijing area in the summer of 1996 and drawing hundreds of letters of support from all over China.[7] And by September that year the book had sold some 400,000 copies.[8]

Attacking American cultural, political, and economic imperialism in hyperbole, this book of 400 pages represented the third such book following *Japan Can Say No* by Japanese authors and *Asia Can Say No* by Malaysian Prime Minister. Denouncing U.S. practices against China on issues such as human rights, population, most-favored-nation status, and Taiwan, this book asserted that the U.S. government had no right to act as an international judge telling China what was right or wrong, and that China, capable of confronting the United States on all spheres of international activities, should be prepared to go to war with America. Recounting their personal experiences which had evolved from admiring the United States to scolding the United States, the authors claimed that Washington's unfriendly acts toward China had disillusioned many Chinese citizens, especially the young and educated. "The whole country was angrily opposing the U.S. and an entire generation of Chinese children have had similar genuine feelings."[9]

In late 1996, a new anti-U.S. book, *Yaomo Fa Zhongguo De Beihou* [Behind demonization of China] was completed. One of the authors, Li Xiguang, a visiting Chinese journalist at the *Washington Post* in 1995, held that the coverage of China in the mainstream U.S. media was built on a Cold War theory, American ideology, national interest, and White chauvinism. Such biased information had segregated the American public from the reality of China.[10] Li claimed that he and seven returning scholars from the United States had to express the growing anger of the Chinese intellectual over American activities, and it was the anti-China tendency of mainstream U.S. media that fanned their anti-U.S. sentiment to write this book.[11] This book had become a best seller in Beijing by the end of 1996 after the book *China Can Say No*.

Four Types of Anti-Americanism in China in the 1990s

Unlike the previous anti-Americanism from 1949 to 1979 facilitated only by the Beijing government, the resurgence of anti-Americanism in China in the post-Cold War era came from four major sources: governmental, nationalistic, and problem-oriented, and issue-oriented anti-Americanism. Each was incited by different motives and objectives, none of which was entirely separated from another. Problem-oriented anti-Americanism, for instance, was sometimes a combination of governmental and nationalistic anti-U.S. feelings sometimes.

Governmental Anti-Americanism

Governmental anti-Americanism were feelings among the Chinese conservative leaders. Seeking to avoid admitting any mistakes, these conservatives placed the source of trouble in America and promoted hostility toward the United States in order to hold the country together and to provide a plausible scapegoat for governmental failure and a loss of public confidence in the Beijing government. They used official media to vilify the United States and incite anti-U.S. feeling among the public.

After the People's Liberation Army's suppression of the student movement on June 4, 1989, the Chinese leaders instigated a program of hostility toward the United States in order to mobilize domestic support and to provide a scapegoat for the cause of the student demonstration. The Beijing authorities launched a relentless campaign against "counter-revolution rebellion," claiming that some "black hands" had almost succeeded in overthrowing the socialism during the student movement in 1989. The campaign quickly widened its aim at the convenient target--the

United States which supported the Chinese students and imposed sanctions on China to isolate the Beijing government for suppressing the students on June 4. Deng Xiaoping held the United States partially responsible for fomenting the unrest that caused demonstrations and contributing to their sustenance. "Frankly speaking, the United States was involved too deeply in the turmoil and counter-revolutionary rebellion that occurred in Beijing not long ago," Deng told former President Nixon in October, 1989.[12] Deng's assessment stimulated an outpouring of anti-American invective not seen in the Chinese media since the normalization. China's National People's Congress, meeting in February 1990, chastised the United States for sanctions imposed after the June crackdown.[13] Also, the semi-official journal *Ban Yue Tan,* in a lecture series on patriotism, emphasized China's ability to withstand any threat from the U.S., condemning the United States for imposing sanctions against China after June 4.[14] State sponsored anti-Americanism in China intensified following the 1989 repressions, and the Chinese government attacked U.S. foreign policies toward China in several ways.

First, the Beijing government accused the United States of attempting to overturn the Chinese government by a "peace evolution" tactic. The Beijing leaders claimed that the United States supported the Chinese student movement because America attempted to overthrow the Chinese government through "peaceful evolution." On 3 May, 1990, in the People's Great Hall, Jiang Zemin spoke to 3,000 students stressing the idea that the hostile forces in the United States were continuing to subvert socialist China through this tactic. A wave of attacks targeting the United States began in April, 1991. On 24 April, Renmin *Ribao* [People's daily] in a rare frontal attack on America openly regarded the United States as the major hostile driving force abroad against China. This was the first time the Washington government was labeled as an enemy by a major official newspaper in China.

Official media attacks intensified on American sponsorship of "peaceful evolution" after August. On 19 August 1991, a hard-line coup against Gorbachev failed, signaling the total collapse of Communism in Soviet Union and the death of the Soviet Union itself. The Chinese government asserted that the U.S. government had added fuel to the flames in Moscow and further blamed that the United States had been stepping up the implementation of their "peaceful evolution" scheme against the last Communist giant, China. The official national network also broadcasted extensively the scenes of chaos in the Eastern European countries in order to convince many Chinese that China must resist U.S. "peaceful evolution."

Secondly, the Chinese government condemned the new hegemonism which was the nature of the post-Cold War foreign policy of the United States and which had some characteristics such as interfering with other countries' internal affairs and exporting the American system and values. To the Chinese conservative leaders, power and interest are still the two key concerns for understanding world politics today. The end of the Cold war did not bring a lasting peace to the world as people hoped. Rather, conflicts of national interests became more intense and the world was not tranquil. The post-Cold War U.S. global strategy was expansionist in nature because of its superior power. The global politics of the United States appeared to have an impact on the Chinese leaders. In January, 1991, the United States engaged in the Gulf War against the Iraqi. During the war, Bo Yibao, vice-Chairman of the CCP's Central Advisory Commission, accused the United States of planning to create a "world domination" when he spoke to the Shanxi delegates of the Chinese National People's Congress. Some officers in the CCP advocated establishing a new pact with Russia against U.S. imperialism.[15]

The Chinese military leaders took a firm stand unanimously opposing U.S. hegemonism. and openly lobbied for a more aggressive defense policy to resist American expansion.[16] During both the 14th CCP Congressional sessions in 1992 and the National People's Congress (NPC) sessions in 1993, high-ranking military officers wrote a letter to the CCP's Central Committee Political Bureau and the chairman of the NPC's Standing Committee, saying that China must oppose U.S. power politics and strike back at US intervention and subversion in China. In May and June 1993, the Central Military Commission's Liu Huaqing, Chang Zhen, Chi Haotian, and others delivered anti-U.S. speeches attacking Washington's hegemonism policy to the armed services, military academies, and military scientific research units while making inspections.[17] In 1993, a new book, *Zhongguo Yuhe Dajing Xia Yi Chang Zhanzheng* [How China will win the next war in the future], was published and circulated among high-ranking military officials. This book considered the United States as the major enemy of China and encouraged the Chinese military forces to be prepared for a war with Americans in the future.[18]

The Chinese conservative leaders were becoming more hostile toward America. On 1 April 1994, the CCP Central Committee Secretarial held an extremely important conference in Beijing attended by the secretaries and propaganda chiefs of the party committees of all ministries, state commissions, provinces, municipalities, and autonomous regions. During the conference, General Zhang Wannian claimed, "When facing blatant interference by the U.S. hegemonists and their open support for the activities of hostile elements . . ., we have to strengthen our power in order to defeat the challenge from hegemonism and colonialism."[19] Thirdly, the Beijing government attacked the containment policy of the United States. After 1989, the Chinese leadership believed that the U.S. government already had a long-term strategy of containment. At the beginning of 1992, the Chinese Communist Party issued an internal document which claimed the United States had become more arrogant after the triumph of the Persian Gulf War and the collapse of the Soviet Empire and had a plan to destroy Socialist China. In addition to using the "peaceful evolution" tactics, the Bush administration had renewed the containment policy of China in order to blockade, isolate, and destroy China. The document claimed Bush's recent visit to Singapore, South Korea, and Japan was a part of this containment policy which had been used against the Soviet Union during the Cold War.[20]

In 1993 the official media began to attack the Clinton administration, and in January, the official journal *Renmin Luntan* said that Clinton had established a new policy toward China. He and his advisers had developed seven strategies for containing China, playing the Taiwan card, strengthening the Japan-United States Security Treaty, promoting the Tibet independence movement, internationalizing the Hong Kong issue, and others. [21]

Finally, the official criticism of the United States was also directed at American cultures and people. The official media played up contradiction within U.S. society and serious domestic problems in order to create a negative of American society and prove the "superiority of socialism." The propaganda campaign was ominously useful. Evidently, many Chinese people generally accepted the official anti-American propaganda concepts and had a negative perspective of American cultures, values, society, and ideology.

Nationalistic Anti-Americanism

Since 1989 there has been a rise of Chinese economic nationalism. The demands for economic nationalism by the Chinese resulted from the strong demands of economics. China was living in a post-Cold War world in which economic nationalism was surging. The growth of China's population meant tens of millions of new job-seekers came into the market each year. If the economy did not grow rapidly, the risk of social unrest would be huge. China needed to develop overseas markets, to enter the World Trade Organization, and to exploit the oil in the South China Sea. Economic nationalism would create a sense of internal cohesion and unity against foreign economic influence and pressure.[22]

The expansion of Chinese economy also promoted economic

nationalism in China. In the 1990s, China's economy continued to grow at a rate of 10% every year and trade with other countries increased rapidly. The trade between China and the United States had made remarkable progress. Since 1979 bilateral trade had achieved an annual average growth rate of 20% increasing from US$2.5 billion in 1979 to US$40.8 billion in 1995. Bilateral trade accounted for 14.5% of China's total imports and exports and 4.3% of that of the United States. As Wu Yi, minister of Foreign Trade and Economic of China, said, "The United States has been China's third largest trading partner, and the United States has identified China as the most important emerging market offering the greatest potential."[23]

China's booming economy created a huge potential market for the United States as well as for Europeans. The result was that China was becoming more nationalistic at home and more vocal abroad, especially in its dealing with the U.S., for many Chinese believed that the United States and other industrialized countries needed the market in China. Millions of Chinese liked to eat at McDonald's, KFC, or Pizza Hut restaurants, watch U.S. movies, and puff on Marlboro cigarettes, but they said they could do without America. As Mr. Ren Jie, shipping executives at the five-star China World Hotel in eastern Beijing, told *The Wall Street Journal* that his friend "could smoke local cigarettes without any problem. . . but U.S. cigarette companies have a big market here." He also said that he did not like America's annual hue and cry over human rights and China's most-favored-nation status." Mr. Ren's friend added, "The U.S. film industry will be the most vulnerable if the U.S. imposes sanctions against China [over the piracy row] and China retaliates with counter-sanctions."[24] Obviously, China's huge economic gains in recent years had bolstered its confidence and the Chinese spoke out and commanded respect from the United States. At the Xicheng District Communist Party School, school official Wang Youngming said, "Our country is a great country with a big population and a long history . . . I feel our potential for making progress is endless."[25] Hang Yuejiao, a Beijing trade officer, said that the United States should not dictate timetables to China because it was not the leader of China, after reprimanding the Washington government for failing to show respect to the Chinese representatives during talks on China's piracy problem.[26] The anti-American sentiment is an expression of new self-confidence and nationalism which was commensurate with China's growing economic power.

The post-Tiananmen China's nationalism is a pro-commerce economic nationalism. After 1989, the Chinese leaders were forced to accept that real socialism meant economic development and that the only way for China's survival was an export-led and manufactures-based economic strategy. More people attempted to make more money by exportation of their products to the world. The rise of China's economy was a rise of trade deficit unfavorable to the United States. In 1993, U.S. trade deficit with China was $22,777.1 millions, and it jumped to $29,504.2 millions in 1994. Following Japan, China was ranked the second largest trade deficit country in the U.S. trade. Disturbed by its huge trade deficit with China, the United States has increasingly put pressure on Beijing to open China's markets to American goods. Many Chinese complained that the United States was trying to impose its goods on China, and anti-American rhetoric now focuses on trade issues to a considerable extent. Liu Baiyue, General Manager of Guangdong Enterprises in Guangdong Province, groaned that "China is struggling to build up an economy that seems to be very competitive in world markets, but Americans are threatening China's new prosperity with harsh protectionism."[27] Hang Shiliang, deputy director-general of the Independent China Center for International Studies, moaned to a U.S. journalist, "We don't do anything to harm U.S. China relations, but now U.S. puts so much pressure on China - first human rights, then the economy. What for?"[28] Many Chinese believed that U.S. economy policy toward China aroused their anti-American feelings. It seems that anti-Americanism grew worse and more extensive in China because of United States' pressure on China's economy.

Problem-Oriented Anti-Americanism

Problem-oriented anti-Americanism is a pattern of outbursts against American policies with which another country disagrees. It also resulted from the policy disagreements of two countries pursuing their respective national interests. This type of anti-U.S. sentiment is also intensified by the United States' often heavy-handed approach to the specific problems between two countries involved.

The U.S. government's approach to the Taiwan and Tibet problems in the 1990s was one of the examples. The military suppression of the students at the Tiananmen Square in 1989 had a very negative effect on millions of Americans sitting before their televisions. After 1989, the Beijing administration continued to persecute political dissidents, reduce freedom of assembly and freedom of press, and carry out no political reforms, in spite of the achievements of its economic reforms. In addition, the United States was angered by some of China's policies such as intellectual property piracy, nuclear proliferation, and missile exportation, among others. Anti-Beijing forces were taking shape in America in the 1990s. Several long-term anti-Beijing Congressmen were brought onto the foreign relations committees of both the Senate and the

House Representatives, and the most-anti-Beijing U.S. Congress was established. Senator Jesse Helms, who was strongly anti-Communist and pro-Taiwan, took charge of the powerful Senate Foreign Relations Committee, and Benjamin Gilman, an old friend of Tibet's exiled leader, Dalai Lama, was in charge of the House Foreign Affairs Committee. In the 1990s, Congress passed a number of resolutions against the Chinese government and the White House took tougher policies toward Beijing than ever before.

In September, 1992, the Washington government disregarded repeated pressure from the Chinese government and blatantly decided to sell 150 sophisticated and highly functional F-16 fighters to Taiwan. This event caused much anger among high-level CCP leaders who responded strongly and quickly and made an effort to stir anti-U.S. winds. The Minister of Foreign Affairs completed a Five-Point proposal and submitted it to the State Council for approval. This proposed that China must immediately lodge a serious protest with the U.S. government against its violation of the China-U.S. joint communique, and the Chinese ambassador to Washington should be called back for an indefinite time. Thereafter, the official media took the advantage of U.S. fighter sales to Taiwan to stir up feelings of hatred of America by condemning the U.S. government for playing the "Taiwan Card," hurting Chinese feelings, interfering in China's internal affairs, and creating an openly hostile relationship between Beijing and Washington.[29]

In April, 1995, both the Senate Foreign Relations Committee and the House of Representatives' Foreign Affairs Committee unanimously approved a resolution calling on Clinton to allow Taiwan President Li Tenghui to visit the United States. The resolution was adopted by both the Senate and the House of Representatives in May. Many congressmen probably did not understand the historical origins of the Taiwan problem and the current status of the China-Taiwan relations, but they strongly supported the Taiwan government because Taiwan was a democratic and capitalist country while main China was a totalitarian and Communist one.   Pressured by Congress, Washington allowed Taiwan's President Lee Tenghui to visit the United States in June, 1995, in a private capacity. The Beijing government was not notified through U.S. ambassador to Beijing or Chinese ambassador to Washington. The Chinese government learned of this very important decision only from the Taiwan newspapers. Clinton's assistant secretary in the Department of State still asserted that Washington would not made the decision to give a visa to Lee during the press conference in Hong Kong one day before Clinton granted a visa to Lee.

Lee's visit to the United States annoyed the Chinese people. Although insisting that it still maintained a "One China" policy, the Washington government did not understand that it was challenging China's most fundamental interests of national sovereignty and domestic order. The Beijing government lodged a strong protest against the U.S. government, and the Sino-U.S. relations reached its ebb since 1979. China's official media interpreted Lee's visit to the United States as a U.S. plot to split China and a big step toward Taiwan independence. Ordinary Chinese were quick to agree and believe that the United States was aiding Taiwan's independence aims. This interpretation also served to promote the anti-U.S. feelings. Once again, resentment of Americans became a valid course that the Chinese could accept. A computer science student at Qinghua University angrily said that while invading the island would be "too much, because a lot of ordinary people would be killed. Maybe assassinating Lee Tenghui would be better." Posters such as "Down with U.S. Imperialism" were found on many university campuses in Beijing, and young students applied to the public security bureau for permission to stage a demonstration at the U.S. embassy in Beijing.[30]

American activities during the Taiwan crisis further irritated the Chinese. In March, 1996, the Chinese armed forces conducted large-scale military exercises including the use of missiles on the Taiwan Strait in order to scare the Taiwanese not to vote for Li Tenhui during the president election campaign. To deter a feared China's attack on Taiwan, Clinton ordered U.S. aircraft carriers to sail for Taiwan, defending the Nationalist government. As a result, America-bashing was widespread in China. The Beijing government lodged a strong protest against the Clinton administration. Some Chinese even encouraged the China navy to use missiles to attack U.S. warships during the military exercises.

The United States' approach to the problems of Tibet was another source of anti-U.S. feeling in China. In 1990, the Senate and House passed a Joint Resolution on March 23 urging the President to issue a proclamation designating May 13, 1990, as the "National Day" in "Support of Freedom and Human Rights in China and Tibet," and calling on the people of the United States to observe such a day with appropriate ceremonies and activities. In an effort to provide humanitarian assistance to Tibetan refugees in India, Congress authorized 1,000 special visas for Tibetans under the Tibetan Provisions of the U.S. Immigration Act of 1990. The Tibetan U.S. Resettlement Project began in 1990.[31]

In 1991, Congress invited the Dalai Lama to the United States. The Chinese government was particularly sensitive to persistent allegations from human rights organizations that it had engaged in widespread violations in Tibet. As a result, in March, the Chinese consul general's office in New York sent letters to the presidents of schools, including

Harvard University, Massachusetts Institute of Technology, and Cornell University, calling the Dalai Lama "an exile who engages in political activities aimed at splitting the motherland." The letters suggested the Dalai Lama's appearance be canceled and hinted that Sino-America cultural exchanges could be harmed by such engagements.[32] The pressure campaign was part of a longtime policy of the Beijing government when accused of flagrant human rights abuses in Tibet, and was done to discourage international recognition of the Buddhist leader of the world's six million Tibetans. It came at a time when members of Congress, many of whom were still angry about the Chinese army's 1989 massacre of pro-democracy demonstrators, were considering whether to extend China's preferential trading status.

Congress adopted the State Department's Authorization bill on March 23, 1991. This bold bill contained a provision sponsored by Senator Pell declaring Tibet to be an occupied country whose true representatives are the Dalai Lama and the Tibetan government-in-exile. It also declared Tibet (including the areas inhabited by ethnic Tibetans in the provinces of Sichuan, Yunnan, Gansu and Qinghai) an occupied country under the established principles of international law; and that "Tibet's true representatives are the Dalai Lama and the Tibetan government-in-exile."[33]

When the Dalai Lama was invited to visit the United States again, on April 27, 1992, Vice President Al Gore received the Dalai Lama at his office, and in order not to anger China, Mr. Clinton casually dropped into Al Gore's office for a few minutes while the Dalai Lama was there.[34] This 50-minute meeting was significant because it marked the first time senior U.S. officials allowed the Dalai Lama to enter the White House through the front door and spent so much time discussing human rights issue with the Dalai Lama. The Dalai Lama spokesman said Clinton had told the Tibetan leader that he would help the Tibetans.

On May 8, 1993, President Clinton announced the renewal for one year of China's MFN status in an executive order. It was conditional on China making "overall, significant progress" with respect to human rights, including "protecting Tibet's distinctive religious and cultural heritage." He became the first American President to list improvement of human rights in Tibet as a condition for renewal of China's most-favored-nation trading status.[35] For the first time in decades, Tibet reappeared on the agenda of bilateral U.S.-China relations and was integrated into U.S. China policy.

In 1995, American legislators pushed through several measures on Tibet, establishing "the Voice of America Tibetan" service, referring to Tibet as an occupied sovereign country under international law, and appointing a special U.S. envoy with ambassador rank to Tibet. America's new measures on Tibet made the Chinese government and people to think that the United States was not only interfering China's internal affairs, but was promoting the independent movement of Tibet under the pretext of concern about the Tibet human rights problem. As an editorial by the official Chinese news agency Xinhua wrote in September 1995, "Covertly, the U.S. government and Congress have been backing activity of the Dalai Lama for a long time."[36] Under this circumstance, the official criticism of the United States made sense to the Chinese became Washington was playing the Tibet card against China. The external hostility was real and an external threat to China's territorial integrity existed.

Event-Oriented Anti-Americanism

In the 1993, two major events helped to start the resentment of America in China. On 15 July 1993, the Chinese cargo ship *Yinhe* left the port of Dalian in Northeast China for Abbes, Iran, with the load of thiodiglycol and thionyl chloride. On July 23, the American Embassy alleged at the a conference with the Chinese Foreign Minister that *Yinhe* was carrying two banned materials which might be used for making chemical weapons and Beijing had to stop this exportation. Otherwise, China would face sanctions imposed by the United States according to American laws.

But Beijing claimed that Washington's allegations were totally unfounded and full of self-contradictions. First, contrary to American allegations, the container ship in fact left the port of Tianjin instead of Dalian on July 7 rather than on July 15. Second, this ship was bound for the port of Kuwait and would be impossible to go to Abbes port because it could not handle container ships. Third, thirty containers were leaving for Iran, but they were carrying stationery, metal fittings, machinery spare parts, and dye stuff which would be unloaded in Dubai, the United Arab Emirates, and then were transported to Iran. There were no chemical products, chemical weapons, or even nuclear weapons on this containers. Finally, the Chinese officials claimed that China, a signatory to the Chemical Weapons Convention which would not become effective until 1995, had promoted the control of the transfer of thiodiglycol and thionyl chloride, formulating as early as 1990 the policies to ban and to control these materials.

Therefore, the Chinese government refused to order *Yinhe* to come back China. The U.S. warships and military airplanes started on August 1 to follow *Yinhe* on the high seas and to take aerial photos. Washington also informed the Gulf countries of the alleged chemicals on the ship and forced these countries not to allow the Chinese ship to enter their ports. At the same time, the Washington government continued to make further representations with the Chinese government, asking Beijing either to order *Yinhe* to return to the Chinese port or to let Americans go abroad the ship and carry out inspection.

With its normal navigation severely interrupted, *Yinhe* was compelled to stay adrift on the high seas in the Gulf area and began to suffer serious fuel, food, and water shortages. The ship finally was to drop anchor on the high seas off the Hormuz on August 3. Under this serious situation, the United Arab Emirates sent to the Chinese a tugboat with 60 tons of water and 60 tons of fuel. The United States, however, claimed that the Iranians was sending a ship to help the Chinese and warned the Chinese sailors not to enter the Iranian Port.

Due to the American interruption, *Yinhe* could not arrive in its port of destination Kuwait and unloaded its materials according to its schedule, and the Chinese seamen were suffering. In order to solve this crisis, the Chinese government on August 4 suggested an inspection by the third party of the cargo on the ship which the U.S. government suspected. At the same time, the Kingdom of Saudi Arabia promised to let the Chinese ship enter the Damman Port and send inspectors to join the Chinese inspectors in examining *Yinhe*. American government would also send representatives to join the examination as the Saudi Arabia's technical advisors. Expects from three sides agreed on August 26 to conduct a special examination of the materials destined for Iran and check the containers that American were questioning about. The three parties also promise to sign and publish the examination report in the end.

The inspection started on August 28. The inspectors opened one container after another but they discovered no materials which the U.S. government claimed. The U.S. inspects then required inspection of the cargo transported from Hong Kong to Iran, but they found no banned chemicals either. Finally, American experts asked to check all the cargo on the ship. Insisting the American group had gone back on its own words with its unreasonable request, the Chinese inspectors were reluctant to let Americans check all the containers on the ship at first, but finally allowed all cargo's checked. American experts failed to find the chemical materials on the ship. The report of inspection signed by three parties declared on September 14 that there was nothing the U.S. government accused of on *Yinhe*.

The Chinese government lodged a strong protest against the United States and used this event to accuse Washington of damaging China's reputation under the pretext of controlling chemical weapons proliferation, criticize the U.S. navy of violating the international laws, and condemn U.S. hegemonism and power politics.[37] Without doubt, this event angered many Chinese too.

At the same time, another event happened. After the Tiananmen Crisis, sports became a national obsession and pride in China's athletes had unified the Chinese in spite of the political wounds of June 4 that had then divided Chinese society. Believing that the 2000 Olympic Games would be a golden opportunity for this unification, the Beijing government began the Olympic bid campaign in 1993 with the support of Deng Xiaoping. The Chinese government wanted the Olympic Games for several reasons. During the campaign, the Chinese representatives promised the International Olympic Committees (IOC) that 300 million Chinese citizens would take part in the torch relay--which would have been a memorable spectacle. In its bid, the Chinese leaders, including Deng Xiaoping, hoped that the Olympics would boost its economy and world standing, just as the 1988 Games did for South Korea and the 1964 Olympics did for Japan. The official media often claimed the rest of the world should give China a chance because all Chinese within and outside China wanted Beijing to host the Games, and Beijing should have an opportunity to host the Games.[38]

But the U.S. Congress did not want IOC to give the Beijing a chance. On 26 July, 1993, the US House of Representatives adopted a resolution against China's bid because Congress did not want the Chinese government to have "a huge propaganda victory when it routinely tortures [and] severely restricts freedom of assembly and expression," said U.S. Senator Bill Bradley, a Democrat from New Jersey, and past Olympic basketball gold medalist and professional player.[39] No doubt this resolution had impact on the members of the IOC.

On 23 September, Sydney edged out Beijing by 2 votes, 45 to 43, ending the most politicized race to host an Olympics ever. The International Olympic Committee's decision to deny Beijing the 2000 Olympics was an added humiliation to the Chinese government. Chinese officials sat in stunned silence after their hopes to host the 2000 Olympics were dashed by a come-from-behind victory for Sydney. When defeat came, the Beijing government expressed "respect" for the decision and urged people to "display the demeanor of a great and proud country, but noted that "international prejudice, misgivings, and hostility against China had not been completely eliminated." The official media contributed this defeat to the United States. As *Tahung Bao*, the official Chinese newspaper in Hong Kong, claimed that "U.S. Congressmen went so far as to pass a resolution adding political colors to the Olympic Games in order to block China's bid to host the Games. U.S. Congress should understand that today's China was no longer controlled by hegemonist and colonialist."[40]

The defeat was a serious blow to the pride and ambition of the ordinary Chinese too. One disappointed Beijing native sounded off, "Some foreigners still think we have pigtails and women have bound feet. They really don't understand us."[41] "If China had won the bid, my company would be able to operate in a more relaxed surrounding. There would be more business opportunities with the influx of foreign investment," said a young businessman and consultant, who was a leader during student demonstrations in 1989. [42] "It really hurt China's feelings," Lu Zhifang, a Beijing lawyer, said to the reporters of *Far Eastern Economic Review* in Beijing.[43]

The eventual failure of the Chinese bid was seen as a catastrophe orchestrated by U.S. bullies. Most Chinese believed that America was responsible for the Chinese's failure to win the games. Hang Shaowei, a student at the Beijing Sports College said to an American reporter, "I feel a little bit angry, American has no rights to interfere in the [International Olympic Committee] decision."[44] A Beijing lawyer said that "That [failure of the China's bid] was the moment when the Chinese started believing that the U.S. wanted to contain China."[45] Demonstrations were banned because of fears of anti-American resentments. Security was increased in Beijing just in case protest broke out. Actually, before the Internal Olympic Committee's announcement, the U.S. Embassy had notified the Chinese Foreign Ministry that it needed official protection for US institutions in Beijing because they had already learned that many people had indicated if Beijing failed in its 2000 Olympic bid they would blame America first.[46] Anti-U.S. sentiment was rising among the Chinese, especially among the Beijing residents in October, 1993.

Conclusion

Anti-Americanism was evident in China in the 1990s. It was particularly strong among the youth, the college students, and those people in Beijing area. Anti-Americanism was initially promoted by the Beijing government after the Tiananmen crisis and the end of the Cold War in order to solve domestic problems and survive in the crisis. It permeated into the Chinese society under the influence of powerful official propaganda.

Like anti-Americanism in other Asian countries as well as in Latin America, Chinese anti-Americanism expressing a strong resentment of U.S. political and economic dominance was natured by past humiliation and a new self-confidence which was commensurate with China's rapid economic expansion and military power. As a rising power, the Chinese wanted to be treated equally and fairly by the United States and a change in the post-Cold War world order from two superpower domination to multi-power domination.

It seemed that anti-Beijing Congress and some Washington's policies toward China   provided another basis for the rise of Chinese anti-Americanism. American politicians may claim that their fire was directed at the Chinese government in Beijing, but they did not understand the minds of the Chinese in the post-Cold War ear. Although the Chinese government was not popular at all in China and many Chinese might not like their government's policies because of its corruption, dictatorship, and incompetence, they did not have any other choice. They still had only one government -- Beijing representing the interests of the Chinese. To many Chinese, U.S. unfriendly attitude and policies toward the government in Beijing was directed toward the Chinese too.

Notes

1.   For the study of Anti-Americanism, see *Anti-Americanism in the Third World*, Rubinstein and Smith, eds. (New York: Praeger, 1985), *Anti-Americanism in Europe,* Rob Kroes and Maarten van Rossem, eds. (Amsterdam: Free University Press, 1986), and Paul Hollander, *Anti-Americanism: Critiques at Home and Abroad, 1965-1990* (Oxford: Oxford University Press, 1992).

2.   For the scholar study of this anti-Americanism campaign in China, see Kenneth Lieberthal, *Revolution & Tradition in Tientsin, 1949-52* (Stanford, CA: Stanford University Press, 1980).

3.   Yu Wentao, "TV Series Tells about Beijingers in New York," *China Daily,* 13 October 1993.

4.   Xu Jilin, "Wudu zhi houde jiazhi anshi--zai shuo '*Beijingren zai Niuyue,*'" [Values implied by a Misreading--Further View of A Beijing Native in New York], *Wenwei bao*, 13 November 1993.

5.   Zha Xiduo, "Youse Yanjinglide Xiyangjing-Beijingrende Niuyue men," [The West Through coloured glasses--Beijing people's New York dreams], Jiushi niandan yuekan [The Nineties Monthly], No. 2 (1994), pp. 16-17.

6.   Fan Yuan, " Neither does Beijing Want to Cut Off Diplomatic Relations with the United States Nor Try to Defend its Territorial Integrity by Force," *Ming Bao* (Hong Kong), 10 July 1995, p. C3.

7.   "China Saying No," *The Economist,* 20 July 1996.

8.   .Joseph Kahn, "Chinese Writers Increasingly Blast Anti-U.S. Bestseller," *The Wall Street Journal*, 19 September 1996, p. A18. This book had become the best seller, but some Chinese also criticized it.

9.   Rone Tempest, "Just Say 'No' to U.S., Young Chinese Urge," *Los Angeles times*, 5 July 1996, p. A5; Patrick Tyler, "Rebels's New Course: A Book for Yankee Bashing," *New York Times*, 4 September 1996, p. A4.

10. Li Xinguang, "US Media: Behind the Demonization of China," *Beijing Review*, 21 October 1996.

11. "The Rising Nationalism in the Press Circle in China," *China Times* (Taiwan), 1 January 1997, p. 3.

12. As quoted in Daniel Southernland, "Deng Says U.S. Involved in Democracy Movement," *Washington Post,* 1 November 1989.

13. Xinhua News Agency," China's NPC and CPPSS Against U.S. Congress Sanctions Amendment, " BBC *Summary of World Broadcasts--Far East,* 6 February, 1990, A1/1.

14. See " Independence--a base for a strong and rich China," *Ban Yue Tan* (Beijing), No.9 (15 May 1990), pp. 19-21.

15. Willy Wo-lap, "Impact of War on Sino-U.S. Relations Viewed, *South China Morning Post* (Hong Kong), 27 February 1991, p. 15; "He Xin Claims Gulf War Turning Point for U.S., *Hong Kong Standard,* 15 March 1991; Shih Yen, "He Xin' Paper to CCP Leadership With Regard to US attempt to turn China into Chaos and to Overthrow China," *Baixing* (Hong Kong), No. 244 (16 July 1991), pp. 3-4.

16. Chris Yeung, "Bo Yibao Accuses U.S. of World Domination," *South China Morning Post,* 4 April 1991, p. 11.

17. Chen Shaopin, "China Never Surrenders to Hegemonism," *Ching Pao* (Hong Kong), No. 7, 5 July 1993, p. 42.

18. See *China Times* (Taiwan), 16 January 1997, p. 4.

19. "Military Advocates Tough Policy against the U.S.," *Zheng Ming*, No. 199, 1 May 1994, pp. 10-12.

20. "Party Warns of Renewed U.S. 'Containment Policy'," *Kyodo* (Tokyo), 8 January 1992.

21. Gu Dexin, "Clinton's Seven Strategies of Conspiracy toward China," *Renmin Lutan*, No. 6, 15 January 1993, pp. 40-41.

22. For details of the public patriotic sentiment in China, see James Watson, "The Renegotiation of Chinese Cultural Identity in the Post-Mao Ear," in Jeffrey Wasserstrom and Elizabeth Perry's *Popular Protest and Political Culture in Modern China*, (Boulder: Westview Press, 1992) and Edward Friedman, "Reconstructing China's National Identity: Southern Alternative to Mao-Ear Anti-Imperialist Nationalism," *The Journal of Asia Studies*, vol. 53, No. 1 (February 1994), pp. 67-91.

23. Wu Yi, "China-US Trade Balance: An Objective Evaluation," *Beijing Review*, 10 June 1996, p. 10-13.

24. Kathy Chen, "Anti-US Sentiment Surges in China, Putting a Future Strain on Relations," *The Wall Street Journal*, 15 May 1996, p. A11.

25. Robert Greenberger, "Nationalist Fervor, Bolstered by Economy, Chinese Are Resisting Policies of the West," *The Wall Street Journal*, 23 June 1995.

26. Kathy Chen, "Anti-US Sentiment Surges in China, Putting a Future Strain on Relations," *The Wall Street Journal*, 15 May 1996, p. A11.

27. Interview with Liu Baiyue in Guangzhou on July 9, 1996.

28. Kathy Chen, "Anti-US Sentiment Surges in China, Putting a Future Strain on Relations," *The Wall Street Journal*, 15 May 1996, p. A11.

29. See "A Look at America's Antagonistic China Policy," *Takung Bao* (Beijing's official newspaper in Hong Kong), 7 October 1992; Wu Jin, "On

China's Threat theory," *Renmin Ribao*, 10 October 1992.

30. See Fan Yuan, "Neither does Beijing Want to Cut Off Diplomatic Relations with the United States Nor Try to Defend its Territorial Integrity by Forces," *Ming Bao* (Hong Kong), 10 July 1995, p. C3; Nayan Chanda, Kari Huus, "The New Nationalism," *Far Eastern economic Review*, 9 November 1995, pp. 21-26.

31. This project was to establish twenty U.S. sites to bring 1,000 Tibetan refuges living in Nepal and India to the United States from 1990 to 1993. In order not to offend the Beijing government, these new Tibetan immigrants were allowed to enter into the United States not as refuges but as "qualified displaced Tibetans." For more details of this project, see "Strangers in a Strange Land," *Utne Reader*, March 1993, pp. 94-96 and "Quiet Tibetan Influx," *New York Times*, May 14, 1992, p. B1.

32. "China Frowns on Dalai Lams's U.S. Visit," *Washington Post*, Friday, April 5, 1991.

33. This bill was signed into law by President Bush on October 28, 1991. See US Congress Foreign Relations Authorization Act, Fiscal Years 1992 and 1993. As a result, in April 1992, when Senators Pell and Boren applied for visas to visit Tibet, China refused to issue permission to them to enter Tibet, saying the visit would not be appropriate at that time. Speculation in the press was that the two Senators were denied entry because of their efforts to attach human rights conditions to renewal of China's Most Favored Nation trading status, and because of Senator Pell's long time vocal criticism of Beijing's policies in Tibet.

34. During his visit to the United States, Dalai Lama was the first guest to enter the Holocaust Museum in Washington, which opened to the public on 26 April. This event also angered the Beijing government, see "Lukewarm Welcome: Dalai Lama gets cautious reception in Washington," *Far Eastern Economic Review*, May 13, 1993, p.13.

35. In November 1993, the White House further appealed to Beijing to begin substantive negotiations with the Dalai Lama or his appointed representatives. See "Don't Flinch on Tibet," *New York Times*, March 11, 1994.

36. *Keesing's Record of World Events* (Longman), vol.41, no.9, 1995.

37. See *Renmin Ribao*, August 9, 1993, p. 1; September 5, 1993, p. 1.

38. See *South China Morning Post*, 2 August 1993; *South China Morning Post*, 6 August 1993; see also Editorial, "US Politicians do not have a Right to Intervene in Olympic Games," *Wenwei Pao* (China's official newspaper in Hong Kong), 9 August 1993.

39. Editorial, *Boston Herald* (Boston, Massachusetts), 25 September 1993.

40. "We Have Hopes in the Future in Spite of Our Loss ," *Tahung Bao* (Hong Kong), 24 September 1993, p. 2.

41. See editorial, *The Tampa Tribune* (Tampa, Florida) 29 September 1993.

42. Sheila Teft, "Rejected and Dejected, China Tries to Rebound, " *The Christian Science Monitor*, 27 September 1993, p. 4.

43. Nayan Chanda, Kari Huus, "The New Nationalism," *Far Eastern Economic Review*, 9 November 1995, pp. 21-26.

44. Sheila Teft, "Rejected and Dejected, China Tries to Rebound, " *The Christian Science Monitor*, 27 September 1993, p. 4.

45. Nayan Chanda, Kari Huus, "The New Nationalism," *Far Eastern Economic Review*, 9 November 1995, pp. 21-26.

"Beijing: Ready for Olympic Vote," *Ming Bao* (Hong Kong), 24 September

About the Contributors

CHEN Jiafang has received his Ph.D. from Mississippi State University in 1992. His research interests include demography, social change, and human behavior in both China and America. He has intensively studied homicide and suicide in the United States.

CHEN Weixing is an assistant professor in the Department of Political Science at East Tennessee State University. He has published articles in the *Journal of East Asian Affairs, Modern China, Pacific Affairs,* and *Journal of Contemporary China.* His research interests include the political economy of rural industrialization and ideology.

DENG Xiaogang, who received his Ph.D. from the State University of New York at Buffalo, is an assistant professor in the Sociology Department at the University of Massachusetts at Boston. His research interests include social control, comparative criminology, and quantitative methods. He is currently studying the effects of shame and self-control on deviant behavior.

Jessie X. Fan is an assistant professor of family and consumer economics in the Department of Family and Consumer Studies at the University of Utah. Her primary research interests are in household consumption and saving behavior and applied econometrics, including estimation of complete demand systems, credit use under uncertainty, and the relationship of ethnicity and consumer expenditure patterns.

HONG Zhaohui, associate professor of history at Savannah State University in Georgia, is the author of *The Themes of the Social Economic Transition: Reinterpretation of Modernization* (1994) and *Changing Reputations of Land Speculation on Western Development* (1995). He is also co-editor of *In Searching of A Chinese Road Towards Modernization: Economic and Educational Issues in China's Reform Process* (1996); *Image, Perception, and Making of U.S.-China Relations* (1997); *China-U.S. Relations toward the 21st Century: Reflections of Chinese Scholars in the United States* (1998); and *China Development at the Turn of the Century* (1999) (forthcoming). He has published more than 40 refereed articles on China's reform, comparative modernization, and U.S. economic history.

LI Jian received her Ph.D. in Anthropology from Southern Illinois University at Carbondale. She is a research associate in the Anthropology Department at Southern Methodist University. Her research areas include ethnicity, Chinese Americans, and gender in East Asia. She has published numerous articles and reviews in journals such as *Anthropological Quarterly*.

LI Xiaobing is an assistant professor of history and the associate director of the Western Pacific Institute at the University of Central Oklahoma. He is a co-editor of *Re-interpreting U.S.-China-Taiwan Relations* (1998), *China and the U.S.; A New Cold War History* (1997), *Major World Events in the 20th Century* (1994), and *Western Pacific Journal*, and the author of *Diplomacy through Militancy* (1993). He was the CHUS President and is the 1997-99 ACPSS President.

LIU Guoli received his Ph.D. from the State University of New York at Buffalo. He is an assistant professor in the Political Science Department at the College of Charleston. He is the author of *States and Markets: Comparing Japan and Russia* (1994). His research interests include political culture, international political economy, foreign policy analysis, and comparative politics with a focus on Russia and China.

XIAO Jing Jian is an associate professor of consumer economics and personal finance in the Consumer Affairs Program at the College of Human Science and Services, the University of Rhode Island. His current research interests include family saving and investing behavior, personal financial planning, and consumer behavior in China.

XU Guangqiu, who received his Ph.D. from the University of Maryland, is an assistant professor of history at Northwest Arkansas College. He is the author of more than 10 articles published in both China and America. His teaching and research interests are Sino-American relations in World War II and U.S. China policy. He was the ACPSS organizational director.

XU Xiaohe received his Ph.D. in Sociology from the University of Michigan in 1994. He is an assistant professor in the Department of Sociology, Anthropology, and Social Work at Mississippi State University. He has published many articles in journals such as *Journal of Marriage and the Family, Journal of Comparative Family Studies, International Journal of Sociology of the Family, Social Indicators Research,* and *Journal of Gender, Culture, and Health*. His research interests include family, social change, and comparative family systems.

XU Yinzhou is a professor of Marketing and the Vice President of Guangdong Commercial College in China. His major research interests include retail industry and consumer markets in China.

YU Yanmin received her Ph.D. in Mass Communications from the School of Public Communications at Syracuse University in 1993. She is an assistant professor at the University of Bridgeport. Her research interests include media and foreign policy, media and Sino-U.S. relations, investigative reporting, international and intercultural communication, and journalism ethics.

ZHANG Baohui is an assistant professor of Government at Daemen College. He received his Ph.D. in Political Science from the University of Texas at Austin. His research interests include the politics of economic reform and theories of democratization. His publications have appeared in *Comparative Political Studies, Governance,* and *Studies in Comparative Communism.*

ZHANG Jie is an assistant professor of sociology in the Department of Sociology at the State University of New York College at Buffalo. He received his Ph.D. in Sociology from Brigham Young University in 1992. He has co-authored *Introduction to Contemporary Social Psychology* (1995) and *Principles and Applications of Social Psychology* (1994). He is also the author of numerous book chapters and journal articles. Dr. ZHANG Jie is the 1997-99 Executive Vice President of ACPSS.

ZHANG Lening is an assistant professor of sociology at Saint Francis College. His current research focuses on substance abuse and crime. He is continuing work on the comparative study of crime and criminal justice in the U.S. and China. His recent works appear in *Justice Quarterly, Sociological Forum, Criminal Justice and Behavior, Journal of Research in Crime and Delinquency, Alcoholism: Clinical and Experimental Research,* and *Journal of Studies on Alcohol.*